Land
of
Golden
Dreams

Land of Golden Dreams

of Golden Dreams

California in the Gold Rush Decade, 1848–1858

Peter J. Blodgett

Huntington Library
San Marino, California

NOTE TO THE READER

Beyond standardizing punctuation and capitalization
to enhance the clarity of a few passages from
manuscript letters, all quotations are transcribed
verbatim from the original sources, all of which reside
in the collections of the Huntington Library.

Published by the Huntington Library Press
1151 Oxford Road, San Marino, California 91108
http://www.huntington.org

This book was published in conjunction
with the exhibition *Land of Golden Dreams:
California in the Gold Rush Decade, 1848–1858,*
at the Huntington Library from September 28, 1999,
through September 10, 2000.

Supervising Editor: PEGGY PARK BERNAL
Editor: CHRIS KELEDJIAN
Designer: DANA LEVY
Printer: Toppan Printing Company, Hong Kong

ISBN:0-87328-183-7 (cloth)
ISBN:0-87328-182-9 (paper)

Library of Congress Cataloging-in-Publication Data

Blodgett, Peter J. (John), 1954–
      Land of golden dreams: California in the Gold Rush decade,
      1848–1858 / Peter J. Blodgett.
            p.   cm.
      Includes bibliographical references and index

      1. California—Gold discoveries. 2. California—Gold discoveries—Picto-
rial works. 3. Frontier and pioneer life—California. 4. Frontier and pioneer
life—California—Pictorial works. 5. Gold mines and mining—California—History—19th century. 6. Gold mines and mining—California—History—19th
century—Pictorial works. I. Henry E. Huntington Library and Art Gallery. II.
Title.
F865.B6523   1999   99-39377
                                            CIP

COVER: Detail from title page of G. A. Fleming, *California: Its Past History, Its Present
Position, Its Future Prospects*, London, 1850.

BACK COVER: *The Miners' Ten Commandments,* letter sheet published by Sun Print.

PAGE 1: Detail from cover illustration of the *Overland Monthly* (February 1898).

FRONTISPIECE: Daguerreotype of gold miners at Gold Rush diggings, c. 1850.

Contents

FOREWORD   *7*

ACKNOWLEDGMENTS   *8*

I THE ADVENTURE BEGINS   *11*
Paths to El Dorado
A Society on the Brink: Mexican California before the Gold Rush
Gold Fever

II DAYS OF '49   *35*
Planning the Trek to El Dorado
The Great Migration
Life in the Gold Country

III CALIFORNIA TRANSFORMED: ORGANIZING A NEW SOCIETY, 1850–58   *79*
Accommodating Social Change
Defining a New California: The Constitution of 1849 and Political Life

IV THE LEGACIES OF EL DORADO   *111*
Building the Commonwealth: Gold Discovery and California's Development
Making Sense of It All: Interpreting the Gold Rush Experience

CHECKLIST OF THE EXHIBITION   *139*

INDEX   *144*

This exhibition has been made possible through the generous support of

Dr. and Mrs. Peter Bing   Mr. and Mrs. Charles T. Munger

Wells Fargo

Institute of Museum and Library Services
Library Services and Technology Act

The Times Mirror Foundation

Mrs. Helen Smetz

Dorothy Clune Trask Murray Foundation

The GenCorp Foundation - Aerojet

With special appreciation to the lenders to the exhibition

Mrs. Ellen Ellis

Martha and Roy Tolles

Historical Services Department, Wells Fargo

Foreword

WHILE THE WORLD POINTS TO THE YEAR 2000 in anticipation of a new millenium, closer to home the year also marks the sesquicentennial of California's statehood. California entered the Union on September 9, 1850—fewer than three years after the discovery of gold at Sutter's sawmill on January 24, 1848. Such a transformation in so short a span of time seems remarkable itself but not unanticipated, given the great interest shown by the English, French, Russians, and Americans during the 1830s and 1840s in exploiting Mexican California's abundant natural resources. Even before the discovery of gold, the Englishman Sir George Simpson wrote in 1847 that "the English race, as I have already hinted, is doubtless destined to add this fair and fertile province to its possessions on this continent. . . . The only doubt is, whether California is to fall to the British or the Americans." Gold only hastened what some saw as inevitable.

In contemplating California's fate, Simpson referred to what was "destined" to happen. "Manifest destiny" became the cliché of many American historians in the late nineteenth and early twentieth centuries who saw the acquisition of California as both the logical and appropriate conclusion to the conquest of North America begun two centuries earlier by the first European colonists. The Huntington's exhibition *Land of Golden Dreams* takes a broader look at the impact of the Gold Rush on California, the nation, and the world. Like other contemporary historians, Peter Blodgett, curator of Western American historical manuscripts, examines the complete social fabric of California in the decade 1848–58 and its radical transformation, catalyzed by gold discovery, from "a captured Mexican province to the thirty-first state of the American Union." He notes that "the events of the Gold Rush would remain a touchstone for generations of later Californians."

Unflagging supporters make it possible for the Huntington Library to examine major themes through exhibitions of its holdings. Once again Dr. and Mrs. Peter Bing and Mr. and Mrs. Charles T. Munger have stepped forward, this time to make our extraordinary resources on California history available to the public. They are joined by Wells Fargo Bank and the Times Mirror Foundation in support of the production of this exhibition and catalog. We are grateful to everyone who has given us this opportunity to reflect upon the last 150 years of California history so that we can understand where we are now and where we will go in the next century.

DAVID S. ZEIDBERG
Avery Director of the Library

Acknowledgments

ALL EXHIBITION PROJECTS, no matter their size or subject, are collaborative endeavors by their very nature, relying as they do upon the insights, skills, and abilities of many professionals to achieve a common purpose. Development of the Huntington Library's special exhibition *Land of Golden Dreams: California in the Gold Rush Decade, 1848–1858* particularly exemplifies such collaboration, having involved scores of individuals over an eighteen-month period. It gives us great pleasure to have the opportunity here to publicly acknowledge their many contributions to the ultimate success of the exhibition in all its dimensions, including this catalog.

Although drawn almost exclusively from the Huntington's magnificent holdings on the Gold Rush, *Land of Golden Dreams* has benefited from the loan of various historical artifacts that supplement the documentary record. We express our profound appreciation to Mrs. Ellen Ellis of Pasadena, California, Martha and Roy Tolles of San Marino, California, and Beverly Smith, manager of the historical services department, and her associates Marianne Babel, Robert Chandler, Keri Koljian, and William Sander of Wells Fargo Bank in San Francisco, California, for their unfailing generosity as lenders. Special thanks are also due to Claudine Chalmers, Gary Kurutz, Frank Q. Newton, and the Wells Fargo historical services department for their assistance in suggesting many potential exhibition items.

The sesquicentennial of gold discovery and the great rush to California has inspired much fresh research into these topics in recent years, which allowed the Huntington to convene a panel of eminent scholars to serve as an exhibition advisory committee. Janet Fireman (the Los Angeles County Museum of Natural History), Gary Kurutz (the California State Library), Susan Johnson (the University of Colorado, Boulder), Malcolm Rohrbough (the University of Iowa), Elliott West (the University of Arkansas), and Richard White (Stanford University) gave unstintingly of their knowledge and expertise in the history of California during the Gold Rush era. Susan Johnson and Malcolm Rohrbough in particular devoted many hours to discussions about the complexities of Gold Rush California during research trips to the Huntington. Other distinguished historians, including William Deverell, Howard R. Lamar, Amelia Montes, Martin Ridge, and David Wrobel, shared their insights into aspects of the California experience. Many of these individuals also read and reviewed the text for the exhibition catalog, offering valuable advice and constructive criticism. Thereafter, Peggy Park Bernal, director of the Huntington Library Press, editor Chris Keledjian, and designer Dana Levy brought their many talents to bear upon the manuscript to produce this attractive volume.

At the Huntington, many staff members invested great amounts of time and energy in addressing the many tasks entailed in this exhibition. Within the library division they include, in the office of the librarian, David Zeidberg, Avery Director of the Library, and his assistant, Melanie Pickett; in the rare books department, Alan Jutzi, chief curator of rare books, Tom Canterbury, Erin Chase, Cathy Cherbosque, Aimee Dozois, Lisa Libby, Kate McGinn, and Jennifer Watts; in the manuscripts department, Brooke Black, Kristin Cooper, Christine Fagan, Lita Garcia, and Dan Lewis; in the preservation and photographic services department, Susan Rogers, chief preservation officer, Patricia Cornelius, Manuel Flores, Betsy Haude, Barbara Quinn, Shelly Smith, John Sullivan, and Devonne Topits. Those from other parts of the institution include, in the research and education division, Robert C. Ritchie, Keck Foundation Director of Research, Susan Lafferty, and Carolyn Powell; in the development division, Marylyn Warren, vice president for financial development, Catherine Babcock, Lisa Blackburn, Ava Moeller, and Peggy Spear. Three members of the library division deserve very special thanks for their unflagging commitment to this project: Jennifer L. Martinez, curator of Western American history, who not only ably undertook the responsibilities of that position during the run of the exhibition but who also eagerly tackled innumerable Gold Rush-related dilemmas; Mary L. Robertson, William A. Moffett Chief Curator of Manuscripts, whose keen mind and unflappable temperament helped resolve many of the difficulties inherent in exhibition work; and Lauren Tawa, exhibitions preparator, whose marvelous sense of color and design, combined with her meticulous attention to detail, made possible the transformation of abstract vision into concrete reality.

To Sara S. (Sue) Hodson, the Huntington Library's curator of literary manuscripts, the exhibition curator owes his greatest debt of all. Despite the unyielding demands of her own very busy professional life, she constantly took a lively interest in every phase of the project and expressed unwavering confidence in its ultimate success. Enthusiastic audience, thoughtful critic, and loving spouse, she made the greatest possible contribution to bringing this "golden dream" to life.

PETER J. BLODGETT

I | The Adventure Begins

"**B**OYS, I BELIEVE I HAVE FOUND A GOLD MINE!" With those words, an obscure carpenter and mechanic from New Jersey named James W. Marshall launched one of the most astounding series of events in American history. Marshall's startling discovery on the morning of January 24, 1848, in the millrace of an unfinished sawmill on the American River perhaps forty miles east of present-day Sacramento would rapidly transform the isolated Mexican province of Alta California into "El Dorado," the land of instant riches and vast fortunes, and propel it into the center of a furor of global proportions. In the decade that followed, a great adventure unfolded upon a broad stage spanning much of the world and involving a cast of hundreds of thousands. Today, one hundred and fifty years later, Americans are still grappling with the consequences of Marshall's discovery, of the ensuing rush to the goldfields, and of California's subsequent admission to the United States on September 9, 1850. To tell the story of that remarkable era, we will pay particular attention to the many dreams inspired by the sudden discovery of California's golden possibilities, to the conflicting aspirations that those dreams frequently represented, and to the influence that such conflict exerted upon the development of Gold Rush California.

As Marshall inspected the millrace that fateful January morning, the tiny particles glinting beneath the water's surface represented hitherto unimagined possibilities for the thirty-seven-year-old, who, like thousands of other Americans in the 1830s and 1840s, had come west in stages from the East Coast, reaching California in the summer of 1845 after successive sojourns in Indiana, Illinois, Missouri, and Oregon. Trained by his father as a wagon builder, he gained further experience during his western travels as a farmer, a wheelwright, and a carpenter, developing a comfortable familiarity with various mechanical arts. Equipped with such an eminently practical background, Marshall found employment soon after his arrival in Mexican Alta California, joining the service of aspiring land baron John Augustus Sutter.

German-born and Swiss-educated, Sutter had struggled throughout his adult life to reconcile his great ambitions with his general lack of business acumen and his poor sense of judgment about potential business partners. Even before abandoning his home and family in the Swiss community of Burgdorf in 1834 to seek more attractive prospects in America, he had compiled an impressive record of financial improvidence with his dry goods firm of Johann August Suter and Company. After his arrival in the United States, Sutter spent the next five years pursuing commercial ventures that brought him across the continent from Missouri to the Oregon country and beyond to Hawaii (then known as the Sandwich Is-

**Henry W. Bigler,
manuscript autobiography, 1898.**

(Huntington Library: HM 57034)

Henry W. Bigler, one of the workmen employed to build Sutter's sawmill on the American River, witnessed Marshall's discovery of gold there in January 1848. Fifty years later, he wrote this account of the moment when Marshall cried out, "Boys, I believe I have found a gold mine!"

OPPOSITE >

Capt. Sutter's Account of the First Discovery of the Gold, letter sheet published by Britton & Rey.

(Huntington Library: RB 48052 #94)

During the 1850s, the San Francisco publishers Britton & Rey printed and sold this letter sheet to capitalize upon Sutter's and Marshall's growing celebrity. It bears Sutter's version of the discovery, a portrait of Marshall, and a view of the mill itself and was intended as illustrated stationery that emigrants might use for letters to friends and family back home.

Piece of wood from the original sawmill of John A. Sutter.

(Wells Fargo)

Nothing remains today of Sutter's original sawmill at the site of gold discovery in Coloma. Only a few pieces of the structure, such as this scarred fragment, appear to have survived the intervening century and a half.

lands) before voyaging to Alta California on Mexico's northern frontier in 1839. Once there, the gregarious Sutter applied his considerable reserves of charm and persuasiveness to securing a substantial land grant from the administration of Governor Juan Bautista Alvarado.

Having convinced Alvarado that planting a colony in California's interior would create a reliable bulwark against foreign intruders and hostile Indians, Sutter established himself on a large tract encompassing more than forty thousand acres of grasslands in the region of the Sacramento River, at the northern end of California's great Central Valley. Christening his domain "New Helvetia" in honor of his native Switzerland, he erected as his headquarters a large adobe compound soon known universally as "Sutter's Fort" just east of the junction of the Sacramento and American Rivers.

From within its walls, Sutter directed a growing array of agricultural enterprises throughout the 1840s that eventually included fur trapping, wheat farming, fruit growing, and stock raising, producing the raw materials that his workshops turned into leather, flour, brandy, salt beef, and woolen blankets. In doing so, Sutter both harvested the bounty of the existing flora and fauna of the Sacramento Valley and turned large portions of its landscape to new uses by introducing the domesticated crops and beasts familiar to Euro-American civilization. To raise the grapes, shear the sheep, slaughter the cattle, tan the hides, and weave the cloth, however, Sutter had to exploit the human resources of the

Capt. Sutter's account of the first discovery of the Gold.

"I was sitting one afternoon," said the Captain, "just after my siesta, engaged, by-the-bye, in writing a letter to a relation of mine at Lucern, when I was interrupted by Mr. Marshal a gentleman with whom I had frequent business transactions – bursting hurriedly into the room. From the unusual agitation in his manner I imagined that something serious had occurred, and, as we involuntarily do in this part of the world, I at once glanced to see if my rifle was in its proper place. You should know that the mere appearance of Mr. Marshal at that moment in the Fort, was quite enough to surprise me, as he had but two days before left the place to make some alterations in a mill for sawing pine planks, which he had just run up for me, some miles higher up the Americanos. When he had recovered himself a little, he told me that, however great my surprise might be at his unexpected reappearance, it would be much greater when I heard the intelligence he had come to bring me. 'Intelligence,' he added, 'which, if properly profited by, would put both of us in possession of unheard-of wealth — millions and millions of dollars, in fact.' I frankly own, when I heard this that I thought something had touched Marshall's brain, when suddenly all my misgivings were put at an end to by his flinging on the table a handful of scales of pure virgin gold. I was fairly thunderstruck and asked him to explain what all this meant, when he went on to say, that according to my instructions, he had thrown the mill-wheel out of gear, to let the whole body of the water in the dam find a passage through the tail race, which was previously too narrow to allow the water to run of in sufficient quantity, whereby the wheel was prevented from efficiently performing its work. By this alteration the narrow channel was considerably enlarged, and a mass of sand & gravel carried by the force of the torrent. Early in the morning after this took place, Mr. Marshal was walking along the left bank of the stream when he perceived something which he at first took for a piece of opal – a clair transparant stone, very common here – glittering on one of the spots laid bare by the sudden crumbling away of the bank. He paid no attention to this; but while he was giving directions to the workmen, having observed several similar glittering fragments, his curiosity was so far excited, that he stooped down & picked on of them up. 'Do you know,' said Mr. Marshal to me, 'I positively debated within myself two or three times whether I should take the trouble to bend my back to pick up one of the pieces, and had decided on not doing so when further on, another glittering morsel caught my eye – the largest of the pieces now before you. I condescended to pick it up, and to my astonishment found that it was a thin scale of what appears to be pure gold.' He then gathered some twenty or thirty pieces which on examination convinced him that his supposition were right. His first impression was, that this gold had been lost or buried there, by some early Indian tribe – perhaps some of those mysterious inhabitants of the west, of whom we have no account, but who dwelt on this continent centuries ago, and built those cities and temples, the ruins of which are scattered about these solitary wilds. On proceeding, however, to examine the neighbouring soil, he discovered that it was more or less auriferous. This at once decided him. He mounted his horse, and rode down to me as fast as it could carry him with the news.

At the conclusion of Mr. Marshals account, and when I had convinced myself, from the specimens he had brought with him, that it was not exagerated, I felt as much excited as himself. I eagerly inquired if he had shown the gold to the workpeople at the mill and was glad to hear that he had not spoken to a single person about it. We agreed not to mention the circumstance to any one, and arranged to set off early the next day for the mill. On our arrival, just before sundown, we poked the sand about in various places, and before long succeeded in collecting between us more than an ounce of gold, mixed up with a good deal of sand. I stayed at Mr. Marshall's that night, and the next day we proceeded some little distance up the south Fork, and found that gold existed along the whole course, not only in the bed of the main stream, where the had subsided but in every little dried-up creek and ravine. Indeed I think it is more plentiful in these latter places, for I myself, with nothing more than a small knife, picked out from dry gorge, a little way up the mountain, a solid lump of gold with weighed nearly an ounce and a half.

Notwithstanding our precautions not to be observed, as soon we came back to the mill we noticed by the excitement of the working people that we had been dogged about, an to complet our disopointment, one of the indians who had worked at the gold mine in the neighbourhood of La Paz cried out in showing to us some specimens picked up by himself, – Oro! — Oro — Oro !!! –

PORTAIT. OF Mr. MARSHAL, TAKEN FROM NATURE AT THE TIME WHEN HE MADE THE DISCOVERY OF GOLD IN CALIFORNIA

VIEW OF SUTTER'S MILL OR PLACE WHERE THE FIRST GOLD HAS BEEN DISCOVERED

Lith. & Pub. by Britton & Rey San Francisco. Cal.

[Sutter's Saw Mill]
Monday April 16 1849.
The first discovery of gold was in digging this mill race.

William Rich Hutton, pencil and watercolor drawing entitled *Sutter's Saw Mill,* **April 16, 1849**.
(Huntington Library: HM 43214 #90)
William Rich Hutton, an itinerant land surveyor and mapmaker, produced dozens of pencil and watercolor drawings of California scenes during his sojourn there between 1847 and 1853.

region as well, following the models of other contemporary frontier entrepreneurs such as the Hudson's Bay Company in the Pacific Northwest, the Russian-American Company in Alaska, and the rancheros of Mexican California. Sutter assembled large work gangs of Indian laborers from the neighboring Miwok and Nisenan peoples, recruiting hundreds of men and women for seasonal and permanent employment. When possible, he hired workers and paid them with such goods as clothing, blankets, or iron cookware; when he could not recruit enough hands with such inducements, he swept through the surrounding countryside with his private army and dragged reluctant Indians off to work on his lands or in his fort under armed guard. At all times, he stood ready to use force to punish horse thieves and runaways and to forestall open opposition.

Even with an expanding Indian workforce supplying indispensable muscle power, Sutter at first found his dreams of empire hobbled. Desperately short of such artisans as blacksmiths, millwrights, and carpenters who could forge tools, build shops, and train workers, he could make little progress toward ensuring New Helvetia's self-sufficiency. Sutter's dilemma began to ebb, however, as the flow of overland immigration to Mexican California from the United States increased during the 1840s. As more and more emigrant parties passed through New Helvetia after crossing the Sierra Nevada range, such experienced craftsmen as James Marshall found their abilities in demand with Sutter. Often self-described jacks of all trades, Marshall and other men like him tackled many different tasks for Sutter; such versatility made Marshall a logical choice, therefore, to superintend the construction of a sawmill that Sutter planned to guarantee his dominion a supply of finished lumber cut from the forests of the

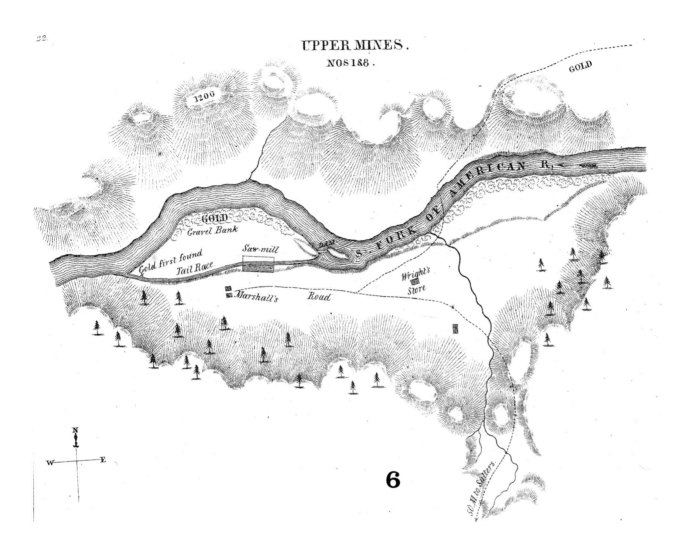

UPPER MINES.
N^OS 1&8.

1200

GOLD

S. FORK OY AMERICAN R.

GOLD
Gravel Bank

Gold first found
Tail Race

Saw-mill

Wright's Store

Marshall's Road

50 M. to Sutters

N
W — E

6

"Upper Mines" and "Lower Mines or Mormon Diggings," in Colonel Richard B. Mason's report on gold in California to the War Department published in *Message from the President of the United States to the Two Houses of Congress … Dec. 5, 1848*, Washington, D.C., 1848.
(Huntington Library: RB 248140)

Colonel Richard B. Mason, American military governor of California, toured the "diggings" in July 1848 and noted with amazement that thousands of miners already were hard at work. His report to the War Department in Washington, D.C., included these maps of the earliest goldfields.

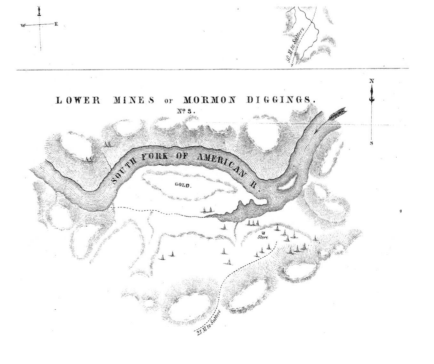

W — E

50 M. to Sutters

LOWER MINES or MORMON DIGGINGS.
N° 3.

N

SOUTH FORK OF AMERICAN R.

GOLD.

Store

S

25 M. to Sutters

HUTCHING'S
CALIFORNIA
SCENES.

THE
CALIFORNIA
INDIANS.

AN INDIAN FANDANGO.

CATCHING GRASSHOPPERS

GATHERING ACORNS,

GATHERING SEEDS.

The California Indians are in stature short, but they are well and stoutly formed. Their features are coarse, broad, and of a dark chocolate color; their hair is black, heavy and matted. In their habits they are unclean, and indolent. Their huts are built of boughs, bark or old canvass, and are smoky, small and dirty. The women do the work, the men the eating, grumbling and sleeping. Their dress consists of any odd and cast-off garments of the whites. Their food is acorns, roots, grasshoppers, weed and flower seeds, grass, clover, wild greens, rabbits, rats, squirrels and fish; but they prefer beef, biscuit and whiskey. The following are their methods of providing for their wants:—

GATHERING ACORNS.—A large cone-shaped basket is carried on the backs of the females, fastened by a band running across their foreheads. The acorns, picked from beneath a tree, are thrown over their shoulders into the basket; they are then dried and stoned, or ground.

DIGGING ROOTS.—This is accomplished by the females and children driving a pointed stick into the ground, and forcing out the roots.

GATHERING SEEDS.—This is done by the females beating them with a bush into a cone-shaped basket.

CATCHING GRASSHOPPERS.—A hole is first dug deep enough to prevent their jumping out, after which a circle is formed of Indians, both old and young, who with a bush beat the insects towards the hole, into which they fall and are taken prisoners. Sometimes the grass and weeds are set on fire, by which they are disabled, and afterwards picked up.

GRINDING ACORNS, &c.—Acorns, berries and flower seeds are reduced to flour, and grasshoppers to paste, by the females pounding them upon a rock with an oblong stone, weighing from six to ten pounds.

COOKING FOOD.—Bowl-shaped and water-tight baskets, holding from two to four pecks, are filled with water, into which flour or meal is stirred; hot rocks are then put into the basket, until the water boils. It is then poured into smaller baskets to cool; when it is about the consistency of paste or mush, and is eaten from the baskets with the fingers. Rabbits, rats, squirrels, &c. are broiled upon a stick, or boiled in the basket until they are cooked. Grasshoppers are gathered into sacks and saturated with salt water; they are then placed in a hot trench and covered with hot rocks for about fifteen minutes, when they are eaten like shrimps; or, after being ground, are mixed with the soup or mush.

FANDANGOES.—These are popular and social gatherings of Indians for dancing, eating, laughing, talking, and learning the traditionary greatness of their noble dead. Any particular tribe, wishing to give a fandango, send messengers to the chiefs of the surrounding tribes, who receive a small bundle of reeds or sticks, which show the number of days before it takes place. Preparations immediately commence upon an extensive scale, by those invited as well as those giving the invitation. Rabbits are snared, grasshoppers and fish are caught; acorns, roots, weed and flower seeds, clover, grass, wild greens and onions are provided in suitable quantities. As each Indian dresses according to his own extravagant notions of paint and feathers, several weeks are sometimes consumed in making head dresses of different colored feathers, nose and ear ornaments, and coat decorations, in every ludicrous variety of style and color. When the day arrives, groups of Indians may be seen wending their way toward the festive scene. In the evening; when all are assembled, the "band"

begins a monotonous "feau, feau," with a reed whistle and wooden castanets—while the dancers keep time by a perpetual "hi hah! hi hah!" until out of breath when they seat themselves to hear from the lips of their greatest chief, or patriarch, the heroic deeds of their warrior ancestors; after which comes the feast. That being over the dancing is renewed, and generally continued until morning, when they finish the remaining eatables and retire to rest under a large tree.

BURNING THE DEAD.—The motive which impels the California Indians to burn their dead, arises from their religious views. They believe in a vast and pleasant camping ground somewhere westward, where Indians live together in perpetual ease and plenty, and which is presided over by a great spirit of unspeakable goodness. They believe also in an evil spirit, who is constantly watching every opportunity to injure them, and who having the power to keep them out of heaven, it is their duty, by conciliation or stratagem, to thwart. They believe, also that the heart is immortal; that while the body is burning the heart leaps out, and if by noises or motions they can attract the evil spirit's attention, the heart escapes to its heaven of rest and is forever safe; but if the body is buried, the evil one keeps continual guard over the grave, and when the heart would escape, it is made prisoner, and is thenceforth employed to annoy their living relatives. When an Indian is known to be dying, his head is lifted gently upon the lap of some relative, and his eyes softly closed; while those who are standing around recite in a low monotonous chaunt the virtues of the dying. The moment his heart has ceased to beat, the sad tidings are conveyed to his relatives, and the low chaunt is changed to mournful wailing, and beating upon their chests, with streaming eyes, they apostrophize the spirit of the departed. The corpse is now prepared for burning, the knees being forced toward the chin upon the breast, and the limbs and body bound firmly together into the smallest possible compass; it is then wrapped in a blanket and placed upon the back on the ground, with the face exposed; every sound is hushed, and both men and women sit in silent groups around the corpse for about twenty minutes, when all simultaneously rise — the women to renew their wailing, the men to build the funeral pyre. When this is about two feet in height, every sound again ceases, and, amid a death-like stillness, the men lift the corpse upon the pyre, after which it is completly covered with additional fire-wood. The oldest and dearest relative then advances with a torch and fires the pile. When the first curl of smoke is visible, the discordant howlings of the women become almost appaling. The men stand in sullen and unbroken silence, while the nearest relatives, having poles in their hands, commence a frantic dance around the burning body, occasionally turning it over that it may consume more speedily, and give the heart a better chance to escape, while, with waving of cloths and hideous noises, they are attracting the attention of the evil one.— Meanwhile all the personal property of the deceased is cast into the fire, his relatives frequently adding their own valuables, even to the scanty garments upon their persons, that he may want nothing in the great camping ground. When the whole is consumed, the ashes are scraped together, and a rude wreath of flowers, weeds and brush is placed around them. A portion of the ashes being mixed with some pitch, is spread over the faces of the relatives, as a badge of mourning, which is allowed to remain till it wears off which is generally about six months.

GRINDING ACORNS, &c.

MODE OF TRAVELING.

BURNING THEIR DEAD.   Excelsior Print.

COOKING FOOD

Sierra foothills. Thus, in August of 1847, Marshall and a crew of laborers set to work at a site on the south fork of the American River, about forty miles east of Sutter's Fort, known to the local Indians as "Coloma." Over the next few months, as work on the mill proceeded, little of note occurred until Marshall's discovery of gold in the winter of 1848. Thereafter, nothing at Coloma would be the same, offering a foretaste of what lay ahead for all of California.

A Society on the Brink: Mexican California before the Gold Rush

As news of Marshall's find circulated, a mania for gold began to spread across California through the winter and spring of 1848. Walter Colton, the United States Navy chaplain who had been elected alcalde of Monterey, later wrote in his 1850 account *Three Years in California* that, as news continued to arrive from the mines on the American Fork through the month of June, "the doubts, which had lingered till now, fled. . . . The excitement produced was intense; and many were soon busy in their hasty preparations for a departure to the mines. . . . All were off for the mines, some on horses, some on carts, and some on crutches, and one went on a litter" (p. 247). As it took root, this growing compulsion for gold accelerated the disruption of Mexican California's established patterns of economic, political, and social relations that had characterized the previous decade and a half. During the 1830s and especially the 1840s, repeated struggles among various factions of the province's upper class for political ascendancy and the volatile nature of Mexican California's economic lifeblood (the commerce in cattle hides and beef tallow) already had thrown many aspects of life for its Hispanic residents (the *Californios*) and the original Californians, the Indian peoples, into tumult. Meanwhile, the increasingly obvious desire of an expansionist United States to acquire California had further undermined the wavering grasp of the Mexican republic upon its distant outpost.

The region known in 1848 as Alta California was itself the legacy of a process begun nearly eighty years earlier in 1769. Driven by worries of possible Russian or British encroachments upon its North American possessions, the Spanish empire established its first permanent presence along the coast of California near present-day San Diego in order to prevent any incursions into its colonies by its European rivals. The agricultural possibilities of the region and the extensive population of native peoples (totaling perhaps three hundred thousand at the time of European contact) seemed to offer great opportunities for colonization on behalf of Spain and missionary work on behalf of the Catholic Church. Located at a great distance, however, from the heart of New Spain, California proved difficult to resupply and generally unattractive to potential settlers. Thus hindered, the colony grew haltingly through the remainder of the eighteenth century and the early decades of the nineteenth, first under the flag of the Spanish monarchy and then, after the overthrow of Spanish colonial rule in 1821, under that of Mexico. By the end of the Spanish era, the number of colonists probably did not reach thirty-five hundred; by 1848, the province's non-Indian population totaled perhaps fourteen thousand.

The ensuing changes in Alta California's governance sparked even greater changes in the economic and social life of the province. Abandoning the prohibitions imposed by Spain upon commerce with foreign countries, for example, Mexico opened California's ports to trade with merchants from Great Britain and the United States. California cowhides and beef tallow soon began to flow across the oceans to factory towns on both sides of the Atlantic in exchange for all kinds of manufactured goods, including shoes made from hides sent in earlier shipments. As a result, communities such as Monterey, Santa Barbara, and San Diego throughout the 1830s and 1840s played host to Britons

The California Indians, letter sheet published by Anthony & Baker.
(Huntington Library: RB 48052 #103)
The gold seekers who swarmed into the foothills of the Sierra Nevada after 1848 encountered not an empty wilderness but a landscape inhabited by thousands of California Indians. As this 1854 letter sheet suggests, many of the argonauts were both fascinated and repelled by Indian cultures.

"Indian Woman Panning Out Gold," engraving in *Hutchings Illustrated California Magazine* 3, no. 10 (April 1859).
(Huntington Library: RB 420)
Many early gold seekers hired crews of Indian laborers to work the deposits for them. Grasping the value that Euro-Americans put upon gold, other Indians began to hunt for it on their own account.

Drawn by Capt. Smyth, R.N.

CALIFORNIAN MODE OF CATCHING CATTLE,
WITH A DISTANT VIEW OF THE MISSION OF ST JOSEPH.

Lith'd by L.M. Lefevre

"Californian Mode of Catching Cattle, with a Distant View of the Mission of St. Joseph," engraving in Alexander Forbes, *California: A History of Upper and Lower California…*, London, 1839.

(Huntington Library: RB 401667)

Long important to the economy of colonial Alta California, cattle raising became its economic lifeblood after Mexico achieved independence from Spain in 1821. Both the missions and the land-owning rancheros who succeeded them found a ready international market for cowhides and tallow.

California Vaqueros, Returned from the Chase, letter sheet published by Anthony & Baker.

(Huntington Library: RB 48052 #188)

California ranchos depended upon work crews adept with horse and lariat to manage the cattle herds. Many of the tools and practices devised by the *vaqueros* would be inherited by the American cowboy in later years.

CALIFORNIA SCENES,
DRAWN FROM LIFE AND ENGRAVED EXPRESSLY FOR "THE PACIFIC."

CALIFORNIA VAQUEROS, RETURNED FROM THE CHASE.

William Rich Hutton, pencil and watercolor drawing entitled *Trying Out Tallow, Monterey,* 1848?

(Huntington Library: HM 43214 #61)

In this watercolor, William Hutton captured an essential part of California's cattle trade. The Indian laborers "try" or melt down the fat of the cattle in cauldrons over open fires to produce the substance known as "tallow" that would be used in products such as candles or soap.

William Rich Hutton, pencil and watercolor drawing entitled *Santa Barbara Mission from the Hill,* 1852.

(Huntington Library: HM 43214 #35)

The twenty-one missions established in Alta California between 1769 and 1821 formed the cornerstone of Spanish colonization. Deprived of their lands and their special status by the Mexican government after 1833, they still exercised a powerful hold on the imagination of many travelers, in this case William Rich Hutton.

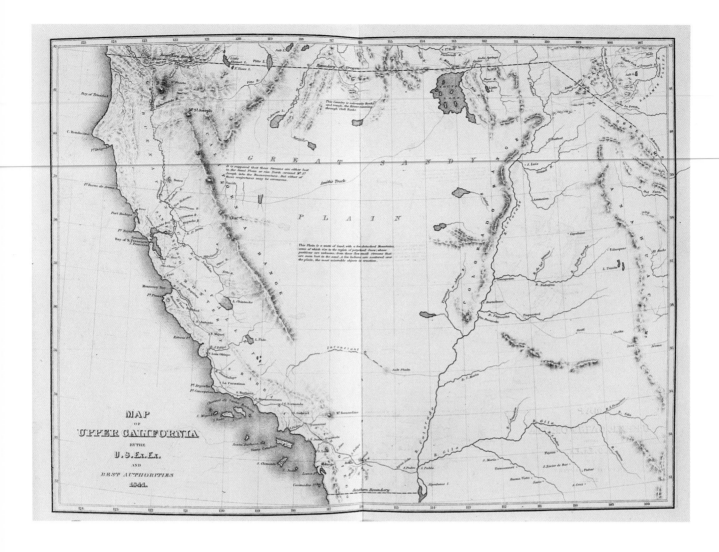

**"Map of Upper California … 1841,"
in Charles Wilkes, *Narrative of the
United States Exploring Expedition,*
vol. 5, Philadelphia, 1845.**

(Huntington Library: RB16211)

Increasing American awareness of and
interest in Alta California during the
early 1840s encouraged various writers
and explorers to probe its geography,
economy, and society. This map of
Upper California, first published in
1845, resulted from an 1841 visit by
Lieutenant Charles Wilkes's United
States Exploring Expedition.

and Americans of various backgrounds and classes, from ordinary seamen and retired ship's
captains to shopkeepers and resident agents for English or American businesses.

For most of those sojourners, very little about Alta California resembled the landscape
or the society back home, wherever that might be. Exotic and intriguing to some, life in
Mexican California evoked disgust and dismay among others. Richard Henry Dana, writing in his celebrated *Two Years before the Mast* (1840) about his service as an able-bodied
seaman in the hide trade, condemned it as a place "at the ends of the earth; on a coast
almost solitary; in a country where there is neither law nor gospel" (p. 112), while characterizing its inhabitants with no less harshness, declaring that "the men are thriftless, proud,
and extravagant and very much given to gaming; and the women have but little education,
and a good deal of beauty, and their morality, of course, is none of the best" and lament-
ing that "in the hands of an enterprising people, what a country this might be! we are
ready to say. Yet how long would a people remain so in such a country?…If the 'California fever' (laziness) spares the first generation, it always attacks the second" (pp.
214–16). Sir George Simpson, a high official of the British Hudson's Bay Company
who toured Alta California in 1842, observed acidly in his 1847 *Narrative of a Voyage round the World* that "sooner will the Ethiopean whiten his skin than the Californian lay aside his indolence" (p. 408). Other foreign visitors, however, found
California and its opportunities sufficiently attractive that they began to settle there.
Although comparatively few in numbers, perhaps three hundred or so in the aggre-

MONTEREY - CAPITOL OF CALIFORNIA.
Published by C. S. Francis & C°. N. York.

Sketched by J. W. Revere U. S. N.   *Lith. of W^m. Endicott & C°. N. York.*

"Monterey—Capitol of California," engraving in Joseph Warren Revere, *A Tour of Duty in California; Including a Description of the Gold Regions,* **New York, 1849.**

(Huntington Library: RB 662)

As the official port of entry for Alta California, Monterey remained the province's commercial hub right up to the time of the Mexican-American War. Merchant vessels from Europe and the United States called there frequently as they plied their trade up and down the coast.

gate, they did begin to play a notable part in the province's economic and social life. Many of them, such as Americans Abel Stearns and Alfred Robinson, English-born Henry Dalton, and Hugo Reid from Scotland, by converting to Catholicism and accepting Mexican citizenship, became eligible to buy property of their own. Their subsequent marriages, often to daughters of prominent local families, only strengthened the significant role they played in provincial affairs

The commercial activities pursued by this first wave of Anglo-American emigrants drew California deeper and deeper into an international marketplace during the 1830s and 1840s, despite the province's continuing physical isolation from Mexico. At the same time, the continued presence of a small but growing population from such far-flung locations as New England and the British Isles created an oddly cosmopolitan core of emigrant merchants and landowners within a relatively insular and provincial society. Many of them watched international affairs quite closely, especially in the 1840s, as they followed the economic expansionism of Great Britain, America's principal rival, and the frequently quarrelsome course of Mexican-American relations.

Thomas O. Larkin, Massachusetts-born merchant who came out to Alta California in 1832, proved a particularly diligent observer of international issues due to his frequent financial dealings with the province's Mexican administration and his appointment in 1844 as American consul in California. Writing on April 18, 1843, to a fellow transplanted American, Abel Stearns, landowner and merchant in the vicinity of Los Angeles, Larkin passed along

William Rich Hutton, pencil drawing entitled *San Francisco (from the Hill Back)*, 1847.

(Huntington Library: HM 43214 #81)

The tiny village of San Francisco contained barely six hundred people when William Rich Hutton sketched it in 1847, although its residents included such prominent California merchants as William A. Leidesdorff.

Lansford W. Hastings, *The Emigrants' Guide to Oregon and California...*, Cincinnati, 1845.

(Huntington Library: RB 1782)

A vocal and energetic advocate of American expansionism, Hastings produced the first substantial guidebook describing the journey across the continent to Oregon and California. His enthusiasm spurred other Americans to join the ranks of emigrants headed west in the 1840s.

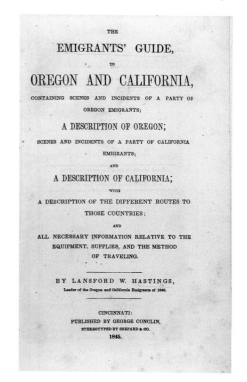

word of English military success in the so-called Opium War against the Chinese empire, noting that they "have faught much in China and succeeded in making a treaty [by which] a new and great trade has opened in China to English goods." "The Yankees," he noted with evident satisfaction, "will of course see to it, as their Interest is concerned." Turning to matters closer to home, Larkin also discussed the unquiet state of Mexican domestic politics and the likely effect of new Mexican tariff legislation upon Alta California's own economic circumstances. Through the exchange of such letters, expatriates such as Larkin, Stearns, Dalton, and others shared information of common interest about the political and economic questions of the day that affected them.

Most of the Anglo-American expatriates had maintained some ties to the mercantile world of the hide and tallow trade, since so many of them had come to California as part of it. As they settled into their new lives on the Pacific Coast, however, many of them also became part of the larger Californio society around them, especially as they began to join the landowning class. Their large grants, known as *ranchos,* gave them a stake in the cattle trade that remained at the heart of the province's economic and social life. The holders of these grants, referred to as *rancheros*, benefited from the dissolution of the great mission tracts decreed by the Mexican government in 1833. Successive provincial governors in Alta California, seeking to court the region's leading citizens, had awarded large grants to friends and potential political allies, bolstering the fortunes of a well-to-do and politically influential landowning class. With vast amounts of acreage now released to private ownership, the hide and tallow trade with British and American merchants mushroomed dramatically through the 1830s and early 1840s. Much of the income generated for the rancheros from this trade went back immediately to those same merchants to pay for the often lavish way of life maintained by the rancheros as the outward sign of their position at the top of Alta California's social hierarchy.

Accompanying the rise of the rancheros in the late 1830s and into the 1840s, relations between the Mexican citizenry and California's Indian peoples grew more complicated. Exposure to unfamiliar European diseases and destruction of many familiar habitats in the course of colonization had already

William Rich Hutton, pencil and watercolor drawing entitled *Los Angeles from the South*, 1848.

(Huntington Library: HM 43214 #27)

As the provincial government continued to transfer mission lands in Alta California to private ownership during the 1830s, a great cattle-raising empire developed around the pueblo of Los Angeles in the southern districts of the province.

had a drastic impact upon the peoples of California's coastal regions. As Spanish sovereignty over California ended in 1821, the total Indian population had fallen by perhaps one-third to two hundred thousand. Now, dissolution of the missions beginning in 1833 had distributed substantial quantities of land to the mission Indians whose lack of familiarity with the buying and selling of property left them ill-equipped to deal successfully with land-hungry Mexican and American rancheros. As a result, large numbers soon were convinced to sell off their lands, often at prices far below market value. Bereft of other resources, many of the former mission Indians, trading upon their skills as ranch hands (*vaqueros*) or artisans acquired while in service at the missions, found employment on the ranchos or in the pueblos.

Given the province's minuscule non-Indian population, the new rancheros depended as thoroughly upon an Indian labor force as had the mission fathers, especially since the proliferation of ranchos ensured that Alta California would remain essentially agricultural in nature. For some of them, Indian labor even became a commodity, used like wheat or cattle or lumber to discharge debts and settle accounts. John Sutter and the San Francisco merchant William A. Leidesdorff frequently traded in laborers as well as other goods, with Sutter noting his regrets in one letter of May 11, 1846, that "it layed not in my power to send you the 10 Indians this time, as I had only a few new hands from the mountains here" but that "in harvest time You can select them while they are all coming here to work."

As the trade in the abundant natural resources of its ranchos pulled California into the global market, it also helped to realign many of the province's economic ties away from its

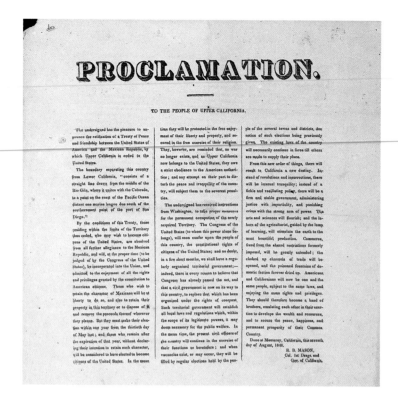

Pio Pico, autograph letter to Thomas O. Larkin, June 29, 1846.
(Huntington Library: HM 37548)
In this scorching protest written to American diplomatic agent Thomas O. Larkin, California Governor Pio Pico denounced the "treacherous" seizure of the town of Sonoma and the "criminal" proclamation of an independent republic two weeks earlier by a band of disgruntled American settlers.

Richard Barnes Mason, broadside entitled *Proclamation. To the People of Upper California,* Monterey? 1848.
(Huntington Library: RB 35682)

When news of the peace treaty between the United States and Mexico reached California in August 1848, military governor Richard B. Mason proclaimed that "a new destiny" was at hand for all its people under a benevolent American regime.

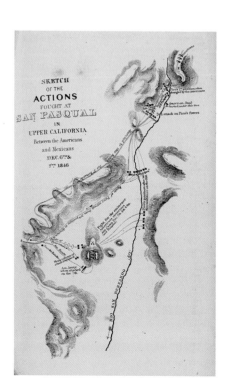

U.S. Army Corps of Topographical Engineers, *Notes of a Military Reconnaissance from Fort Leavenworth..., to San Diego,* Washington, D.C., 1848.
(Huntington Library: RB 195294)
On December 6, 1846, a force of Californio horsemen commanded by Andrés Pico badly mauled General Stephen W. Kearny's Army of the West at San Pasqual near present-day San Diego, inflicting a temporary setback to American military efforts to occupy Alta California.

mother country, the Mexican republic. Unfortunately, distracted by chronic financial and political instability, Mexico proved unable to respond to this challenge, further eroding the Californios' loyalties, which were already strained by the republic's routine neglect of the military and political needs of its northern frontier. As prominent Californios grew more aggressive in demanding a role in guiding the province's destiny, struggles for political power grew more frequent and the political lifespan of provincial governors grew shorter through the 1840s.

Against the backdrop of such bitter internal squabbling, the province's fate also became enmeshed in the imperial ambitions of various foreign powers during that same decade. Although Russian expansion south from their Alaska colony subsided following John Sutter's 1839 purchase of their outpost

Page. 72.

Sketched by J. W. Revere U. S. N.   Lith. of Wm Endicott & Co. N. York.

SUTTER'S FORT – NEW HELVETIA.

Published by C. S. Francis & Co. N. York.

**"Sutter's Fort—New Helvetia,"
engraving in Joseph Warren
Revere, *A Tour of Duty in California;
Including a Description of the Gold
Regions*, New York, 1849.**

(Huntington Library: RB 662)

After the outbreak of war between
Mexico and the United States, John A.
Sutter's trading establishment on the
Sacramento River was commandeered
as an American outpost in July 1846.
Sutter and many of his employees were
enrolled into John C. Frémont's battal-
ion of California volunteers.

at Fort Ross north of San Francisco Bay, both England and France viewed California's abundant natural resources and its strategic position on the Pacific Coast with considerable interest. Many observers would have agreed with Sir George Simpson, who commented that "the
English race, as I have already hinted, is doubtless destined to add this fair and fertile province
to its possessions on this continent…. The only doubt is, whether California is to fall to the
British or the Americans" (*Narrative of a Voyage round the World,* p. 409). Lansford W.
Hastings, author of *The Emigrants' Guide to Oregon and California* (1845), perhaps the first
major guidebook to capitalize on the growing enthusiasm for these two faraway destina-
tions, proclaimed that "there is no country, in the known world, possessing a soil so fertile
and productive…and a climate of mildness, uniformity and salubrity; nor is there a country in my opinion, now known, which is so eminently calculated, by nature herself, in all
respects, to promote the unbounded happiness and prosperity, of civilized and enlightened
man" (p. 133). In the end, however, it would be the undisguised desire of many Americans
for Mexico's northern provinces, including California, that would finally swamp Alta
California's political ties to Mexico.

Throughout the 1840s, this increasing fascination with California propelled a small
but steady parade of American emigrants who came by way of an overland crossing rather
than by sea aboard the merchant ships from the East Coast of the United States. Trickling
illegally into Mexican California across the Sierra Nevada, perhaps six or seven hundred established themselves in the province by 1845. Many settled in the inland valleys, often in the

William P. Reynolds, autograph letter to his brother John Reynolds, December 27, 1848.

(Huntington Library: HM 4157)

As 1848 unfolded, further news of gold discoveries inspired an international frenzy. William Reynolds, writing on December 27, noted that "the long sought for *El Dorado*" had been found, attracting thousands from Mexico and Latin America.

R. V. Sankey, *The Good Time's Come at Last, or the Race to California. A Comic Song Written to a Golden Measure and Dedicated to the Master of the Mint by One of the Golden Fleece*, London, 1849.

(Huntington Library: RB 1221)

This English "comic song," with its satirical title illustration, reflected the obsessive fascination that gold fever exerted upon the popular consciousness in many countries.

vicinity of Sutter's Fort where some of them found work helping Sutter build his New Helvetia dream. Unwilling to abandon their American citizenship or their Protestant faith to become citizens of Catholic Mexico, they nonetheless hungered after land of their own. Dissatisfied with the unfamiliar mechanisms of Mexican law and government, they chafed under what they regarded as "foreign" rule. Some even threw themselves into the province's political upheavals, seeking to obtain political advantage by backing a winning side in one of the frequent Californio revolutions. More than a few, however, fixed their gaze upon American annexation as their permanent salvation, echoing the sentiments of Alfred Robinson, a Boston merchant active in the hide trade who had made his home in California, when he wrote in the conclusion to his book *Life in California* (1846) that "in this age of 'Annexation,' why not extend the 'area of freedom' by the annexation of California? Why not plant the banner of liberty there, in the fortress, at the entrance of the noble, the spacious bay of San Francisco? ... It must come to pass, for the march of emigration is to the West, and naught will arrest its advance but the mighty ocean" (pp. 225–26). Thus, as war between Mexico and the United States seemed ever more likely, these restless newcomers watched for an opening.

By the middle of June 1846, some concluded that their moment had arrived. Although confirmation of a formal declaration of war could not yet be obtained, rumors of hostile encounters between Mexican and American troops in Texas had already been circulating. As the United States Navy's Pacific Squadron under the cautious command of Commodore John Sloat edged closer to opening a war in California, a band of American insurrectionists captured Mariano

Kimball Hale Dimmick, diary entry beginning May 25, 1848.

(Huntington Library: HM 4014)

Gold fever spread all over California during the spring of 1848, infecting nearly all exposed to it. Late in May, United States Army Lieutenant Kimball Dimmick recorded the "tremendous excitement" that swept through the troops in the garrison at San Jose, inspiring mass desertions.

Vallejo, chief military commander in the northern part of the province on June 14. These self-described revolutionaries, although rather unclear as to their final goals, did proclaim a republic in the Northern California community of Sonoma under a banner emblazoned with a California grizzly, forever identifying this event as the "Bear Flag" Revolt. William B. Ide, a recent emigrant from New Hampshire who had taken a prominent role among the opponents of the provincial administration, published a proclamation from his headquarters in Sonoma which asserted that, "oppressed by a military despotism" and "threatened … with extermination," he and his companions had taken up arms to overturn the unnamed despots and establish "a Republican Government" that would "secure to all civil and religious liberty; … encourage virtue and literature; … and leave unshackled by fetters, agriculture, commerce and manufactures."

With Commodore Sloat's bloodless seizure of Alta California's principal ports, the short-lived Bear Flag Revolt evaporated, making way for American occupation of the province. A steady stream of proclamations issued not only by the Bear Flaggers but by Sloat, his successor Commodore Robert F. Stockton, and Californio leaders José Castro and Pío Pico made the initial phase of California's conquest more a war of words than of bullets and bayonets. Renewed Californio resistance brought about a bloodier series of confrontations that finally culminated in the battle of San Pasqual in late December 1846 and the American recapture of Los Angeles in early January 1847. Although another year and more would pass before news of the Mexican-American War's formal conclusion by the treaty of Guadalupe Hidalgo in February 1848 would reach California, American occupation of this Mexican province proceeded uneventfully. Unbeknownst to all parties was the ferment that would be set off in the winter and spring of 1848 as word of the gold strike on the American River circulated through the territory.

Gold Fever "The whole country, from San Francisco to Los Angeles, and from the sea shore to the base of the Sierra Nevadas, resounds with the sordid cry, *'gold,* GOLD, GOLD!' while the field is left half planted, the house half built, and everything neglected but the manufacture of shovels and pickaxes." So saying, the San Francisco-based newspaper the *Californian* sourly announced suspension of further publication on May 29, 1848, for lack of subscribers, proclaiming itself a victim of gold fever. By that date, just four months after Marshall's discovery, hundreds of Californians who suffered from that affliction had already fled toward the Sierra foothills in search of a golden cure. Abandoning homes, jobs, and all their daily routines, they swarmed over the hills, canyons, gullies, and streams surrounding Coloma in pursuit of riches.

As the *Californian* noted in its valedictory issue, the allure of gold proved irresistible and the grasp of gold fever unshakable. In its earliest stages, however, the fever almost seemed to lie dormant in the vicinity of Coloma, confined to those who had been personally exposed to the contagion on January 24. Both Marshall and Sutter, though exhilarated by the discovery, proposed to keep this news confidential for a few more weeks, hoping to see the sawmill and a proposed gristmill to completion. Worried that a sudden influx of gold miners might derail these construction projects and overwhelm any claims they might make on the site, Marshall and Sutter enlisted the cooperation of the members of the work crew with promises of time off to collect gold for themselves. At the same time, in an effort to secure their rights to exploit this find, Marshall and Sutter also negotiated a lease for various uses of the land surrounding Coloma with leaders of the Yalisumni Nisenan, a tribal community with which Sutter had had previous dealings.

Unfortunately for Marshall's and Sutter's plans, too many people already had seen gold from the American River for the discovery to be concealed for very long. Even before Marshall's workmen put the finishing touches on the mill in early March, further details began to fly about by letter and by word of mouth. The refusal of California's military government to sanction their proposed arrangement with the Nisenan only cemented their failure to secure pride of place in exploiting the bonanza. On March 15, the first notice appeared in the *Californian*, reporting that "gold has been found in considerable quantities" in the tailrace of Sutter's mill and observing that "California, no doubt, is rich in mineral wealth" which would offer "great chances here for scientific capitalists." Subsequent commentary bore an ever-more passionate tone as news of the amounts of gold discovered and the relative ease with which it could be dislodged traveled further and further.

By the summer of 1848, various observers concluded that much of California had succumbed to a violent case of gold fever. Across the Pacific, as ships from California brought word of these events along with their cargoes to Hawaii, the *Sandwich Islands News*, in its June 22, 1848, issue, commented with bemusement that "it would appear that the California people are running wild after minerals," that more than five hundred people had already dashed to the diggings, and that every artisan in San Francisco had departed save for a lone blacksmith, "who is constantly employed in making little pickaxes at five to ten dollars each." Other trading vessels carried reports of Marshall's find to the British colony of Hong Kong from which the details spread throughout southern China in the spring and summer of 1848. And in Monterey, Colonel Richard B. Mason, commander of American occupation forces and military governor of California, set out on an expedition to the gold district. With a small party in tow, Mason toured the region of the American River in early July to gauge for himself and for the government the significance of this phenomenon. In the detailed report he composed a month later and forwarded to the War Department in Washington, he noted estimates that as many as four thousand men (half of them Indians) were working the goldfields where they

Casse frères, à St. Gaudens.   à Paris, chez A. Bes et F. Dubreuil, imp. édit. rue Git-le-Coeur, 11.   (Déposé)

TRAVAIL EN CALIFORNIE.

Débarqués sur cette terre privilégiée, tous les travailleurs saisissent leurs instruments et fouillent à l'envi le sol dans tous les sens; ici, les rochers soulevés par la pioche, cèdent la place à des lingots d'or; là sous le racloir s'éparpille ou s'entasse le minerai ; et, chaque jour les mêmes travaux produisent les mêmes fruits, et chaque jour le coffre-fort s'emplit.

L. Scherer, lithograph entitled *Travail en Californie*, Paris, 185-?

(Huntington Library: RB 183903)

Untroubled by their lack of first-hand information, many illustrators in Europe and the United States produced imaginative conceptions of life in El Dorado to feed an insatiable public curiosity. This French lithograph portrayed gold mining as a delicate enterprise carried out under swaying palm trees.

extracted between thirty thousand and fifty thousand dollars of gold per day. Such events, he wrote, had "entirely changed the character of Upper California. Its people, before engaged in cultivating their small patches of ground and guarding their herds of cattle and horses, have all gone to the mines or are on their way thither."

Dispatched to Washington in the charge of one of Colonel Mason's officers, his report (and an accompanying tea chest filled with gold samples) wended its laborious way by land and sea toward the nation's capital. Traveling in less-formal channels, other versions of the news flowed north as far as the Oregon country and south to Mexico through the summer and fall. Stories first published in the San Francisco newspapers, often carried by merchant ships bound out of that port, appeared in Peruvian and Chilean newspapers by early November, confirming rumors that had been floating in Latin American cities for weeks. Other newspaper accounts, carried by ubiquitous American merchantmen, traveled as far as Australia's shores just prior to Christmas 1848, where they aroused an interest in mining the wealth of the New World through commerce as well as through prospecting. Captivated by this news, American settlers from Oregon, Mexicans from the northern province of Sonora, and Peruvian and Chilean adventurers joined the growing tide of migration. Before year's end, perhaps six to eight thousand newcomers had reached California, raising the former Mexican province's population to approximately twenty thousand people. Lieutenant Cave J. Couts, enroute to California with a detachment of the United States Army's Second Dragoons in the autumn of 1848 after service in the Mexican-American War, repeatedly observed the steady flow of gold

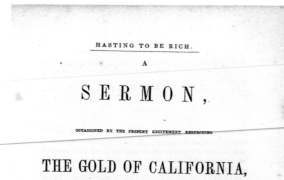

Elisha L. Cleaveland, *Hasting to Be Rich: A Sermon, Occasioned by the Present Excitement Respecting the Gold of California...*, New Haven, 1849.

(Huntington Library: RB 55506)

Despite the overwhelming popular enthusiasm aroused by the news from California, dissenting voices were heard. Many clergymen such as the Reverend Elisha Cleaveland of New Haven, Connecticut, warned that the heedless pursuit of wealth would lead the fortune seeker into iniquity and bring only "sorrows, tears, and blood."

seekers from Mexico. Writing in his diary on December 1, he remarked that "persons, Mexicans, from Sonora, are passing us daily on their way to the abundancia, the gold mines. This is all we can hear, the Mines!" Just over two weeks later, as the column approached Los Angeles, Couts reported that "the mania that pervades the whole country, our camp included, is beyond all description or credibility. The whole state of Sonora is on the move, are passing us in gangs daily, and they say they have not yet started." William Reynolds, writing from San Francisco to his brother John back home in Boston on December 27, 1848, nicely summarized the character of the stampede to California that had unfolded in the eleven months since Marshall's discovery: "Nearly all the Foreigners have left the Sandwich Islands [for California], and thousands are pouring in from all parts of South America, Guatimala and Mexico and when the mail steamers commence running which will be by Feb. next there will no doubt be thousands from the Atlantic States, if they credit it, for it is certainly almost incredible, were it not for the gold to speak for itself."

East of the Mississippi, in the settled reaches of the United States, word of the stupendous discovery in the nation's newest possession penetrated the public consciousness slowly, being dismissed on occasion as "golden exaggerations" created to promote emigration to California. Publication of the first news received about the discovery in the August 19, 1848, issue of the *New York Herald* inspired no frenzy, despite the author's "prophetic vision" that the discovery in California would produce wealth in vast amounts reminiscent of the magnificent treasure captured by the Spanish conquerors of the Aztecs in Mexico and the Incas in Peru three hundred years earlier. Subsequent appearances, however, of letters from other Californians such as Walter Colton and especially Thomas O. Larkin, men of substance holding responsible positions of civic trust, began to arouse considerable interest. On October 15, Archibald Gillespie, formerly an officer with the American forces of occupation, writing from New York to Abel Stearns in Los Angeles, observed that "the public in general are mad about California, & the late news about El placer has made many adventurers look towards that region. But there are very many solid people about to emigrate to California. . . . The emigration next spring overland will be very large, many families have already rendezvous'd upon the frontier."

News from California thus had begun to capture the nation's fancy as 1848 dwindled away. As further details of Colonel Mason's report and his treasure chest began to leak out in late November and early December, however, it became an astonishing national obsession. With the inclusion of Mason's report in President Polk's annual message to Congress on December 5, 1848, the news about California received official validation. "The accounts of the abundance of gold in that territory," the President wrote, "are of such an extraordinary character as would scarcely command belief were they not corroborated by the authentic reports of

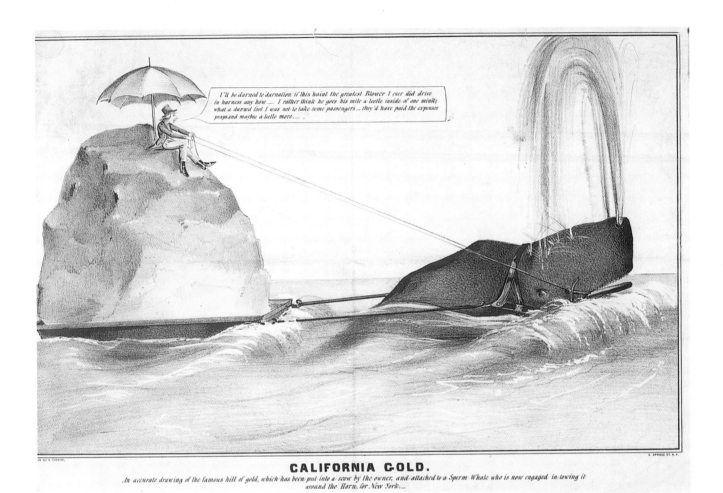

CALIFORNIA GOLD.

An accurate drawing of the famous hill of gold, which has been put into a scow by the owner, and attached to a Sperm Whale who is now engaged in towing it around the Horn, for New York.

N. Currier, lithograph entitled *California Gold*, New York, c. 1850.

(Huntington Library: RB 10285)

The incredible tales of fortunes found in California invited both awe and ridicule. This farcical cartoon portrayed a stereotypically ingenious Yankee hauling his golden reward home from El Dorado.

officers in the public service" (p. 10). Sweeping away the last doubters under a flood tide of enthusiasm, leading newspapers took up the cry only days after publication of the President's message. "The gold fever continues to rage in all sections of our country," reported the *Pennsylvania Inquirer and National Gazette* on December 15, noting further that "if half be true that is told of the gold region of California, the field is indeed a tempting, a glittering one." The *Weekly Yankee* of New York City only two weeks later on December 30 commented that "the new land of Ophir seems to have entirely filled the vision of our people, and naught but the golden harvests to be there reaped, are heard of. . . .Turn where you will, the gold fever appears to rage. The mechanic, the merchant, the sailor, the clerk, the idler, . . . are all hastening to the shores of the Pacific." And in the *Charleston Courier* of South Carolina on January 7, 1849, an editorialist wrote that it must be admitted that "[California's] rich mineral products have produced a state of excitement the like of which the memory of man does not compass. . . .The Almighty Dollar fever is at its height in every section of the country." To any reasonable observer, it was clear that America would enter the new year of 1849 prostrated by the gold malady.

Among the thousands of Americans who fell victim to this powerful affliction, most could envision only one remedy; a pilgrimage for their health to California where they would break the grip of this fever by amassing a fortune. For all but the most ardent gold seekers, however, the complexities of actually leaving home, friends, and family raised troubling questions. Both publicly and privately, many voices spoke out in opposition to the lure of El

FOR CALIFORNIA.—The barque *Maria*, Capt. BAKER, cleared at Boston on Monday for San Francisco, with a large assorted cargo and twenty-two passengers, among whom is Mr. GEORGE H. DAVIS, of Worcester, (Mass.) son of Hon. JOHN DAVIS. The Maria has on board, among other articles, a house, painted, and in complete order for immediate erection on her arrival out.

The fine ship *Edward Everett*, owned by the Boston and California Mining and Trading Company, cleared for the same port on Tuesday. She has one hundred and fifty passengers.

The brig *Forest* also cleared on Tuesday for the same port. She has forty-five passengers, mostly mechanics, of the old Bay State. The F. has a library on board, partly furnished by her owner, and the remainder by the American Home Missionary Society.

We observe from the papers that at Boston some twenty vessels are yet up for the Gold Region, besides as many more at New York, Philadelphia, and Baltimore.

At Charlestown (Va.) there is a company forming for California, which already numbers twenty-five young men.

COLD WEATHER.—At Saco (Me.) on Monday morning the thermometer stood at sixteen degrees below zero.

The Thermometers in these parts are not long enough to show such cold as they have at Saco. But, only yesterday morning at daylight, the thermometer stood as low as 4° above zero, and was not higher during the day in a northern exposure in the open air than 15°.

SUPREME COURT OF THE UNITED STATES.

THURSDAY, JANUARY 11, 1849.

CHARLES S. MOREHEAD, Esq., of Kentucky, and HARRIS W. PATRICK, Esq., of Athens, Pennsylvania, were admitted attorneys and counsellors of this court.

No. 17. Bridget McLaughlin, appellant, vs. the Bank of Potomac. On appeal from the Circuit Court of the United

---

INCIDENTS IN CALIFORNIA.

Extract of a letter from an Officer in the Navy to his friend in Washington, dated

"SAN FRANCISCO, DECEMBER 28.

"You would be surprised that in this region an enthusiasm could be excited by any thing. The gold mines in this neighborhood have stirred up the natives to a galvanic activity. This little village is literally deluged with gold, and common laborers are refusing to work in the mines for a hundred dollars a day. The stories told you will take it for granted must be all fabulous; but were you to see the vast quantities hawked about the streets for sale, you would look upon the tale of the 'Arabian Nights' as quite a probable narrative. There seems to be no exhausting the vein, which is said to extend over a district as large as Virginia.

"To give you some idea of the state of things here, I will mention the prices of a few of the necessaries of life. Flour has been selling at $300 per barrel, pork 70 cents per lb., brandy $60 per gallon, and washing $6 to $8 per dozen, and most other things in proportion.

"The officers are becoming nervous and excited, while the men desert by the dozen.

"Young B., of Baltimore, is hard at work making his fortune, and will return in a year or two a rich man. I saw Dr. M., also of Baltimore, and he is also coining money; he is highly popular and esteemed, and I think is the first man in the place.

"I trust J. will not take it into his head to emigrate. Gold hunting is a most dangerous amusement. The mortality is really frightful among the diggers, and the poor beggarly-looking creatures returning from the mines have no doubt paid dearly for their peck or two of gold."

Dorado, cautioning the prospective emigrant and warning of the moral and practical hazards that lay ahead for the argonauts.

In many communities, opposition coalesced in the columns of local newspapers and in the pulpits of the churches. The New York City newspaper *Sunday Times and Noah's Weekly Messenger,* as it considered the spectacle of gold fever on December 7, 1848, summarized with approval the cautionary words of the *Philadelphia Public Ledger* in a column entitled "A Sober Glance at California." Applauding the *Ledger*'s application of "the test of experience and the standard of common sense to the visions of exhaustless wealth," the *Messenger*'s columnist warned that "we must know more about this golden calf, set up for universal admiration, before we fall down and worship it." Echoing such concerns, the *Presbyterian* in Philadelphia wrote discouragingly of "the Gold Region" on January 6, 1849, forecasting "the dangers to be encountered from the unprincipled and reckless class of men which would be gathered together [and] who have completely given themselves up to one of the most absorbing and fearful passions, the lust of wealth, by which the devil hurries men into every species of wickedness." The Reverend Elisha Cleaveland of New Haven, Connecticut, to drive home his point forcefully, preached a sermon in January 1849 upon the folly of "Hasting to Be Rich," reminding his audiences of the warning in the Book of Proverbs, chapter 28, verse 20, that "a faithful man abounds with blessings; but he that maketh haste to be rich, shall not be innocent." By falling victim to "the excessive love of money," the gold seeker would eventually fall into "unprincipled and vicious conduct" and a "covetousness" that would propel him into "idolatry." Those who pursued instant wealth would give in to "the love of money, … a passion tell to be also highly acceptable to our readers.

INTERESTING FROM CALIFORNIA.

FROM THE CALIFORNIA STAR OF DECEMBER 2.

WINTER IN THE MOUNTAINS.—We are glad to learn that many of our citizens have abandoned the unwise project of wintering in the mountains, and returned, or are preparing to return, to their homes. We are every day more convinced of the error those already encamped in the several mountain diggings have committed, and our fears are for even *life*, in many places, as the forfeit of imprudence. We conversed with a gentleman recently arrived from the mines, and who has pretty accurately calculated the chances favorable to a stay in that region this winter, who is prepared to speak influentially in the matter, and from very fair experience. The prospect is a frosty and a starving one. It does not convey to our understanding one inducement to remain upon the mining ground this winter, or encourage any attempt to dig for gold after the setting in of the rains. The stuff will not be taken in quantity sufficient to render desirable a residence in the mountains during the season, and as for establishing a rightful claim to any particular section by precedence, many may make a grand and glorious *faux pas* in the business, let us observe.

At the "dry digging," where most are located, snow, it is said, falls to the depth of two or three feet. The weather is extremely cold, and the various streams intersecting the mountains become swollen and rendered almost impassable. This will prevent travelling, and we hope no camp in that remote section is destitute of its winter supply of provisions.

LATEST FROM THE MINES.—About 800 souls is it calculated, will winter at the "dry diggings" alone. On Juba and Feather rivers, preparations are being made to pass the winter, by a great number. Houses are constructed and supplies stored, but a scarcity of provisions for the coming season prevails in every camp. At Juba a settlement has been formed near the upper "diggings"—150 houses have been erected, constructed chiefly of logs, and hopes entertained of passing a comfortable winter. Upon the Middle Fork, at the newly-discovered "diggings," the worthy citizens of Drydiggings-*ville* are employed almost to a man, it is said, in mining, and with fair success. The diggers are mostly of the Oregon emigration. From $5 to five ounces per day is the stated yield. The gold is large and extremely beautiful, quite free from sand and pebbles. The usual process of taking it is by throwing up dykes and turning the water from its channel, or draining portions of the river's bed. In the eddies of the main stream it can be seen in great abundance, and at a depth of 25 and 30 feet in many places. At this aggravating distance it is quite harmless. Kanakas have dived with a desperation becoming pearl fishers, but "no go."—the gold yet remains unfingered. Washing for gold has been generally given up for the season. The water is cold, and Jack Frost is regular in his morning visits. As we have before stated, very little gold will be gathered after the commencement of the rains.

SCARCITY OF DWELLINGS.—Houses and shanties are so scarce that an occupant of a ten by twelve, who has the shanty on a lease of $10 per month, was offered $30 per month to move out, by a recent arrival. In consequence of the large number of passengers arriving from abroad by every vessel, we fear that a vast deal of suffering will be experienced by hundreds without shelter, when the rains commence, which must be close at hand. Lumber is scarce, and at the enormous price of $125 per 1,000 feet, while quantities are lying ready for shipment at all the Embacaderas on this bay, at Bodega and Santa Cruz, to say nothing of the abundant supplies we might obtain from Columbia river and Sitka, if we had the vessels. Our citizens hope to obtain some relief from Com. Jones, by his throwing open the coasting trade of Oregon and California *temporarily* to foreign flags, and thereby enabling them to obtain articles of first-rate necessity—lumber and provisions—at moderate cost.

MARRIAGE.

**"Interesting from California,"
in the *National Intelligencer*,
Washington, D.C., March 8, 1849.**
(Huntington Library: RB 111337)

To satisfy the appetite of their readers for anything related to the land of gold, many American newspapers also exchanged articles with their California counterparts, making columns headlined "Interesting from California" or "Latest from the Mines" regular features.

of amazing strength [that] sweeps away the barriers of truth and morality...and hurries on its subject through a career of detestable fraud, ending, not seldom, in open and infamous crime" (pp. 7–8). The Reverend Edward Beecher of Boston, preaching a sermon on January 25, 1849, to the members of the New England and California Trading and Mining Association just before their departure, condemned the "inordinate desire to obtain any kind of earthly wealth," warning against such excitements "that destroy the balance of the mind, the power of sober forethought, sagacious calculation, and enlarged views." In his text, reprinted in the *Boston Daily Times* of January 29, he urged the voyagers to "take at least as great pains to secure the eternal treasures of heaven" unsullied by any "base alloy of avarice, selfishness, luxury and vice."

During the winter of 1848/49, in thousands of homes all over the United States, these same arguments and others were taken up and deployed by anxious wives, siblings, parents, and acquaintances to convince prospective emigrants to abandon their ambitions. Warnings about the dangers to life and limb as well as the temptations of wickedness that awaited the gold miners so far from home rang in their ears. Families debated who would care for aged or infirm mothers and fathers, who would take responsibility for the management of farms and small businesses left unattended, and how the costs of the journey would be defrayed. Before coming to a resolution, angry words might be exchanged and tears shed. In the end, though, overcoming all obstacles and wearing down all resistance, they made the decision by the thousands to set off for the land of gold.

Before their departure, many of the gold seekers felt compelled to justify their choice yet again, whether to themselves or to others, in the diaries, journals, and letters that chronicled their travels. Some, like Francis Clark, a physician bound for California with an emigrant company aboard the ship *York*, chose to emphasize the adventure that lay before them. Writing to his aunt Abigail Wells on March 14, 1849, the eve of sailing, he admitted, "You will ask why I go at all....The people of Wells are very friendly to me and my prospect was encouraging. Still it was a hard one. I am in the prime of life, have no family & here is a chance for Enterprise and it seems right to embrace it." Dr. Thomas L. Megquier of Winthrop, Maine, while acknowledging the allure of fortune for others, professed that more modest goals commanded his attention. In a letter to family friend Milton Benjamin on February 21, 1849, Megquier asserted that "the having of gold there, does not excite me in the least, I was, & still am, determined If I live, to get some money & a competency. I do it for my families' sake. If I die in the cause it cannot be said that I did not try." Daniel Robinson, writing to family back east on March 12, 1849, as he prepared for the transcontinental journey, reflected the kind of optimism that led most of the argonauts to think quite well of their prospects: "I have not the slightest doubt in my mind that any young man of steady habits may go to California and tend strictly to his interests cannot fail to become rich." And, of course, there were many like Edward Gould Buffum, a member of Colonel Jonathan D. Stevenson's New York Regiment of Volunteers stationed in California during the Mexican-American War, who, upon his discharge from the army in 1848, took up the prospector's pick and pan in search of nothing but treasure. Describing his career as a gold seeker in *Six Months in the Gold Mines* (1850), Buffum wrote that "the stories from the mines breathed the spirit of the Arabian tales, and visions of 'big lumps' floated before our eyes" (p. 17). Whatever their specific motive, however, many adopted for themselves a name harkening back to the mythology of ancient Greece, as one song of the period put it: "Like Argos of the ancient times, / I'll leave this modern Greece: / I'm bound to California mines, / To find the Golden Fleece." Emulating the hero Jason and his crew, the modern "argonauts" prepared for their great quest.

II | Days of '49

Planning the Trek to El Dorado

For most argonauts, of course, no matter how fiercely the gold mania burned within them, setting out at once for El Dorado was simply impossible. All across the American continent, from the passes of the Sierra Nevada to the country roads of the Midwest and Northeast, winter weather in January 1849 had closed down most of the feasible overland routes to California. Along the Atlantic coast, ice-blocked harbors hampered the organization of seaborne ventures. While a few parties from the southern-most states began their trek by land or sea just before or after the New Year, nearly all emigrants faced an unavoidable delay, during which they began planning their expeditions.

Confronted by a journey into the unknown of staggering proportions, many would-be gold seekers immediately cast about for sources of reliable information outlining the means of travel available and the actions that would be required to reap their fortunes once they reached California. Recognizing an attractive market when they saw one, many editors and publishers stepped forward into the breach. Rushing their words into print as quickly as possible, they unleashed a torrent of newspaper articles, travel accounts, and guidebooks that the argonauts devoured in huge quantities. Following the appearance of a handful late in 1848, many more publications poured forth throughout 1849 from presses in the United States, England, France, Germany, and beyond.

This copious literature, as it flourished in the months after President Polk's confirmation of gold discovery, derived from many different sources, though nearly all of it shared certain common purposes. Especially in the final months of 1848 and the beginning of 1849, before many firsthand accounts had surfaced from the gold country, literary entrepreneurs set to work with scissors, paste, and stacks of previously published volumes. Brief pamphlets such as Ely Sherwood's *California: And the Way to Get There* (1848) or George Foster's *The Gold Regions of California* (1848) routinely reproduced lengthy excerpts from the official letters and reports of Colonel Mason, Thomas O. Larkin, William H. Emory, and John C. Frémont, while others, such as Henry Simpson's *The Emigrant's Guide to the Gold Mines* (1848), wove together passages from the observations of travelers like Edwin Bryant in his book *What I Saw in California* (1848). From other publishers came reprintings of Bryant's work and other popular narratives of western travel, including those by Frémont and Thomas J. Farnham (author of the 1844 volume *Travels in California*), sometimes expanded with selections from government documents, maps of the gold country or the overland trails, or illustrations of scenes from the western regions. The resulting "new" versions, such as the "pictorial edition" of Farnham's book, retitled *Life, Adventures, and Travels in California* (1849), were also offered up to meet the clamor of prospective argonauts for facts, figures, and directions.

Overseas, similar demands, rising in intensity as 1849 wore on, were met with similar

< Detail from "Chagres River," lithograph in Frank Marryat, *Mountains and Molehills, or, Recollections of a Burnt Journal,* London, 1885.

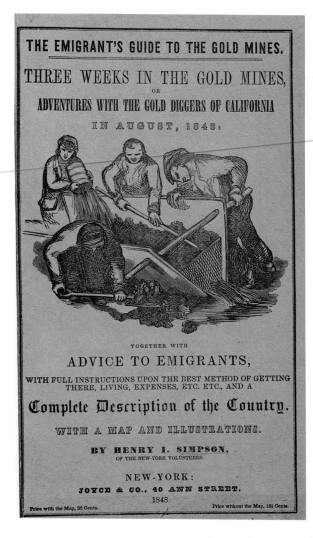

THE EMIGRANT'S GUIDE TO THE GOLD MINES.

THREE WEEKS IN THE GOLD MINES,
OR
ADVENTURES WITH THE GOLD DIGGERS OF CALIFORNIA
IN AUGUST, 1848:

TOGETHER WITH

ADVICE TO EMIGRANTS,

WITH FULL INSTRUCTIONS UPON THE BEST METHOD OF GETTING
THERE, LIVING, EXPENSES, ETC. ETC., AND A

Complete Description of the Country.

WITH A MAP AND ILLUSTRATIONS.

BY HENRY I. SIMPSON,
OF THE NEW-YORK VOLUNTEERS.

NEW-YORK:
JOYCE & CO., 40 ANN STREET.
1848.

Price with the Map, 25 Cents.   Price without the Map, 12½ Cents.

Henry I. Simpson, *The Emigrant's Guide to the Gold Mines,* New York, 1848.

(Huntington Library: RB 2598)

With gold fever circling the globe, a great demand arose for reliable information about the routes to California and about mining techniques. The first guidebooks, such as this 1848 pamphlet attributed to Henry Simpson, often contained little more than excerpts from previously published newspaper articles and government reports.

measures. Publishers eager to tap into the ready audience for Gold Rush treatises commissioned translations of current titles and compiled extracts from United States government documents while waiting for the first English, French, or German voyagers to produce their observations of travel to and life in California's mining camps. Even as Bryant's *What I Saw in California* went through seven American editions by 1850, enterprising publishers in England, France, Holland, Belgium, Sweden, and Australia brought out edited versions as well during the same two years. While the works of few other individuals achieved such popularity as a source about conditions in California, many European publishers, like their American counterparts, freely reproduced in part or in whole Colonel Mason's report of his expedition to the goldfields as well as selected examples of correspondence from other representatives of the American government on the Pacific Coast. Guides such as Bruno Schmölder's *Neuer praktischer Wegweiser für Aswanderer nach Nord-Amerika* (Mainz, 1848) and its 1850 English translation, *The Emigrant's Guide to California,* Charles Bouchacourt's *Notice industrielle sur la Californie* (Paris, 1849), and even the Russian G. K. Blok's *Kratkoe geografichesko-statistichesko opisanie Kalifornii* (Saint Petersburg, 1850) might quote liberally from or at least rely heavily upon the writings of Mason and Larkin and even Frémont's celebrated 1845 report of his travels across the continent. No doubt the publishers, like their American colleagues, believed that the official status of such documents would lend the guidebooks and travel accounts in which they were published an extra degree of credence that would boost sales. The competition for commercially attractive texts grew sufficiently intense that some titles, such as Foster's *The Gold Regions of California* or Schmölder's *Neuer praktischer Wegweiser,* might appear in various foreign versions having been translated, edited, and sometimes even pirated with the original authors left unacknowledged.

Only months after Marshall's discovery, would-be emigrants throughout much of the world thus had access to a considerable body of literature about every aspect of life in California, including its golden riches. So compelling a topic did California remain that a steady stream of titles added to this literature year after year, continuing well into the 1850s. For those argonauts too impatient or anxious to wait for the publishing world, however, most could find great doses of California dispatches in the newspapers of the day. Especially in America, from small-town weeklies to the great metropolitan dailies, newspapers in the winter of 1848/49 blanketed their readers with stories from El Dorado.

Like their counterparts in the publishing houses, the press in the first months of the great excitement gathered in and reproduced every official text to give the greatest credibility possible to the incredible accounts appearing in their newspapers. Needing to meet a daily or weekly deadline, however, they also collected every available scrap of information from the widest possible range of sources. Struggling to feed the undiminished appetite of their readers for news about the gold country, they picked up articles from other newspapers at home or abroad, printed the anecdotes of sea captains returned from voyages to the Pacific Coast, and editorialized about the likely impact of the gold mania upon the economic, political, moral, and spiritual health of the gold seeker and the American republic as a whole.

Prospective emigrants who turned to their newspapers for facts and advice in preparing for their great adventure found much to absorb as the winter months of 1849 ebbed away. Many of the papers filled their columns with stories from emigrants on their way to the gold-

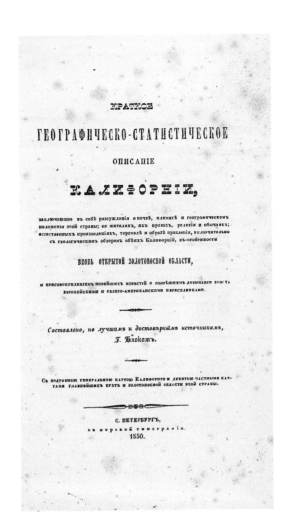

G. K. Blok, *Kratkoe geografichesko-statistichesko opisanie Kalifornii*, Saint Petersburg, 1850.

(Huntington Library: RB 880)
The allure of California caught hold everywhere, prompting the Russian government to produce this short geographical and statistical survey of California in 1850.

***Colección de artículos, noticias I capítulos de carta con respecto a California...*, Santiago, 1849.**

(Huntington Library: RB35621)
Newspapers in such Latin American nations as Chile and Peru voraciously consumed articles about gold fever from periodicals in California. Translated into Spanish and republished for South American audiences, compilations such as this Chilean pamphlet stoked the excitement in those countries.

fields and from those who were already hard at work digging for their golden reward. Gold fever even spilled into other corners of many papers, as every merchant and manufacturer under the sun tried to find some way of associating his products with the California obsession. Side by side with notices advertising passage to the golden shores of California by steamer or sailing vessel were others offering "Fever and ague and disinfecting liquid," "India Rubber Outfits," or "preserved meats...not equalled in the country...which we guaranty to be as sweet and nutricious as any freshly cooked meats that can be produced." Advertisers trumpeted everything from lessons in Spanish to "camp hampers" filled with pots, pans, and plates, from six-barreled Allen pistols and rubber tents to watertight "California" bags and portable houses made out of galvanized iron. Californians-to-be were urged to buy maps and charts, canteens and Bowie knives, shirts and socks, and boots and holsters while being reminded to ensure that friends and families would not forget them by having a daguerreotype photograph taken before their departure. And for those who chose to stay behind, new business opportunities could be had in purchasing the inventories of shopkeepers who, in the throes of gold fever themselves, joined in the cry, "Ho for California!" Some cagey retailers, blessed with a sharp sense of humor and an eye to the unmistakable allure of the word "California" in any setting, made light of the frenzy by reminding readers that "the excitement at the Decatur Clothing Mart...was intense beyond all description. The Gold Fever was up to the highest pitch, and well it might be, for the bargains in Clothing that were being sold to the crowd of customers, were truly astonishing" or that "we, who are friends to the public health and public

WHAT I SAW IN CALIFORNIA:

BEING THE

JOURNAL OF A TOUR,

BY THE EMIGRANT ROUTE AND SOUTH PASS OF THE ROCKY MOUN-
TAINS, ACROSS THE CONTINENT OF NORTH AMERICA, THE
GREAT DESERT BASIN, AND THROUGH CALIFORNIA,

IN THE YEARS 1846, 1847.

"ALL WHICH I SAW, AND PART OF WHICH I WAS."—*Dryden.*

BY EDWIN BRYANT,
LATE ALCALDE OF ST. FRANCISCO.

NEW YORK:
D. APPLETON & COMPANY, 200 BROADWAY.
PHILADELPHIA:
GEO. S. APPLETON, 148 CHESNUT-STREET.
M DCCC XLVIII.

Carl Meyer, *Nach dem Sacramento*, Aarau, Switzerland, 1855.

(Huntington Library: RB 931)

Artists commissioned to illustrate various guidebooks often exercised the same creative license as lithographers and engravers. The cover of Meyer's primer to the gold country emphasized the exotic peoples and places that the argonaut would encounter.

Edwin Bryant, *What I Saw in California...*, New York, 1848.

(Huntington Library: RB 32838)

Although written about an 1846 transcontinental expedition, Bryant's informative and well-written account achieved great success after the discovery of gold, running through many editions in America, England, and Europe as well as numerous pirated versions.

good, would therefore respectfully recommend, that every emigrant should supply himself with WRIGHT's INDIAN VEGETABLE PILLS."

As the public fascination with California in the United States, Europe, and elsewhere persisted into the 1850s, articles about El Dorado remained a staple of the popular press just as publication of new guides to California and new accounts by returning travelers continued unabated. The relationship of quality to quantity in this rapidly expanding literature, unfortunately, proved an elusive one. By dashing many books or articles into print to satisfy that curiosity, various editors, authors, and publishers grasped the opportunities presented by the marketplace but distributed a good deal of intelligence and guidance that ultimately proved of questionable accuracy or reliability. Whatever their failings, however, many of these writings radiated with the glow of golden visions held fast by the authors. Some were simple and straightforward, such as the sentiment expressed in Simpson's *The Emigrant's Guide to the Gold Mines*, cast in the form of a letter, which the writer concluded by urging his friend back home to "come out and gather a fortune. I have already thirty thousand dollars, and intend, God willing, to come home with what will do me for life, and enable me to live like a Nabob" (p. 39). Others, like the journalist writing in the *New York Herald* during December 1848, already could foresee far broader consequences, imagining that "the western portion of our territory will, in a few years, rival the Atlantic coast in opulence, in population, [and] the extent of its commerce," due entirely to the "gigantic mineral discoveries" in California.

"California. Medicines Suitable for California," in the *Boston Shipping List,* May 2, 1849.
(Huntington Library: RB 54472)

"California! Mexican Saddles" and "Blunt's New Chart of California," in the *Boston Shipping List,* May 2, 1849.
(Huntington Library: RB 54472)

With thousands of people preparing to depart for California in the winter and spring of 1849, merchants in cities and towns in every part of the United States advertised a staggering variety of goods, either for personal use or for speculation in "the California market."

Whether haunted by the tantalizing dream of uncovering a personal fortune or dazzled by the image of an American empire on the Pacific Coast, the authors of these newspaper stories, guidebooks, and travelers' sagas reflected the excitement and amazement already felt by many Americans and stimulated similar feelings in thousands more around the globe. For those individuals inclined to chase their dreams, this wealth of written accounts also served as the fount of wisdom from which they drew up plans for their own expeditions to El Dorado. A flourishing trade grew up in guidebooks and travel accounts that focused specifically upon the *journey* to California. To enlighten the inexperienced traveler, many of these works included details about everything from packing the proper supplies for a six-month journey to selecting successful gold-finding machinery. First and foremost, though, many discussed the merits or deficiencies of one or more of the principal routes to the realms of gold. Among the argonauts, once they had made the decision to head for California, no other choice would be more troublesome than that of choosing a particular path to riches.

The Great Migration

Of course, for some travelers, practical considerations intervened to limit the range of their choices in such matters. Frenchmen, Chileans, Australians, and Chinese among others had no option other than to entrust themselves to the maritime passenger trade that sprang up during 1849 and especially 1850 between their ports and San Francisco. Americans suffering from gold fever, by contrast, could select from a great variety of routes, each with its specific advantages and drawbacks. Some of these journeys might pass entirely by sea, some might be

CALIFORNIA OUTFITS,

Very desirable and well adapted for all persons going to California, Gold Diggers, Traders, Exploring Parties, &c., at low prices.

THE BOSTON BELTING Co.,
No. 1 Morton Block, Milk st.,

Are now prepared to offer a large and complete assortment of

PATENT METALLIC,
—OR—
Vulcanized Rubber Goods,

Of all the Different Varieties,

And made expressly to stand the climate of California, being entirely unaffected by heat or cold, and perfectly adapted to meet the wants of Gold Diggers, Exploring Parties, Traders, emigrants, and all others going to that *El Dorado.*

AMONG THEIR ARTICLES ARE

PORTABLE BOATS, WHITE RUBBER TENTS, AIR BEDS,

Tent Carpets,	Money Purses,
Camp Blankets,	Saddle Bags,
Air Mattresses,	Pails, Buckets,
Air Pillows & Cushions,	Life Spars,
Provision Bags,	Wading Boots,
Water Bottles,	Wading Pants,
Gold Pouches,	Gun Cases,
Drinking Cups,	Coats, Cloaks,
Life Preservers,	Ponchos, Pants,
Floats, Canteens,	Leggins, Wallets,
Knapsacks,	Gloves, long or short,
Clothing Bags,	Mittens, Overalls,
Haversacks,	Pants with Boots,
Tarpaulins,	Figured Carpets,
Sou'westers,	Horse Covers,
Caps with Capes,	&c., &c.

All of which being manufactured of the Metallic Rubber, are *Warranted* not to decompose.
mh22—3m

——A Printed List (for patrons of this establishment) of necessary articles, required for six months, one, two, or three years' Outfit, together with prospectus explanatory of various routes, can be had by post-paid application, addressed to "Oak Hall."——When a large company or club desire it, one of my Travelling Agents will be despatched to their orders.——Together with the above, we have an extensive stock of every grade of Clothing, adapted to those who have not caught the "Gold Fever," and prefer to remain at home.

RECAPITULATION OF ABOVE ARTICLES,
WITH PRICES ATTACHED.

Spanish or California Cloaks, for double purpose, Blankets or Cloaks	6 50 to 15 00
"Feather River" Mining Coats,	5 50 to 12 00
Capt. Sutter's Long 'Mining Waistcoats,	3 00 to 3 50
Linen sacks, or Thin Coats -	75 to 1 25
Thin Pants, adapted to that climate,	50 to 2 00
Vests, of various patterns, -	50 to 1 50
Oil suits, adapted to the voyage out, and the rainy season	1 75 to 3 25
India Rubber Coats or Capes,	6 00 to 8 00
India Rubber Pants,	3 00 to 3 50
India Rubber Life Preservers,	50 to 1 00
Isthmus Bags for Pack Mules,	1 75 to 2 25
Canteens, for drink, -	25 to 1 00
Travelling Bags, -	1 00 to 2 00
Gold bags, -	50 to 1 00
Tents of various patterns, (one can be seen pitched at Oak Hall Rotunda,)	8 00 to 40 00
Hemp Hammocks, for slinging in the open air -	1 75 to 2 00
Mattresses, -	1 00 to 2 50
Blankets, -	1 00 to 2 50
Musquito Bars, for protection from various insects that infest the mineral region,	
Fancy striped Travelling shirts,	50 to 2 75
Red Flannel shirts, Drawers, &c.	75 to 1 25
Blue Flannel shirts, -	1 25 to 1 50
Cravats or stocks, -	17 to 1 00
Pocket Handkerchiefs, -	25 to 75
Fine shirts with Linen Bosoms, Collars and Wristbands, -	75 to 1 50
California Caps -	25 to 1 00
Tampico Hats, -	75 to 1 00
Pocket Knives, -	17 to 1 50
Bowie Knives, with Belts for Pistols complete, -	5 00 to 6 00
Dirks, or Large Knives, -	50 to 1 50
Belt, sheath, and Knife, complete,	37 to 75
Tin Cup, Plate, spoon, &c., all for	50
Pistols, Revolvers, &c., -	3 00 to 12 00
Travelling Trunks, -	2 00 to 3 50
Travelling Bags, (very handy in travelling to the mines from San Francisco) -	1 00 to 1 50
Umbrellas for the rainy season,	37 1-2 to 1 50
Clothes, Hair, and shoe Brushes,	17 to 50
Fancy soaps, per cake, -	3 to 12 1-2
Pocket Combs, Pocket Mirrors, &c.,	3 to 25
Specie Belts, -	50 to 1 50
Socks of Woolen, Cotton, Linen, &c,	12 1-2 to 50

SMITH'S
California Gold Washer.

PATENT APPLIED FOR.

THIS machine has been examined by gentlemen familiar with washing out gold from the soil, and is pronounced by them to possess decided advantages over any that has yet been produced.—The subscribers, who are agents for the inventor, will be happy to show and explain its operation to any one interested. There may be found at their warehouse a full assortment of MINING TOOLS, necessary to complete an outfit.

PARKER & WHITE,
No. 10 Gerrish Block, Blackstone street.
mh22-tf

For California!

FOR SALE, a large assortment of Shovels, Spades, Hoes, Ploughs, Mining Picks, California Barrow, and other agricultural impliments; Seeds of all kinds; Cambooses and Cooking Stoves, suitable for vessels, families, or the California market, which we offer in large or small quantities, and at extremely low prices.

PROUTY & MEARS,
19 *and* 20 *North Market Street, Boston.*
mh22-3m

CALIFORNIA PASSPORTS
AND CERTIFICATES OF NATURALIZATION,
CAN BE OBTAINED AT THE OFFICE OF
THOMAS ROWEAN,
No. 47 FEDERAL STREET, NEARLY OPPOSITE WILLIAM STREET

THE subscriber having had nine years experience in this line, is confident he can give entire satisfaction, and on more reasonable terms than can be obtained elsewhere.
THOMAS ROWEAN.
Boston, March 22, 1849.   tf

California Bedding
AT MANNING, GLOVER & Co's,
No. 1 Faneuil Hall, *and* No. 2 Market Square,
(OPPOSITE QUINCY MARKET,) - - - - BOSTON.
Please call and examine our goods before purchasing elsewhere.   mh22-tf

---

"California Outfits," in the *California Bulletin,* Boston, April 5, 1849.
(Huntington Library: RB 54464)

"Smith's California Gold Washer," in the *California Bulletin,* Boston, April 5, 1849.
(Huntington Library: RB 54464)
Outfitters and manufacturers set up a great clamor in the columns of newspapers everywhere, encouraging prospective argonauts to equip themselves with everything from air mattresses and mittens to "goldwashing" devices.

made solely over land, and some might combine aspects of both. All required a high tolerance for hardship, tedium, and a certain amount of danger.

To many Americans, especially those from the nation's traditional maritime heartland such as New England and the Middle Atlantic states, a sea voyage seemed like the obvious choice. That voyage, whether begun in a major port like New York or Boston or in a fishing village like Nantucket or Newburyport, spanned a distance of more than thirteen thousand miles. Bearing south into the heart of the Atlantic Ocean, vessels carrying the argonauts traveled along the eastern coast of Latin America until they finally reached the southernmost tip of the continent at Cape Horn. After safely navigating the treacherous channels and ferocious storms that often marked the passage around the Horn, they emerged into the Pacific Ocean to start the even longer leg of the voyage north to California. At the voyage's end, following a trip that might last as long as six months or more, those ships would finally pass through the Golden Gate at the mouth of San Francisco Bay to the port of the same name, where their eager passengers would disembark to continue the trek to the goldfields.

Although a few dozen ships had set out for San Francisco in the autumn and winter of 1848 from ports along the eastern seaboard of the United States, President Polk's December 1848 message clearly inspired shipowners as well as argonauts. During the next two years, at the height of the rush to California, a veritable armada of perhaps fourteen hundred vessels departed from scores of harbors in the United States and Canada alone. Individual argonauts and organized contingents of gold seekers, responding to announcements of imminent sailings,

"Important to Those Going to California," in the *National Intelligencer,* Washington, D.C., January 2, 1849.
(Huntington Library: RB 111337)

"The Gold Seeker's Manual," in the *National Intelligencer,* Washington, D.C., March 15, 1849.
(Huntington Library: RB 111337)

"California Goods," in the *National Intelligencer,* Washington, D.C., March 17, 1849.
(Huntington Library: RB 111337)

Gold seekers uncertain about solving the mysteries of finding hidden treasure or worried about the dangers of far-off California could turn to advertisers offering them "practical and instructive" guides, machinery constructed on the finest principles, and sufficient firepower to defeat any adversary.

often flocked to owners or to booking agents, pressing to purchase passage of any kind to California. Some companies of emigrants, having agreed to pool their resources, their abilities, and their labor for their mutual benefit in traveling to and then exploiting California's riches, even chartered an entire craft for the use of their members only. Whatever arrangements they made for the voyage, seagoing emigrants found it an expensive proposition; the price of individual passages might run between five hundred and a thousand dollars as demand escalated, while the cost of memberships in emigrant companies might reach three or four or five hundred dollars per head. Nonetheless, by one reliable estimate, as many as sixteen thousand emigrants reached California by the Cape Horn route in 1849 and nearly twelve thousand more followed in 1850.

Once launched upon their seafaring excursion, those individuals shipping out for California soon realized that they had stepped into an alien world, isolated, self-contained, and extending no more than a few hundred feet in any direction. From the moment they first came on board, they encountered a veritable wilderness of halyards, capstans, fo'c'sles, jib booms, and mizzenmasts whose names and functions were utterly incomprehensible to the uninitiated. Prey to everything from seasickness to being shipwrecked and lost at sea, travelers discovered that this world was fraught with dangers great and small.

In between moments of great anxiety, however, stretched hours, days, and weeks of rarely interrupted tedium. Once acclimated to the regular motions of sea and ship, the passengers were able to take a livelier interest in their surroundings, from the marine life in the ocean

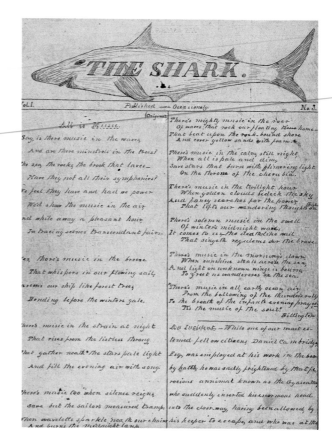

John E. Grambart, journal of a voyage on the brig _Cordelia_, May 2, 1849.
(Huntington Library: HM 17013)
Gold seekers from Europe, Latin America, and Australia traveled to California by sea as did many American argonauts. Hundreds recorded episodes in the seafarer's life, such as John Grambart's experiment with saltwater clothes washing aboard the _Cordelia_ in May 1849.

"The Shark," a handwritten newspaper produced aboard the ship _Duxbury_, August 4, 1849.
(Huntington Library: HM 234)
Argonauts sailing for California might spend eight months at sea before arriving in San Francisco. As one diversion, some ship's companies produced handwritten "newspapers" filled with jokes, cartoons, poetry, and satire, like "The Shark" and "The Petrel" issued to passengers aboard the _Duxbury_ during her 1849 voyage.

around them or the interplay of winds and currents to the arts of navigation and seamanship. Bearing none of the duties or responsibilities that fell to the officers and crew, they could spend hour after hour engaged in learning about such things. Eventually, as shipboard life settled into certain unvarying routines, the novelty of it wore off, leaving the landsmen in search of other distractions to pass the weeks of monotony. For some, the obligatory idleness, combined with the restlessness of their own dispositions, bred frustration that might be directed at anything and everything: the quality and quantity of the provisions or the accommodations; the temperament of captain and crew; or the character and behavior of their fellow passengers. Confronted by the often autocratic disposition of many ship's captains and the miserly investments made by many shipowners for the care and feeding of their customers, some passengers did not hesitate to air their complaints loudly and repeatedly. Writing in his journal aboard the ship _California Packet_ in June of 1850, Lewis Sanger recorded one such episode, provoked by the single-most common cause of distress—dissatisfaction with the ship's supplies of food and drink: "The scene on board to day has been anything but pleasant[.] [I]n every corner you may see three or four passengers cursing and swearing in wild accents against the Steward and his unpalatable preparations which he is pleased to call food. The fault is in him for not having cooked such provisions as are fit to be eaten, while the best and most perishable provisions we have on board are spoiling in the hold of the ship."

For those of a cheerier makeup, other, more-benign diversions helped to relieve the excessive boredom of their voluntary confinement. Many companies of argonauts culled from

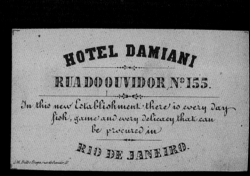

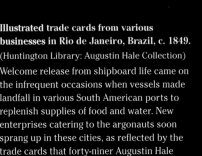

Illustrated trade cards from various businesses in Rio de Janeiro, Brazil, c. 1849.

(Huntington Library: Augustin Hale Collection)

Welcome release from shipboard life came on the infrequent occasions when vessels made landfall in various South American ports to replenish supplies of food and water. New enterprises catering to the argonauts soon sprang up in these cities, as reflected by the trade cards that forty-niner Augustin Hale collected during a stop in Rio de Janeiro.

**Clark Oliver, painting of the ship
Argonaut off Cape Horn, January
1850.**

(Huntington Library: Norton Collection)
Reaching California by sea from Europe
or the United States required every
ship to brave the ferocious gales and
freezing weather that usually swirled
around Cape Horn at the southernmost
tip of Latin America.

their memberships aspiring or accomplished actors, dancers, and musicians to perform in impromptu minstrel shows or stage plays, like those on board the *Leonore* as observed by argonaut Charles Plummer in 1849. Some companies of a more martial bent might don their company uniforms, shoulder their rifles, and put on a military drill, like the "Sea Fencibles" on William DaCosta's ship, the *Duxbury*. Various emigrants experimented with new techniques to improve their domestic arrangements within their frequently crowded and uncomfortable quarters, such as John Grambart's test of a saltwater laundry on the *Cordelia* as he described in his diary entry of May 2, 1849: "I this morning commenced washing my own cloths by taking a Flannel Shirt & making a Rope fast to it threw it overboard & Towed it about an hour & then hung it in the Rigging to dry, it beats all the Washing machines (so far as regards woolen cloths) that was ever invented." And every emigrant waited anxiously for one of the infrequent landfalls when, as their ships took on new supplies of food and fresh water, they might spend a few days ashore. Freed temporarily from the narrow borders of their nautical existence, Americans from New Hampshire, Pennsylvania, or Virginia who might never have traveled more than a few hundred miles from their birthplaces could explore Latin American ports of call such as Saint Catherine's Island, Rio de Janeiro, Valparaiso, and Callao.

The adventures of these wayfarers in such exotic lands also provided part of the substance for perhaps the most common shipboard diversion of all—capturing their experiences on paper. On some ships, handwritten "newspapers," such as "The Shark" and "The Petrel" aboard the *Duxbury,* began to circulate during the voyage, filled with poetry, cartoons, and

California Emigration Society, broadside entitled *Emigration to California!* **Boston, 1849?**

(Huntington Library: RB 82892)

As gold fever intensified through 1849 and beyond, shipowners and brokers in every major American port produced a blizzard of newspaper advertisements and broadsides. Seeing the opportunities presented by the enormous demand for passenger berths, they promoted their own golden visions of El Dorado.

humorous stories intended to lighten the reader's day. Some of the emigrants, like Charles Plummer, crafted lengthy letters to those back home that might be mailed at one of their intermediate stops, delivered to a passing ship bound back for the United States, or posted at their final destination, San Francisco. Still others applied themselves with great diligence to the task of keeping up a diary or journal, like John Grambart on the *Cordelia,* that would constitute a history of their particular voyages. For all who put pen to paper, these chronicles served as the stage upon which they rehearsed the anger, anxiety, delight, disappointment, misery, and excitement provoked by the events of the journey and the prospect of what lay beyond once they reached California.

Even as the first shiploads of American emigrants destined for San Francisco stood out to sea in the winter of 1848/49, other fortune hunters had already set other plans in motion. While many travelers appreciated the certainties of a sea voyage to California (one fixed price for their passage, guarantees of food and accommodations, and a predetermined destination), thousands of others desired nothing so much as the speediest journey possible, opting instead for a trip that would combine travel by sea and by land. After a voyage south from the Atlantic into the Caribbean Sea, they would cross the North American continent by land at its narrowest point, the Isthmus of Panama, and then depart by ship again, bound north to San Francisco.

The isthmian route and others like it (crossing Panama's northern neighbor Nicaragua or crossing Mexico at several different points) offered by far the shortest voyages to the gold country, especially in the Panamanian or Nicaraguan routes. Under the best of conditions, if emigrants encountered no delays in crossing Panama or in obtaining passage from its Pacific coast to San Francisco, they might make the entire journey in six to eight weeks, rather than the four, five, or six months required to navigate around the balance of North and South America. Charges as high as $350 or $400 for through tickets from New York to San Francisco in first-class berths tended to match or fall below costs for the trip around Cape Horn. Moreover, for those who could secure space on the steamers of the United States Mail Steamship Company or the Pacific Mail Steamship Company, food and accommodations for passengers were likely to be significantly better than for most travelers on the longer ocean route. The hundreds who left American ports for Panama in the waning days of 1848 and early 1849 soon were followed by tens of thousands, with anywhere from thirty-five thousand to fifty thousand crossing each year through most of the 1850s by the Panamanian or Nicaraguan paths.

Unfortunately for the earliest argonauts, the best of conditions rarely obtained in the first few years of the rush. Founded in 1848 with contracts from the federal government to carry the mail from the eastern states to the West Coast, both steamship lines were unprepared to cope with the enormous demand for berths from Panama to California after gold discovery. Consequently, as the numbers of argonauts arriving in Panama rose drastically through the winter and the spring of 1849, they completely outstripped the capacity of both the United States Mail and the Pacific Mail's steamers to meet the need on either side of the isthmus. Soon hundreds and then thousands of Americans piled up in and around the port city of Panama, waiting with mounting desperation for the sight of

any ship that might carry them north to California. Mary Jane Megquier, writing on May 14, 1849, from the city of Panama to Milton Benjamin in Maine as she and her husband awaited their escape, observed that "the passengers [have] been pouring in from the states all the while until the town was overrun....The news from the gold regions far exceeds our expectations, every man that goes to the mines picks up a fortune. I have had a lump of pure gold, weighing two pounds in my hand, just as it was dug."

Despite their forced delay, however, those emigrants adrift in the city of Panama at least had overcome the first great obstacle of the journey, the crossing of the isthmus itself. Deposited at the port of Chagres on the Caribbean coast of Panama, all California-bound emigrants then faced the daunting sixty-mile span of rivers, jungles, and mountains that lay between two coasts. By native canoe or, after a few years, by steamer up the Chagres River to the inland town of Gorgona, and then by mule or by foot along mountain and jungle trails, the emigrants with all their attendant baggage trudged on to the city of Panama. To many Americans who had never ventured into tropical lands, everything of earth, sea, and sky left them awestruck. At the start of her voyage toward Gorgona, Mary Jane Megquier wrote to her daughter Angeline on March 20, 1849, that it afforded "the most delightful view in the world, the banks were covered to the edge with the most splendid trees covered with a thick foliage of leaves and flowers the most brilliant hues that could be imagined." Luther Fitch, describing his crossing of the isthmus a year later, observed to his sisters in a letter of July 12, 1850, that "we found the mud Sometimes so deep that we would find some difficulty in extricateing ourselves—occasionally we did come out minus boots. . . .Parrots & Parroquetes are very abundant here and there are many other birds with beautiful plumage. In some places the road is worn into the rock 4 & 6 feet, & the path is so narrow that only one mule can pass at a time."

Drenching rains, oppressive heat, impenetrable jungle growth, mosquitoes, snakes, scorpions, ramshackle hotels, and wretched food notwithstanding, Americans continued to flock to the isthmus through the early 1850s. Again and again, argonauts who had struggled over the difficult crossing found themselves temporarily marooned at the port of Panama, where anxious crowds waited impatiently for the first opportunity to reach El Dorado. "The Office of the Pacific Mail Steamship Company [in Panama City] was announced to be open at 9 o'clock this morning," wrote New Hampshire merchant Stephen C. Davis in his diary on February 25, 1852, of his experience, "but before the door was opened, about 1000 persons were assembled to be the 'lucky ones,' and although we exerted every nerve to maintain our position we found it impossible, as the violent heavings of that excited mass of human flesh could not be resisted by a few men, but when the door opened the crowd rushed for the 'ticket delivery' with frantic efforts, and with such force as to make the building tremble like an aspen leaf."

Sensing, however, that there might be profits to be made from serving the needs of this stream of emigrants, various entrepreneurs arrived in Panama as the 1850s wore on. Better roads, better accommodations for travelers, and better coordination between the United States Mail and Pacific Mail Steamship lines relieved many of the worst aspects of the journey, especially the maddening delays waiting for

CHAGRES RIVER.

Sarah Nichols, autograph letter to Samuel Nichols, April 7, 1849.
(Huntington Library: HM 48291)

Samuel Nichols, autograph letter to Sarah Nichols, May 6, 1849.
(Huntington Library: HM 48272)

No matter which route to El Dorado an argonaut might choose, the agonies of separation and the anxieties felt by those left behind could be devastating, as this sorrowful exchange between one married couple, Sarah and Samuel Nichols, demonstrated.

ships to California at the port city of Panama. The most significant improvement of all, the completion of a transisthmian railroad to move passengers, freight, and mail, came to pass in 1855 after extensive negotiations with the government of New Granada to charter a railroad across its territory in Panama and after six difficult years of construction. The privately owned Panama Railroad began regularly scheduled service that year, reducing the length of time required to cross the isthmus from as much as four or five days to as little as three or four hours. Although contemplated long before the discovery of gold in California, the transisthmian railroad found a ready market for its services among the argonauts each time it opened a new segment during its construction.

Taken as a whole, therefore, this maritime migration grew to vast proportions as gold fever intensified. Ships sailing for San Francisco from the east coast of the United States or from the Isthmus of Panama were joined year after year by hundreds of others that had departed from the west coast of Mexico, from China and Australia, from England, and from the European continent. In the months between April 1849 and January 1850 alone, as many as forty thousand people may have reached San Francisco by sea. While much of the world rushed to the California goldfields by sea, many Americans chose to make their way to El Dorado strictly on dry land.

During the winter of 1848/49, thousands of New Yorkers, Pennsylvanians, Ohioans, Michiganders, Kentuckians, and Missourians sat by their firesides, often in the company of friends and families, puzzling out their plans to hunt for gold in California. To reach the goldfields, however, they turned west across the continent rather than east and south across the Atlantic Ocean toward Cape Horn. For nearly a decade, a small but steadily rising number of emigrants already had been marching west overland to the Oregon country and Mexican California, pioneering the routes and techniques of transcontinental migration. Letters from relatives and former neighbors now living on the Pacific Coast, published accounts of western travelers such as Frémont and Bryant, and such volumes of formal advice to wayfarers as Hastings's *Emigrant's Guide* all contributed details (albeit on occasion contradictory ones) that were applied to organizing for the great trek.

Like so many of the seaborne argonauts, large numbers of overlanders to California gathered together in joint-stock companies, agreeing to pool their resources and thus to share both the risks and the rewards. In small towns and rural counties, such companies often grew out of informal associations of friends and family members; in large cities such as New York or Philadelphia, they could be assembled in response to announcements posted in leading newspapers. By the end of January 1849, their proliferation became the subject of repeated notices in newspapers such as the Washington, D.C., *National Intelligencer*, whose columns observed the preparations of many. Stories in the *Intelligencer*, like those in its peers around the nation, depicted the activities of many eager argonauts, including "Mr. Audubon, Jr., the son of the distinguished naturalist of that name, [who] is to head an overland expedition, getting ready in New York, to start for the mines. They are to go via St. Louis, and contemplate passing through Chihuahua to the region of the Gila" (January 27, 1849). Newspapers in communities all over the United States exchanged details with each other, reporting on the progress of various emigrant companies. In its columns, the *Intelligencer* followed developments across the country. In New England, it observed, "The Springfield Republican states that the Hamden Mining and Trading Company, which originated in Westfield (Mass.)...were ready to take their departure for New York. From that port they propose to ship their heavy baggage around the Cape, and take passage themselves for Matamoros. There they intend to take passage up the Rio Grande to Point Isabel, and strike across the country on foot." In the Midwest, "California companies are forming in Iowa City....The companies propose going overland" and "A. Coquillard, of South Bend, (Indiana,) goes out with a company of five hundred or more persons to San Francisco. He is to start from South Bend about the 1st of April; and for $150 will furnish rations, teams, &c. sufficient to carry 40 pounds of baggage for each person. Tents and camp equipage to be furnished by each individual for himself" (January 30, 1849). In the South, "A party of young men is being formed in Winchester, (Va.) to go to California by the overland route, from Independence (Mo.) and to start on the 1st of April. Each member contributes $300. Twenty names have already been enrolled. A similar company in Charleston has already been formed, to consist of sixty. They had many applicants beyond this limit" (February 6, 1849).

As these and many more companies took shape in the winter of 1849, their planning intensified as argonauts readied themselves for any eventuality in the wilderness. Many of them no doubt must have gone forward with the same confidence expressed by one organizer, a draftsman employed by the U.S. Army's Corps of Topographical Engineers named J. Goldsborough Bruff. Writing to J. T. Ames on January 30, 1849, Bruff boasted that his Washington City and California Company would "carry out every appliance and means of security, comfort and success—I have, for general outfit about $300 per man. (wagons, tents, animals, provisions, &c.) And officers of the U.S.A. travellers, scientific men &c. all concur that ours will be the most efficient party, and on the wisest principles yet started."

For Bruff and his company, like for thousands of other overlanders, the ultimate test of those plans and preparations began with the first signs of spring that year. Through March and April of 1849, they advanced individually or en masse to the jumping-off points for the many routes that carried the overland migration toward California, moving in numbers that staggered the imagination of participants and spectators alike. Alonzo Delano, a young pilgrim on his way to Saint Joseph, Missouri, from his home in Ottawa, Illinois, to begin his

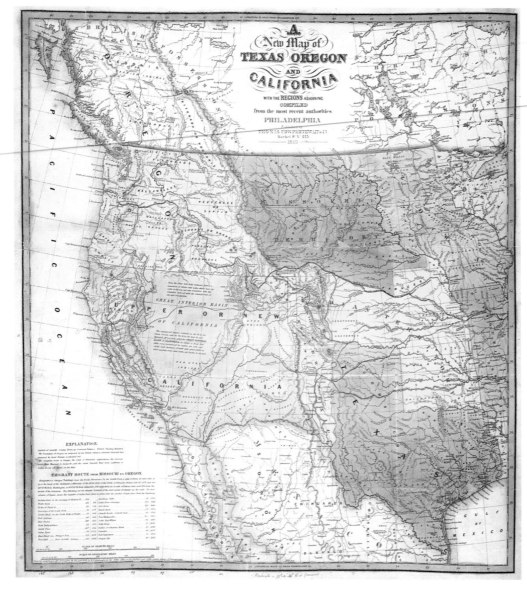

journey, later described in his 1854 account *Life on the Plains and at the Diggings* the sight of this fantastic procession from his vantage point on a Missouri River steamboat: "There was a great crowd of adventurers on the Embassy. Nearly every State in the Union was represented. Every berth was full, and not only every settee and table occupied at night, but the cabin floor was covered by the sleeping emigrants. The decks were covered with wagons, mules, oxen, and mining implements, and the hold was filled with supplies. But this was the condition of every boat—for since the invasion of Rome by the Goths, such a deluge of mortals had not been witnessed, as was now pouring from the States to the various points of departure for the golden shores of California" (p. 15).

A New Map of Texas, Oregon, and California…, **Philadelphia, 1849.**
(Huntington Library: RB 560)
Parties of overland emigrants bound for California needed maps and guidebooks as well as mules and gold pans. This 1849 map traced the various routes that most emigrants followed through the desert Southwest or across the Great Plains and the Rocky Mountains on their way to El Dorado.

Even before setting out on their march to El Dorado, however, the overlanders had already grappled with the question of which path to follow across the continent. What route would lead them to California through the fewest obstacles in the shortest number of days? Should they rely upon the familiar road known variously as the Oregon or California Trail, opened nearly a decade earlier by westering emigrants and stretching from the Missouri River frontier along the Platte River and across the Rocky Mountains at South Pass, to reach the gold regions of Northern California? Or should they strike out along one of the more southerly trails, following routes pioneered in the Santa Fe trade of the 1820s and 1830s or by General Stephen W. Kearny's march to California during the Mexican-American War? Or might they push yet further south, across Mexico's northern frontier states of Chihuahua and Sonora? Balancing such variables as distance, climate, and topography based upon the incomplete or inaccurate information at hand, the overlanding forty-niners flooded into such settlements as Council Bluffs in the Iowa Territory, Saint Joseph and Independence in Missouri, Fort Smith, Arkansas, and Brownsville, Texas, which became the jumping-off points for the trek.

After arriving in these frontier entrepôts, the emigrants had one last opportunity to perfect their arrangements for the great excursion. Patronizing the local merchants who did a

Tremendous hailstorm, on a mountain, after leaving the Platte river.

J. Goldsborough Bruff, pencil drawing entitled *Tremendous Hailstorm,* 1849.

(Huntington Library: HM 8044 #18)

A meticulous observer, forty-niner J. Goldsborough Bruff captured the essence of the overland migration in the diaries and sketches he kept during the journey. His party, the Washington City Company, suffered through many difficult moments such as this towering storm near the Platte River in the early summer.

J. Goldsborough Bruff, pencil drawing entitled *Death of Charles Bishop from Cholera,* 1849.

(Huntington Library: HM 8044 #37)

Especially in 1849, the overlanders faced no greater danger than that of cholera, a disease spread by crowded living conditions and poor sanitation. Cholera outbreaks struck many emigrant parties, resulting in the sad spectacle of trailside burials depicted here by Bruff.

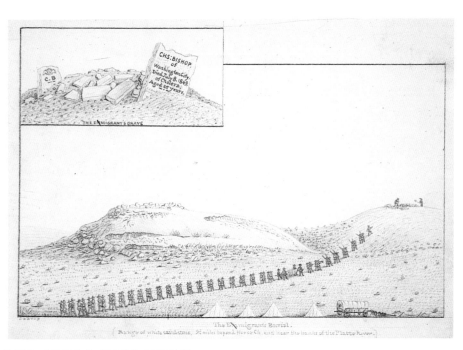

A VIEW from the SUMMIT of INDEPENDENCE ROCK. _
exhibiting the Sweet-water river and Mountains, and
the Washington City Comp? corralled at noon,
July 26, 1849.

J. Goldsborough Bruff, pencil and pastels drawing entitled *View from the Summit of Independence Rock,* **1849.**

(Huntington Library: HM 8044 #60)

As they wound their way across the continent, the overlanders encountered various natural landmarks that denoted their progress. Independence Rock, in present-day Wyoming, attracted much attention in particular since it had become a tradition for emigrants to inscribe their names on its surface.

thriving business as outfitters, the forty-niners could refurbish their equipment, replace lost or damaged supplies, or even prepare themselves completely for the journey. Oxen or mules, packsaddles or axletrees, guides or gunpowder could be found for a price at most of these commercial outposts. City-dwelling gold seekers tried to master the mysteries of handling oxteams or greasing wagon wheels while other emigrants traded gossip about the dangers of marauding Indians or cholera epidemics. Those emigrants crossing on the California Trail waited fretfully on the east bank of the Missouri for the spring grasses to grow up thick and lush over the prairies, conscious that too early a start would starve their livestock while too late a one might strand them in California's Sierra Nevada once winter's first blizzards had blocked the passes.

Finally, with preparations complete and the last vestiges of winter dispersed, parties of emigrants took to the westward trails in the spring and early summer of 1849. Migration had begun as early as March of that year in the southern reaches of Texas; the majority of migrants, however, set out on the northern route along the Platte River by the end of May. Especially on the California Trail, long trains of wagons grouped together in thoroughly organized bodies, like Bruff's Washington City Company, ground across the prairies, covering ten or fifteen miles on a good day. Daniel Robinson, writing to his brother back in Bloomington, Illinois, on May 3, 1849, about his company's departure from Saint Joseph, Missouri, observed that "there were three or four hundred teams waiting to cross the [Missouri] River[.] [W]e had to encamp on the bank of the River and there wait until our turn came to cross[.] [W]e have no feede for our cattle for two days[.] [T]o buy corn in St. Joseph at the present time is out of the question.…Our boys are all in fine spirits[.] [T]hey have escaped the clorea [cholera,] the smallpox[,] and almost everything else but hard work." Driving west across the Great Plains or the deserts of the Southwest in the summer heat, once-inexperienced emigrants (often known by the derisive term "greenhorns") grew accustomed to the daily routines of caring for themselves, their equipment, and their livestock. Though often in contact with other emigrant companies ahead of or behind them on the trails, they were now completely isolated from friends or family back in the States. Only at a handful of such military encampments or trading posts as Fort Laramie, Fort Bridger, or Fort Hall on the California Trail or during infrequent stopovers at such established settlements as Santa Fe in New Mexico or the Mormon enclave of Salt Lake City could they expect to meet other human beings not bound for California.

Such isolation also forced the emigrants to rely upon themselves and their comrades in times of difficulty or peril, especially during the first few years of the rush to California. Disasters of any kind, from disabling injury or illness to a calamitous breakdown, would have to be overcome in almost every case by the resources on hand in the emigrant's own company or in neighboring companies on the trail. Broken bones, gashed limbs, gunshot wounds inflicted by the careless handling of firearms, and outbreaks of cholera or mountain fever might well prove fatal even after medical intervention in an age before antibiotics, the general use of anesthetics, or a comprehensive understanding of infectious diseases. Many emigrants had to perform the sad duty taken up by George M. Murrell on May 8, 1849, when he wrote to his father that "I have some painful intelligence to communicate. Our much esteemed friend James O. Hill died on the morning of the 7th at our encampment 8 miles from Independence [Missouri]. His death was occasioned by cholera….The day he was taken sick was a gloomy day. He did not linger 20 hours….His death threw a gloom and despondency over the whole company which not even the golden dreams of El Dorado could dispel for a time."

Week after week, as the emigrants trudged westward during a journey that regularly lasted four months or more, other disasters both great and small might claim the lives of fellow travelers or at least inspire some to abandon their quest for a golden reward. As Daniel Robinson described his company's experience in a letter home on May 28, 1849, less than a month after leaving Saint Joseph, "Our cattle at night when all were soundly sleeping except the guard broke from the corral and ran in every direction[.] [I]t was so dark that we could not collect them that night….Some of our boys began to think that they had seen the elephant and was almost ready to return home but at this time every man feels like going ahead." Harriet Sherrill Ward, crossing the continent to California in 1853, described the thoroughly miserable night of June 1, early in the journey, when "soon after we retired, the wind commenced blowing a perfect gale, the heavens were overspread with a constant sheet of liquid fire, and such thunder no one ever heard except upon the Platte River." Struggling against the power of the storm, "We soon found that our united strength would fail to hold our Tent down and away it went. We felt like night wanderers indeed, the storm raging with remorseless fury and the water over our ankles." The next morning, she noted, "All the tents in our encampment were down except Mr. Fox's. The young gentlemen were left hatless and coatless and without shelter. Some of them were homesick enough and would have gladly taken their homeward way again."

Stampeding oxen or mules, massive thunder or hailstorms, perilous crossings of flood-swollen rivers, and exhausting treks across long stretches of barren desert challenged the endurance and sometimes threatened the safety of the overlanders. On occasion, such catastrophes might overcome an overlander even before he was fairly launched on the road to El Dorado, fulfilling the worst fears of his loved ones back home. On April 7, 1849, as Samuel Nichols and his son George made their way toward the Missouri River frontier from their home in Buffalo, New York, Samuel's wife, Sarah, prostrate with despair, urged them to abandon their quest. "I cannot live if you go any further," she pleaded with them. "Oh return home sell your things & return to me. Save oh Save my life. I cannot live if You go to California, there is war famine pestilence—murders—& evry evry evil there to await you. have mercy on a poor mother. oh come home. I'm Sick & depres'd…come back Oh come, I fret & weep day & night, a cruel wife was I to let you leave me—remember If You will go on we never meet on earth again. I've prayed but get no relife….If you will go to the grave, I'll go with you. Earth has no charm for me—unless you both will return….George my son beg for me. oh plead with your father ere it is too late to save a fond wife & mother." Just a month later, on May 6, writing from Glasgow, Missouri, Samuel, in his own deep torment, took up the pen: "After becoming a little composed I embrace the first opportunity to communicate to you this sad and afflicting intelligence: Our Lovely George is no more but is numbered with the dead. I have not Language to express my grief on this sollemn occasion. Oh how I have been smitten and god in his providence has visited us moste bitterly. oh remorse remorse my Dear & beloved wife & you my Lovely boys….My Dear & affectionate wife & sons bear upp under this sad affliction oh how heavy it will fall but bear it oh bear it. Let not grief overwhelm you at this most trying time. my Love and prayers for you my dear wife and sons."

For most of the argonauts, however, the journey proved far more tedious than danger-ous, often testing their patience most of all, given their burning desire to reach California's goldfields. Among the more than twenty thousand emigrants who followed just the California Trail in 1849, for example, the best informed estimates suggest that one thousand or less died during the trek, with the largest number probably succumbing to the cholera that plagued the 1849 migration in its early phases. One argonaut, Solomon Gorgas, recounting his experience on the California Trail during the travel season of 1850 in a May 12 letter home to his wife, accurately reflected the experience of many when, after characterizing their jour-ney to date as "very laborious and fatiguing," he went on to observe that "we feel perfectly Safe and at home now" and that he and his fellows did not lack for companionship since "the road is litterally lined with emigrants—Since leaving St. Joseph, I do not think that we have traveled a Single half hour without Seeing a train, or a number of trains either before or behind us—Our three wagons Started out from the River by ourselves, & Soon fell in with plenty of company."

Despite the four months or more that such a journey might entail, however, the hordes of emigrants launched on this journey only seemed to grow in numbers. Writing again to his wife on May 27, 1850, this time from the vicinity of Fort Laramie in present-day Wyoming, Gorgas asserted that "the emigration is extremely large—at this point the officers of the Fort pretend to keep a record of the number who pass[.] [T]hey report as having passed up to the evening of the 26th as follows 5421 men, 45 women, 33 Children, 1509 wagons, 5406 Horses, 1906 mules, 721 Oxen & 52 cows. Thus the officers here say is much larger than last year." By the fall of 1849, perhaps thirty-five thousand emigrants had crossed the continent on one of the various overland routes, followed by possibly well over one hundred thousand in the first three years of the 1850s. Like their comrades tramping through the feverish jungles of Panama or enduring eight months at sea sailing around Cape Horn, the overlanders pressed on year after year, caught up by the lure of adventure or by their hopes for golden prospects in California.

Life in the Gold Country

"I have been up to this Placer and it Surpasses all expectation[.] Men are washing their twenty dollars per day per man with ease and Some have washed even one hundred fifty dollars in one day. . . .It is found in great abundance about the Sacramento river and all its tributaries and as these rivers fall the Gold is found more plenty. . . .I still remain with Mellus & Howard and enjoyed good health until very lately having suffered severely from an attack of the 'Yellow or gold fever' which as has not as yet abated." By the time Henry Richardson wrote this descrip-tion of the gold country for Southern California rancher Abel Stearns on July 9, 1848, many of the first argonauts had already begun to obtain their own golden prospects. Months before the great migrations from the eastern United States or Europe even started to take shape, hundreds and then thousands of gold seekers were scouring hillsides, canyons, and streambeds up and down the Sierra Nevada. Before year's end, as many as five thousand miners had clus-tered at likely sites along a one-hundred-fifty-mile stretch running north to south in the Sierra foothills. Rancheros and townsmen from all parts of Mexican California, Indians from the Sierran tribes, veterans from the United States Army's garrisons in California, Mexicans, Chil-eans, and Hawaiian Islanders (known as "Kanakas") prospected and dug with a vengeance. Halted only by winter's onset in the mountains, these miners resumed work in the following year with the first signs of spring, their numbers greatly augmented by waves of migrants arriving from Latin America, Australia, and the United States. By the summer of 1849, for instance, the San Francisco newspaper *Alta California* estimated that as many as five thousand Mexicans had already made the overland trek while more than fifteen hundred Chileans and Peruvians had come by sea from their homelands. Observing the unfolding frenzy during his own excursion to the gold regions, Southern California rancher Hugo Reid was appalled by what he saw. Writing to his fellow rancher and dear friend Abel Stearns from Monterey on July 14, 1849, Reid noted scornfully that "the whole of the diggings from the numbers and con-

Scene on the Emigrant Trail,
near settlements, Nov. 1849.

tinual movement is well represented by an ants nest.—only the latter possess order & morality which is sadly lacking among the former."

Reid's harsh criticism notwithstanding, the "continual movement" he noticed during the summer of 1849 reflected more than abject confusion and disarray. While some miners raced about helter-skelter in search of "rich diggings," others studied the lay of the land carefully wherever they or their fellows encountered success. Although rarely possessed of sophisticated scientific training in geological principles, some of the original argonauts soon began to assemble considerable practical knowledge about gold's likely hiding places. In particular, realizing the frequent association of gold discoveries with watercourses, they haunted the rivers and streams that drained down from summits of the Sierra Nevada.

Spawned by enormous geologic upheavals dating back millions of years, the principal gold deposits embedded in the quartz rock of California's mountains (known as "veins") thereafter had been subjected to the same gradual erosion that wore layer after layer off the mountains themselves. Over time, as corrosive power of running water carried away fragments of the mountainous terrain, portions of those gold deposits were borne away as well. Drifting along until their heavier weight finally overwhelmed the force of the stream flow, pieces of gold, ranging from substantial chunks to the most minuscule grains, collected amidst the gravels of riverbeds and sandbars or in jagged pockets along stream banks. Eventually, as some rivers carved new channels, abandoning debris-filled dry beds, other gold-bearing deposits became buried in what miners would later describe as the "deep" gravels. Meanwhile,

Indians of the Sierra Nevada mountain
feather river tribe (Diggers)

Indians of N. valley of Feather River
(From life)

J. Goldsborough Bruff, pencil drawing entitled *Indians of N. Valley of Feather River*, 1849.

(Huntington Library: HM 8044 #192)

As argonauts overran canyons, stream-beds, meadows, and forests throughout the gold country, they put great pressure on traditional Indian ways of life during 1848 and thereafter. Despite the fear and disdain most emigrants felt toward Indians, a few like J. Goldsborough Bruff strove to capture at least some vignettes of Indian life.

far downstream from the quartz veins, where flakes and nuggets had finally come to rest, these fugitive gold pieces formed the pockets that Henry Richardson saw miners washing out with pans in the first summer of the Gold Rush.

Many miners coming out from the United States, especially those traveling with organized companies by ship around Cape Horn, had invested ample sums of money in elaborate and ultimately ineffectual machinery intended to uncover this hidden wealth. Upon arrival in the goldfields, however, the argonauts found themselves instead reduced to a far more primitive level of technology. In the early weeks and months, quite a few discoveries could be dug out of crevices or clefts in and around the creeks and streams. Once those had been exhausted, however, gold hunters then faced a much more demanding prospect. To separate finer specimens of gold from dirt, gravel, and other debris, they had to find ways in which to run earth and water together, relying upon gold's unusual weight to pull the ore to the bottom of any receptacle where it would await discovery. Thus individual miners quickly adapted the shallow metal pan in which dirt and gravel would be swirled together carefully with stream water, discarding all the contents except a sandy gold-bearing residue—if the miner was fortunate. After the results of each washing were carefully picked over, the miner would fill his pan from a pile of dirt previously dug up with pickax and shovel, bend back down to the stream beside him, and begin the process again for as many repetitions as his body could stand in a day, for as many days in a row as he could tolerate.

Gold pans, being simple to handle and eminently portable, allowed miners to depart at

John Hovey, "Historical Account of the Troubles between the Chilian & American Miners in the Calevaros Mining District," January 1850.

(Huntington Library: HM 4384)

With the numbers of miners from the United States on the rise beginning in 1849, gold seekers from other nations experienced considerable hostility from their American competitors. Confrontations between Americans and Chileans, Mexicans, or Frenchmen sometimes escalated into pitched battles, as described in this extract from the diary of forty-niner John Hovey.

a moment's notice for new diggings and begin anew somewhere else just as quickly. Restricted to the use of one man at a time, however, they could not take advantage of the gains in efficiency realized in the division of tasks among several men. Eager to find other means that would allow the speedier processing of greater volume to improve the return on their investment of time and labor, miners soon began to improvise and to collaborate. Devices known as "cradles," "rockers," "long toms," and "sluice boxes" appeared in the mining country, with each one improving upon its predecessors in the struggle to separate gold from the sand, gravel, and dirt that usually concealed it. Simple contraptions usually cobbled together from wood and iron, they mimicked the action of natural streambeds, carrying a slurry of earth and water through boxes or troughs lined with small barriers that would catch the heavier particles of gold as they flowed by. Operated by teams of miners who could dig up piles of promising soil, shovel it into the machines, turn the water into them, and sort through the dregs left behind for gold, these machines allowed the argonauts to sift through far greater quantities of earth in a day than an individual miner might have washed in a week.

Miners all over the gold country adopted such advances as quickly as they could, for in these same years they found themselves in a desperate competition. By the fall of 1849, with twenty-five thousand gold seekers flooding over the Sierra Nevada via the transcontinental routes and tens of thousands more streaming through the port of San Francisco, one estimate asserts that the number of miners had increased a remarkable eightfold in just a year to forty thousand. Only a year later, by the close of 1850, that figure rose two and a half times to the staggering total

DEFENCE OF THE CALIFORNIA BANK

Lithograph entitled *The Defence of the California Bank,* **New York, c. 1849.**

(Huntington Library: HEH Print Coll)

The sentiment that California's riches belonged exclusively to Americans found expression in many forms. This political cartoon portrays President Zachary Taylor and General Winfield Scott, heroes of the Mexican-American War, in the symbolic guises of the eagle and the rattlesnake, defending California from a bestiary of European invaders.

OPPOSITE >

G. A. Fleming, *California: Its Past History, Its Present Position, Its Future Prospects,* **London, 1850.**

(Huntington Library: RB 2606)

The color lithograph on the title page of this guidebook gave its English viewers a sense of the labor required in the early stages of the Gold Rush to find a golden reward from the surface deposits known as "placer" gold.

where we could Get good watter & Grass until winter." Lamentably, although Crawford "spent 4 weeks with him" trying to find those "digings," his effort proved unavailing for "he had forgot where his digins was and could not find Eny Gold. I gave him a Good Swet Cusing," Crawford noted caustically, "and had I been able I would [have] whiped him like Hell."

Prospectors like Magruder or Crawford, ranging over hundreds of square miles in search of the next great strike, could ill afford to waste time because of a partner's absentmindedness, for gold mining had its seasons. Like the emigrants who had crossed the continent by wagon to reach California, the miners soon learned to watch for the changes in weather that marked climatic turning points in the year. They watched for the first signs of spring when the warmth of the sun would start to melt the great mountain snowpacks, restoring the streams and rivers that supplied the water for cradles, rockers, and long toms. As summer's hot, dry months approached, they watched the last spring freshets dry up, reducing the quantities of water available. Above all, as the argonauts grew accustomed to California's seasons, they learned that little could be accomplished during the wet, chill months of winter in the Sierra Nevada, when torrential rains might wash out an entire canyon full of diggings and miners with little warning.

To anxious miners, climatic obstacles posed yet one more challenge to realizing the golden reward that had lured most of them to California in the first place. Many, especially among those arriving after 1849, discovered that the search for riches demanded hard, unremitting toil and privation with no assurance of success. Daniel Woods in his *Sixteen Months at the Gold Diggings* (1851), the published account of his expedition to El Dorado, wrote morosely of one January

CALIFORNIA.
Its Past History
ITS PRESENT POSITION
ITS FUTURE PROSPECTS.

SCENE ON A BRANCH OF THE SACRAMENTO.

London.
Printed for the Booksellers.
1850.

Gold nuggets.
(Wells Fargo)

Although it might require enormous effort to find it, much of California's gold surfaced only in tiny fragments whose total worth might range from fifty cents to fifteen dollars after a full day's labor.

day in 1850: "This morning, notwithstanding the rain, we were again at our work. We *must* work. In sunshine and in rain, in warm and cold, in sickness and health, successful or not successful, early and late, it is *work, work, WORK! Work or perish!*…From morning to night is heard the incessant rock, rock, rock! Over the whole mines, in streamlet, in creek and in river, down torrent and through the valley, ever rushes on the muddy sediment from ten thousand busy rockers. Cheerful words are seldom heard, more seldom the boisterous shout and laugh which indicate success, and which, when heard, sink to a lower ebb the spirits of the unsuccessful. We have made 50 cents each" (p. 103). Another miner, writing to his family at home on April 3, 1850, from "Forksvill" on the American River, depicted the type of elaborate mining projects becoming increasingly common in many parts of the gold country. For himself, James McMurphy assured his relatives, "My helth never was better than it is at the present time, while my appetite is first rate, the most of the time I could Eat a dog if it was well cooked & set before me," but he had to admit that he and his companions had made "but very little progress in our canal owning to some reiny wether and the rise of the River[.] [W]hat we have done has required much more labour then we expected when we comensed on the account of the quantity of large Rocks that we found in the bottom…which had to be blasted[.] [T]he lower down we went the more Rocks we found, while at the mouth we had a lege about 20 feet long & 4 feet deep to cut through…it has been managed thus fare very Boyish, every man has a way of his oan & wants to have it."

With steady depletion of the most accessible placer deposits as the number of miners grew and grew, many gold seekers pursued bigger, costlier, and more complicated projects such as McMurphy's canal. Some, such as the Tuolumne Water Company in the county of the same name, sought to provide a more certain supply for long toms and sluice boxes no matter the season through the diversion of natural water courses into man-made ones, requiring the construction of canals, ditches, and flumes. Others diverted rivers and streams entirely, uncovering potentially gold-laden beds for mining operations. And still others actually excavated tunnels and shafts into the earth in search of the veins of gold locked within the quartz rock. These enterprises demanded large crews of laborers, heavy tools and machinery such as winches, pulleys, and drills, experienced engineers to direct everyone's efforts, and significant amounts of outside capital to pay all the bills before reaping any profits. Other capital-intensive ventures appeared: the great iron presses known as "stamp mills," used to crush gold-bearing quartz into tiny pieces, and the mercury mines at New Almaden, New Idria, and elsewhere, whose product proved essential in extracting gold from the quartz rubble. Two inventive miners, working independently of one another, developed the technique known as "hydraulic mining" to channel water from streambeds through narrow canvas hoses capped with iron nozzles. Directing the resulting high-pressure flow onto gold-bearing hillsides, such setups would blast away thousands of cubic yards of earth and carry it through sluices to capture the golden particles. Although many miners continued to devote themselves to the pickax, the pan, or the cradle alone or with a partner or two, the intensification of the mining enterprise represented by river and quartz mining became predominant in the early 1850s.

In these new circumstances, some argonauts found new outlets for their own managerial or mechanical aptitude. Augustin Hale, a New Jersey forty-niner with a less-than-stellar record as a miner and independent businessman, found work in 1856 overseeing the construction of

Mormon Island. 2' view. Apl 1849.

William Rich Hutton, pencil drawing entitled *Mormon Island*, April 1849.
(Huntington Library: HM 43214 #95)
In the spring and summer of 1848, many of the first gold miners lived in fairly primitive conditions, huddled around their diggings in lean-tos or tents, such as this site at Mormon Island, downstream from Coloma on the American River. Exposure to the California winter in the goldfields, however, drove most into more permanent shelter by year's end.

various waterworks at Big Bar in El Dorado County. Applying his talents as a mechanic to the process, he wrote home with great satisfaction on September 15 that "your son A. W. H. has planned and supervised the construction of everything & it is pronounced by all who have visited the Bar to be the best and most extensive work of its kind in the mines....We have four wheels of 8 feet diameter & Buckets or Paddles 10 feet long for driving two Pumps & hoisting Rocks, & a bailing wheel 24 feet diameter for *raising* water for the 'pay sluices.'" Technologically proficient innovators like Hale, pioneering new devices and new techniques to extract gold from quartz veins and deep gravel beds, also excited the enthusiasm and admiration of outside observers. In his *Mountains and Molehills, or, Recollections of a Burnt Journal,* an entertaining account of an 1851 sojourn in California, the English traveler Frank Marryat portrayed them as the men who could realize dreams of golden wealth despite the obstacles imposed by nature: "The popular opinion respecting gold miners, is that of a body of rough, vagabond, long-haired men who work one day with a tin pan and get drunk the next; this is perhaps what they were, to some extent; ...but [with the passage of time] have the mines changed, and the 'vagabond population' stands forth in the shape of engineers, excavators, mechanics, and cunning inventors, and, better still, organized bands of labourers who, under the guidance of these first, bring profit to themselves and benefit to the country generally" (p. 316).

The changes that Marryat and others applauded, however, did not meet with universal approval. Through this process, many once-independent miners were converted to wage laborers, albeit often at a higher wage scale than they ever might have received at home. By

CALIFORNIA MINING
ILLUSTRATED,

BARBER & BAKER, Publishers, cor. J & 3d sts., Sacramento.

The modes of working the gold mines of California are various in different localities, much depending on the character and position of the deposit in which the gold is found. The accompanying views represent the more familiar modes of mining in the WET AND DRY DIGGINGS. The cut on the left representing the Dry or Hill-Diggings, and that on the right the Wet or River Diggings.

Below is the representation of a Quartz Mill, by means of which, the quartz rock containing gold is pulverized by a number of trip-hammers, and the minute particles of gold gathered and amalgamated with quicksilver. This Mill is represented as carried by water power; many of these Mills, however, are worked by steam power.

At the top of the left hand cut, the letter A designates a flume or aqueduct, by means of which water is conveyed in mining regions across the various ravines. The letter B designates a ditch by which the water is conveyed along on the side of the hills. By the aid of these aqueducts and ditches, the water is brought by a gradual fall from the summits of the Nevadas, and the regions of perpetual snows, along the mountain sides, across yawning chasms and frightful ravines, on to the level of the hill tops in the lesser ranges, from whence it is distributed in smaller flumes to various surrounding mining localities, and purchased by the miners at so much the square inch of running water. These enterprises are generally conducted by stock companies, known as DITCH CO's., and are often very expensive, costing many thousands of dollars, and extending fifteen or twenty miles. The letter C designates a pack trail, by which mules laden with provisions reach many places remote and difficult of access and impossible to reach by waggons. The letter D denotes what is known in the mines as the RAILROAD, by which auriferous earth is transported from one place to another, more accessible to water; it is generally conveyed to the bank of some stream, and by means of a slide, as in the cut marked G, dropped to the bed of some creek, into a sluice box, marked J. The sluice box is the most common method in use for separating the gold from the dirt; it consists of a long trough, about 18 inches wide on the bottom, across which, at intervals are small slats or riffles; towards the end or tail piece, the riffles are more numerous, and often contain quicksilver, and designed to catch the small particles of gold, while the dirt and stones of lighter substance pass over and are carried off by the force of a current of water, which is properly graduated for this effect. Ofttimes the box is liable to be filled up by stones, and requires a hand constantly to oversee and keep it from CHOKING. The letter E represents the mouth of a shaft, or a deep well to reach the bed rock and ascertain the richness of the lower stratas of gravel. These are often sunk to the depth of several hundred feet; the water and earth being drawn up by steam power. The letter F designates a reservoir, frequently constructed where water is valuable, near some small rivulet, to gather water that otherwise might escape during the night. H represents a DRIFT or TUNNEL, penetrating into the side of the hill; through this the auriferous earth is obtained and carried out for washing. These tunnels are often very extensive. One hill in California contains upwards of 3 miles of continuous tunneling. The letter I designates the HOSE frequently used to convey water a short distance for the use of a TOM or SLUICE; they are of more service, however, in the use of the hydraulic power, as at K, where, by an elevated head of water, great power is obtained, and a stream forced against the banks with great effect, dislodging and removing immense quantities of earth in a single day. The current is generally sufficient to carry off every thing but the larger rocks, through the sluice box, as at L.

M designates what is termed GROUND SLUICING. A stream of water being turned upon a hill side, and the earth being gathered in the current, passes off, through a riffle box. At the close of the day, and sometimes oftener, the riffle box is cleaned, and the gold, and heavy black sand, with which it is always accompanied, are placed in a pan, in which they are PANNED OUT, and the gold separated from the sand by washing, when it is ready for sale, or the mint.

The engraving on the right represents the manner of obtaining gold in the river-beds. This kind of mining is not so extensively carried on as that of the hill-diggings, though in the earlier days of California mining, the rivers were the principal field of operations; at this day however, they are often very extensively worked, and the river is sometimes seen taken from its bed for miles. River-mining is generally more uncertain than bank-diggings, and it can only be worked for a limited period of time, on account of the seasons. As early in the summer as the water will admit, preparations are made, and the river finally taken from its canal, at an expense of several thousands of dollars. In October the rains usually commence, and the rapid rise of the water generally sweeps every vestige of labor in its course. FIG. 1, in the cut, indicates the flume by which water from a neighboring ravine is preserved at a certain height for mining use and carried across the larger streams. FIG. 2, denotes the FLUME, and 3, the natural BED of the river. These fluming enterprizes are generally undertaken by a number of miners, combining together in stock and labor companies, each share-holder contributing his proportion in labor and money; if a share-holder does not work, he usually employs a substitute, or pays so much per day. FIG. 5, indicates the FOOT-DAM, by which the water is kept from running back into the bed of the stream; the bed is kept dry by means of pumps, worked by hydraulic power, as shown at FIG. 4. Sometimes the continued leakage requires a great number of these to be kept in constant use, day and night. FIG. 6, indicates a BAR, seen at intervals on the rivers and often found extremely rich; many of the bars have been worked over several times, but at this day they are thought to pay but small wages, and are usually left to the undisturbed possession of Chinamen and individual laborers. FIG. 7, designates what is termed a WING-DAM, by which the water is crowded from its course, in order to enable the miner to reach a particular point in the bed of the stream. FIG. 9, indicates the HEAD-DAM, by which the river is gathered up into the flume. It is a difficult work to accomplish, to render these impervious to water, on account of the great pressure they have to withstand; the leakage, as was before mentioned, is taken up by the pumps denoted by the FIG. 10.

QUARTZ MILL.

California Mining Illustrated, **letter sheet published by Barber & Baker.**
(Huntington Library: RB 48052 #2)
With thousands of miners crowding into the gold regions during 1849 and 1850, many of the easily accessible placer deposits were soon exhausted. As a result, gold mining during the 1850s increasingly relied upon elaborate and expensive technological solutions, as pictured in this 1855 letter sheet.

The Mining Business in Four Pictures, **letter sheet published by Britton & Rey.**
(Huntington Library: RB 48052 #9)
Most argonauts arrived in California convinced that diligence and skill in mining would guarantee them success. Their experiences in what one described as "Nature's great lottery" eroded such confidence, however. Many eventually abandoned the mines in disappointment like the two portrayed in this letter sheet satirizing "the mining business."

The Miners, **letter sheet published by Britton & Rey.**
(Huntington Library: RB 48052 #15A)
Miners wrote home frequently and in great detail, explaining the intricacies of their enterprises to their loved ones. Some argonauts also enclosed letter sheets illustrating miners and mining machinery at work, such as this group of white and Indian miners panning in the stream and pumping water into a flume.

THE MINING BUSINESS IN FOUR PICTURES.

GOING IN TO IT.   MAKING SOMETHING.

MAKING NOTHING.   GOING OUT OF IT.

Lith & Published by Britton & Rey. corner of Montgomery & Commercial Sts. S.F.

SUTTER'S FORT

THE MINERS

MOKELUMNE HILL

Lith. & Published by Britton & Rey corn! Comm! & Mont.y St. S. Francisco.

James Wyld, *World on Mercator's Projection, Shewing the Distribution of Gold,* **London, c. 1852.**

(Huntington Library: RB 35008)

The discovery of gold in California and, just a few years later, in Australia, inspired an international fascination with golden possibilities all over the world. English geographer James Wyld surveyed the known resources of the precious metal and the means of extracting it.

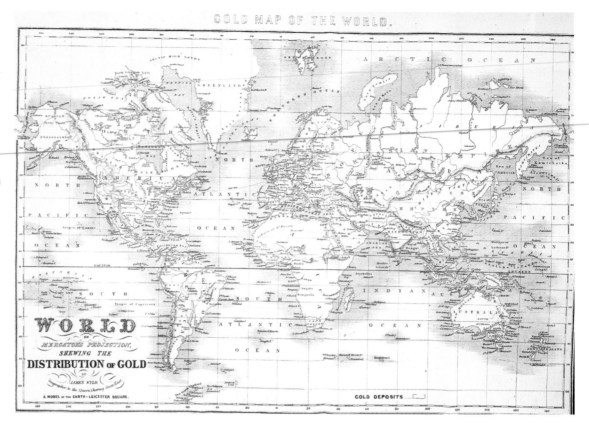

"Mining by Hydraulic Power" and **"Suspension Flume across Brandy-Gulch,"** lithographs in Ernest Seyd, *California and Its Resources: A Work for the Merchant, the Capitalist, and the Emigrant,* London, 1858.

(Huntington Library: RB 27189)

Even as mining techniques evolved, extensive and reliable supplies of water remained crucial for nearly any mining operation. Water companies developed during the 1850s, building large systems of sluices, flumes, canals, and dams to furnish water for all kinds of enterprises including the new method of hydraulic mining.

OPPOSITE >

Hutchings' California Scenes—Methods of Mining, **letter sheet published by J. M. Hutchings.**

(Huntington Library: RB 48052 #81)

By the middle of the 1850s, miners had an impressive arsenal of tactics they could employ to extract gold from its hiding places, with surface mining pursued by individuals giving way to much more elaborate approaches.

SUSPENSION FLUME ACROSS BRANDY-GULCH.

MINING BY HYDRAULIC POWER.

1854, for instance, John Kinkade, one miner who had been chasing a golden dream since 1850, declared to his brother in a letter dated August 8 that "all I have managed to make is a comfortable living. And that is as much as the mining population can average if not a little more. Mining is now Reduced to a system. What is commonly termed placer diggings being principly exhausted. The miners are seeking in the bowels of the mountains for primitive leads.... If he is not successful in finding a leed his only reward is an empty pocket and compleet disgust." The resulting diminution of dreams for many argonauts proved a bitter pill to swallow.

As the technology of mining evolved, other changes came to California's gold country as well, driven in large part by the enormous expansion in the population of would-be miners during the early 1850s. The small clusters of tent camps or log cabins first erected by miners near their claims now

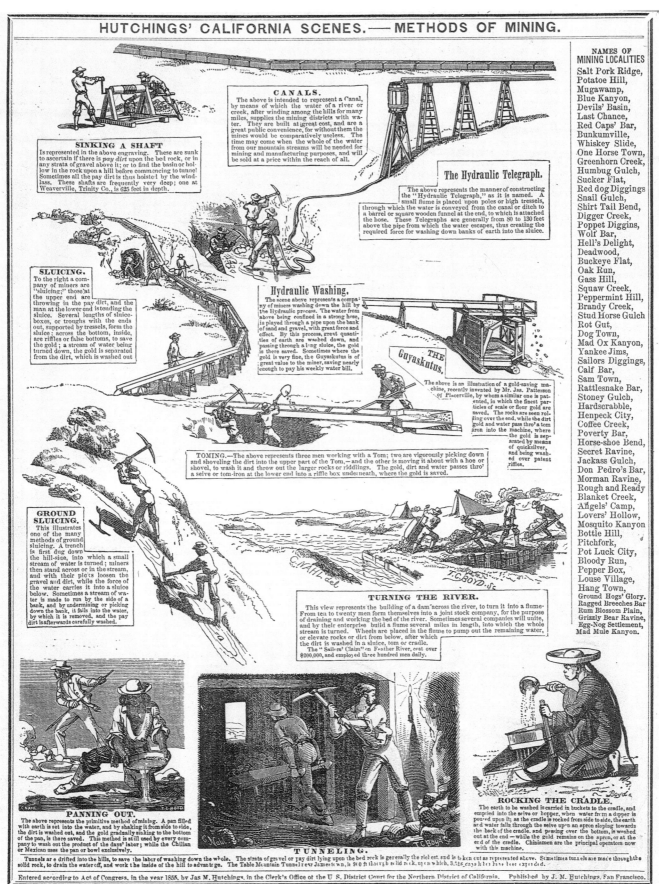

NAMES OF MINING LOCALITIES

Salt Pork Ridge,
Potatoe Hill,
Mugawamp,
Blue Kanyon,
Devils' Basin,
Last Chance,
Red Caps' Bar,
Bunkumville,
Whiskey Slide,
One Horse Town,
Greenhorn Creek,
Humbug Gulch,
Sucker Flat,
Red dog Diggings
Snail Gulch,
Shirt Tail Bend,
Digger Creek,
Poppet Diggins,
Wolf Bar,
Hell's Delight,
Deadwood,
Buckeye Flat,
Oak Run,
Gass Hill,
Squaw Creek,
Peppermint Hill,
Brandy Creek,
Stud Horse Gulch
Rot Gut,
Dog Town,
Mad Ox Kanyon,
Yankee Jims,
Sailors Diggings,
Calf Bar,
Sam Town,
Rattlesnake Bar,
Stoney Gulch,
Hardscrabble,
Henpeck City,
Coffee Creek,
Poverty Bar,
Horse-shoe Bend,
Secret Ravine,
Jackass Gulch,
Don Pedro's Bar,
Morman Ravine,
Rough and Ready
Blanket Creek,
Angels' Camp,
Lovers' Hollow,
Mosquito Kanyon
Bottle Hill,
Pitchfork,
Pot Luck City,
Bloody Run,
Pepper Box,
Louse Village,
Hang Town,
Ground Hogs' Glory.
Ragged Breeches Bar
Rum Blossom Plain,
Grizzly Bear Ravine,
Egg-Nog Settlement,
Mad Mule Kanyon.

SINKING A SHAFT

Is represented in the above engraving. These are sunk to ascertain if there is *pay dirt* upon the bed rock, or in any strata of gravel above it; or to find the basin or hollow in the rock upon a hill before commencing to tunnel. Sometimes all the pay dirt is thus hoisted by the windlass. These shafts are frequently very deep; one at Weaverville, Trinity Co., is 625 feet in depth.

CANALS.

The above is intended to represent a Canal, by means of which the water of a river or creek, after winding among the hills for many miles, supplies the mining districts with water. They are built at great cost, and are a great public convenience, for without them the mines would be comparatively useless. The time may come when the whole of the water from our mountain streams will be needed for mining and manufacturing purposes, and will be sold at a price within the reach of all.

The Hydraulic Telegraph.

The above represents the manner of constructing the "Hydraulic Telegraph," as it is named. A small flume is placed upon poles or high tressels, through which the water is conveyed from the canal or ditch to a barrel or square wooden funnel at the end, to which is attached the hose. These Telegraphs are generally from 80 to 130 feet above the pipe from which the water escapes, thus creating the required force for washing down banks of earth into the sluice.

SLUICING.

To the right a company of miners are "sluicing;" those at the upper end are throwing in the pay dirt, and the man at the lower end is tending the sluice. Several lengths of sluice-boxes, or troughs with the ends out, supported by tressels, form the sluice; across the bottom, inside, are riffles or false bottoms, to save the gold; a stream of water being turned down, the gold is separated from the dirt, which is washed out.

Hydraulic Washing.

The scene above represents a company of miners washing down the hill by the Hydraulic process. The water from above being confined in a strong hose, is played through a pipe upon the bank of sand and gravel, with great force and effect. By this process, great quantities of earth are washed down, and passing through a long sluice, the gold is there saved. Sometimes where the gold is very fine, the Guyaskutus is of great value to the miner, saving nearly enough to pay his weekly water bill.

THE Guyaskutus.

The above is an illustration of a gold-saving machine, recently invented by Mr. Jas. Patterson of Placerville, by which a similar one is patented, in which the finest particles of scale or flour gold are saved. The rocks are seen rolling over the end, while the dirt gold and water pass thro' a tom iron into the machine, where the gold is separated by means of quicksilver, and being washed over patent riffles.

TOMING.—The above represents three men working with a Tom; two are vigorously picking down and shoveling the dirt into the upper part of the Tom,—and the other is moving it about with a hoe or shovel, to wash it and throw out the larger rocks or riddlings. The gold, dirt and water passes thro' a seive or tom-iron at the lower end into a riffle box underneath, where the gold is saved.

GROUND SLUICING.

This illustrates one of the many methods of ground sluicing. A trench is first dug down the hill-side, into which a small stream of water is turned; miners then stand across or in the stream, and with their picks loosen the gravel and dirt, while the force of the water carries it into a sluice below. Sometimes a stream of water is made to run by the side of a bank, and by undermining or picking down the bank, it falls into the water, by which it is removed, and the pay dirt is afterwards carefully washed.

TURNING THE RIVER.

This view represents the building of a dam across the river, to turn it into a flume. From ten to twenty men form themselves into a joint stock company, for the purpose of draining and working the bed of the river. Sometimes several companies will unite, and by their enterprise build a flume several miles in length, into which the whole stream is turned. Wheels are placed in the flume to pump out the remaining water, or elevate rocks or dirt from below, after which the dirt is washed in a sluice, tom or cradle.
The "Sailors' Claim" on Feather River, cost over $200,000, and employed three hundred men daily.

PANNING OUT.

The above represents the primitive method of mining. A pan filled with earth is set into the water, and by shaking it from side to side, the dirt is washed out, and the gold gradually sinking to the bottom of the pan, is there saved. This method is still used by every company to wash out the product of the days' labor; while the Chilian or Mexican uses the pan or bowl exclusively.

TUNNELING.

Tunnels are drifted into the hills, to save the labor of washing down the whole. The strata of gravel or pay dirt lying upon the bed rock is generally the richest, and is taken out as represented above. Sometimes tunnels are made through the solid rock, to drain the water off, and work the inside of the hill to advantage. The Table Mountain Tunnel near Jamestown, is 800 ft through solid rock, upon which, 3,736 days labor have been expended.

ROCKING THE CRADLE.

The earth to be washed is carried in buckets to the cradle, and emptied into the seive or hopper, when water from a dipper is poured upon it; as the cradle is rocked from side to side, the earth and water falls through the seive upon an apron sloping towards the back of the cradle, and passing over the bottom, is washed out at the end—while the gold remains on the apron, or at the end of the cradle. Chinamen are the principal operators now with this machine.

William Rich Hutton, watercolor drawing entitled *New Almaden Quicksilver Mine,* **October 21, 1851.**
(Huntington Library: HM 43214 #73)
For hundreds of years, miners in Europe and South America had taken advantage of mercury's chemical affinity for gold to separate that metal from gravel or crushed rock. California's mercury mines at New Idria and New Almaden played a critical role in many mining efforts.

***The Honest Miner's Songs,* letter sheet published by Geo. H. Baker.**
(Huntington Library: RB 48052 #102)
The argonauts not only shared details of their daily occupation with friends and family but also descriptions of their lives so far from home. Letter sheets like *The Honest Miner's Songs* pictured miners at work, at play, and coping with the demands of domestic life.

proved, in many mining districts, the seedlings from which grew scores of ragtag mining towns. Those towns, in turn, merged into an elaborate network stretching all the way to San Francisco, already claiming for itself the grand title of "Queen City of the Pacific." Across San Francisco Bay and then up the Sacramento, the San Joaquin, or the Feather Rivers flowed a steady procession of sailing ships and steamboats, destined for the smaller port cities of Sacramento, Stockton, or Marysville. Laden with pork, pickaxes, window sashes, flannel shirts, letters from home, and newly arrived gold seekers, these vessels disembarked their cargoes, which then were distributed to Sonora, Columbia, Volcano, Placerville, Coloma, Nevada City, and dozens of other mining towns by stagecoaches, freight wagons, or pack mules.

In the gold camps themselves, the future was always uncertain. Camps located in booming districts might mushroom in size, attracting hundreds or thousands of new residents, including merchants selling goods and services of every description to feed, clothe, house, and entertain the miner while he was in town and to keep him fully supplied when he was in the diggings. Played-out mining claims, conversely, often resulted in the abandonment of whole towns as the miners and the businesses that depended on them moved on to more attractive prospects. Winter or spring floods might inundate an entire town, drowning every home and business in silt and mud, or a sudden blaze might reduce its flimsy wooden shacks to glowing cinders overnight. Facing such volatile conditions, businessmen in any part of the gold country might run into the problems described by Collis P. Huntington, a young shopkeeper originally from Oneonta, New York. Writing to his brother and

Published by Geo. H. Baker.

MINER'S HOME.

MINER COOKING.

LETTERS FROM HOME.

WASHING DAY.

THE HONEST MINER'S SONGS.

The One He Sung at Home.

TUNE—SUSANNAH.

Like Argos of the ancient times,
   I'll leave this modern Greece;
I'm bound to California mines,
   To find the golden fleece.
For who would work from morn till night,
   And live on hog and corn:
When one can pick up there at sight,
   Enough to buy a farm.
    CHORUS.
O California! that's the land for me. [see.
I'm going to California the gold dust for to

There from the snowy mountain side,
   Comes down the golden sand.
And spreads a carpet far and wide,
   O'er all the shining land:
The rivers run on golden beds,
   O'er rocks of golden ore.
The valleys six feet deep, are said
   To hold a plenty more.
    O California, &c.,
I'll take my wash-bowl in my hand,
   And thither wind my way.
To wash the gold from out the sand,
   In California.
And when I get my pocket full,
   In that bright land of gold,
I'll have a rich and happy time;
   Live merry till I'm old.
    O California, &c.

The One He Sings Here.

TUNE—IRISH EMIGRANTS' LAMENT.

I'm sitting on a big quartz rock,
   Where gold is said to grow:
I'm thinking of the merry flock,
   That I left long ago:
My fare is hard, so is my bed,
   My CLAIM is giving out,
I've worked untill I'm almost dead,
   And soon I shall "peg" out.

I'm thinking of the better days,
   Before I left my home:
Before my brain with gold was crazed,
   And I began to roam.
Those were the days, no more are seen,
   When all the girls loved me:
When I did dress in linen clean.
   They washed and cooked for me.

But awful change is this to tell,
   I wash and cook myself:
I never more shall cut a swell,
   But here must dig for pelf.
I ne'er shall lie in clean white sheets,
   But in my blankets roll!
And oh! the girls I thought so sweet,
   They think me but a fool.

SATURDAY NIGHT.

FRIENDS IN THE CITY.

MINER'S EVENING.

MINER'S CABIN.

THE IDLE AND INDUSTRIOUS MINER.

MINER SICK.

MINER'S DREAM.

MINER'S SLUMBERS.

MINER'S CLAIM.

Volcano Calaveras

Gold Hill, Decr. 25, 1852.

My Dear and affectionate Kate:—

As this is Christmas night, and I have nothing better to send you for a Christmas Gift, I thought a letter would be as acceptable as any thing else, for nothing is more gladly received by us than a letter from our dear wives. Last night, being Christmas eve, Sim and I went down to the gambling houses, about fifty yards from our shanty, to see and hear what was going on, and left Joe, at home baking, and while Sim went up to the shanty to attend the bread to let Joe come down to hear the music, the young fellow who attends the store when we get our letters came into the gambling house and told me there was a letter for me, I was off quick, and up to the shanty, with your truly welcome letters of Nov. 16, in short metre; well we read them all over carefully, and while we were reading them a second time, a neighbor of ours brought in a bottle of whiskey, and as it was the night before Christmas he said we should not go to bed without drinking with him, so we made a big dipper full of hot stuff and retired for the night, rejoicing that we had got a letter for our Christmas Gift. A gambling house in this country is just like our hotels at home, only they are licensed as gambling houses, and all kinds of gambling is going on in the open bar-room, and not stowed away in some private room as is the case at home. These houses are what might be called public houses, for it is the first place

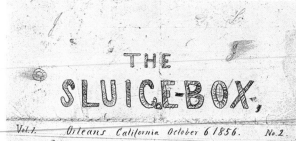

THE SLUICE-BOX.

Vol. 1.   Orleans California October 6 1856.   No. 2.

Published by Frank Ball.

Subscribers,—furnished at four dollars per month or one dollar and a half per single number.

Subscriptions,—invariably in advance.

Adventures of Plug Blunt, Esq.
Continued.

Write

John Eagle, autograph letter to his wife, Margaret, December 25, 1852.

(Huntington Library: EGL 12)

With the passage of time, miners felt the separation from their loved ones ever more keenly. The letters they exchanged with those they had left behind became an indispensable lifeline, as demonstrated in this Christmas 1852 letter from John Eagle to his wife Margaret.

"The Sluice-Box," a handwritten newspaper from Orleans, California, October 6, 1856.

(Huntington Library: Uncataloged manuscript)

Wherever miners might congregate, local newspapers like the handwritten "The Sluice-Box" sprang up to feed the popular taste for news, humor, and gossip.

business partner Solon from Sacramento on March 25, 1850, he complained that, after coming up to Sacramento, he "could do very little as it rained all most insesently and about the first of January the water came up over the City." Trying to recoup his losses, Huntington headed for the mines: "I hired george to stay and sell what goods I had hear while I went to the mines and sold what I had thear but georg as usual did not sell mutch and what goods I sent to the mines I payed very high prices for carrying and goods went down very low so that I did not make mutch of enny thing."

Confronted with such challenges to overcome, mining camps and towns from Sacramento down to the littlest hamlet made every effort to ensure that they provided everything the miner might require. Consequently, restaurants, dry-goods stores, and hardware shops shared the scene in many of these towns with saloons, gambling halls, and brothels, all intending to meet the miner's every need. Describing Sacramento to his brother Solon, Huntington noted that "this place contains about ten thousand Inhabitants and of that number thare is probably about six hundred females and four-fifths of them are Harlots," while among its other attractions were "about fourty gambling Houses," which he observed with a good eye to the bottom line, "pay from one to Eight thousand dollars per month rent." Frank Marryat described the gambling dens in Sonora, near the southern mines, where "the internal decorations were very glittering; chandeliers threw a brilliant light on the heaps of gold that lay piled on each monté table, whilst the drinking bard held forth inducements that nothing mortal is supposed to be able to resist. On a raised platform is a band of music…or if it is a Mexican saloon, a quartet of guitars; and in one house…is a piano, and a lady in

THE WINTER OF 1849.

"The Winter of 1849," lithograph in Frank Marryat, *Mountains and Molehills, or, Recollections of a Burnt Journal,* London, 1855.
(Huntington Library: RB 32560)
Gold Rush towns and cities had taken shape so quickly that few communities were prepared to meet even the most basic needs of their residents. California's torrential winter rains, for example, often reduced them to impassable quagmires, as in this comic view of a San Francisco street.

black velvet who sings in Italian and accompanies herself, and who elicits great admiration and applause on account of the scarcity of the fair sex in this region" (p. 262).

Having such attractions handy, many of these towns became magnets for miners from every surrounding claim, throwing into close proximity a remarkably cosmopolitan array of men and women. Sonora, Marryat wrote, "has a large French population, and to this Gallic immigration is attributable the city's greatest advantages; for where Frenchmen are, a man can dine, which is very important" (p. 263). A half-dozen nationalities might be represented on any street and might be briskly engaged in buying and selling or drinking and gambling. The cosmopolitan character of the crowd, however, never guaranteed tolerance or mutual good will among all parties. As Marryat also observed about Sonora, "The Mexican population predominates…and nearly everything is stamped with their nationality….The American population, between whom and the Mexicans a rooted hatred exists, call the latter 'greasers,' which is scarcely a complimentary sobriquet" (p. 263). When mixed together with the hostility prevalent among many Americans toward foreigners taking gold out of American soil, angry sentiments could flare up, as Enos Christman saw in Sonora during the summer of 1850. In a letter of July 21, Christman wrote to his friend Peebles Pritzer of a series of robberies and murders in the region, attributed to Mexican "guerillas," inflaming passions so deeply that "I fear the Americans will issue an edict and compel every Mexican to leave the country. This I should regret," he continued, "as many of them are good citizens and favorably disposed towards the Americans."

As rambunctious or dissipated as life in the mining camps might be, however, quieter

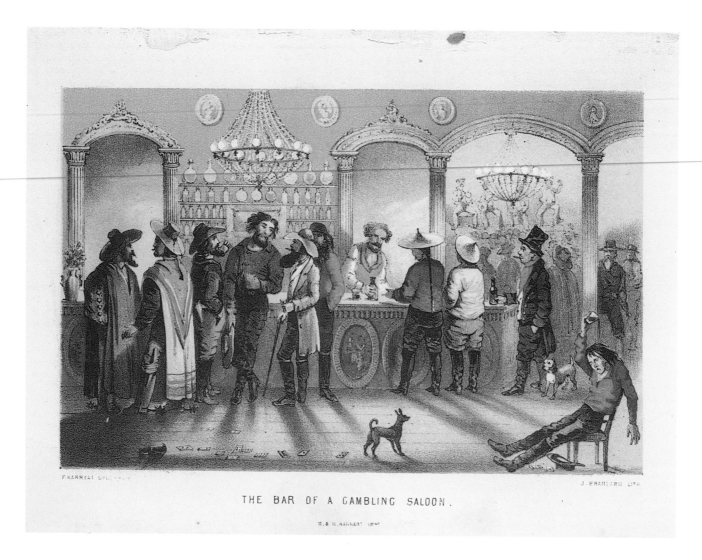

THE BAR OF A GAMBLING SALOON.

**"The Bar of a Gambling Saloon,"
lithograph in Frank Marryat, *Mountains and Molehills, or, Recollections
of a Burnt Journal,* London, 1855.**
(Huntington Library: RB 32560)
The mining camps that blossomed
in the first years of the Gold Rush brought
the miners together for business and pleasure. Often, as in the case of this establishment in Sonora, the camps profited from
the business of pleasure by accommodating miners looking for a spree.

**J. Goldsborough Bruff, pencil
drawing entitled *Indian Lodge
in Lassin's Rancheria...,* 1849.**
(Huntington Library: HM 8044 #155)
During 1849 and 1850, most Indian
laborers had been driven out of the
mining business. Miners often encountered parties of Indians near their
own mining camps, engaged in daily
routines such as the preparation of
the acorn meal that constituted a
staple of most Indian diets.

moments usually prevailed in which the inhabitants just tried to get on with the daily business
of life and anxiously awaited news from home. John Eagle of Pennsylvania, writing home on
Christmas Day, 1852, to his wife, Margaret, from Volcano in Calaveras County, painted a scene of
domestic tranquillity in which, on Christmas Eve, "Jim and I went down to the gambling houses,
about fifty yards from our shanty, to see and hear what was going on, and left Joe at home baking."
Learning that letters from Margaret had arrived that day, Eagle brought them home to read and
share with his companions to their great joy, after which "we made a big dipper full of hot stuff and
retired for the night, rejoicing that we had got a letter for our Christmas gift." Certainly, others

Indian Lodge in Lassin's Rancheria,
Acorns

would have shared the relief expressed
by Lydia Burns to her sister Polly
Burns Hall in 1853, when she wrote
from Placerville that "I am happy to
seate my sevlfe to answer your long
looked for letter...like a drop of
water to a thirsty soul when all hope
is gone it gives new life to the droop-
ing spirits and cheer me here in a
strange land." An issue of a handwritten newspaper called "The
Sluice-Box," published in Orleans

PLACERVILLE.

Lith. & Published by Quirot & C.º corner Montgomery & California St.ª S.Francisco.

#8052

Placerville, **letter sheet published by Quirot & Co.**

(Huntington Library: RB 48052 #41)
Emerging as quickly as they did, many communities took on a rough-hewn appearance at best, as seen in this letter sheet portrait of Placerville east of Sacramento. Such appearances belied the prosperity that many camps enjoyed when the diggings in their particular vicinity flourished.

Bar on October 6, 1856, filled its four pages of columns with news of social events around town, advertisements from local merchants, and satirical commentary about the political developments of the day, in very close approximation of newspapers produced in the larger towns and cities, for example the *Alta California* and the *Sacramento Daily Union.*

Life in the mining camps could also bring moments of unexpected connections between human beings even in the face of the hostility and violence that pervaded relations between them. Charles Plummer, writing to his father back in New England on March 14, 1851, observed that "those who come here *now* Know nothing of '*life in California*' as we found it, for *now* the country not only abounds in the *comforts* of life but many of the *luxuries* are among us. Of the contributors of the *latter,* the Chinese are at the head. There are many of them here, and they are very good citizens,—Though I think that the French population has *increased faster through the country* for the past six months than any other nation." Elias Ketcham, sometime gold miner and merchant, wrote in his diary for February 17, 1853, of his encounter near Pennsylvania Gulch with some Indian women engaged in grinding acorns into meal and of seeing "some indian children…with pieces of pie which they were nibbling apparently with a good relish." Continuing with disgust about the terrible influence exerted upon Indian men by alcohol when they could acquire it from "some vendor of the poison," he scrawled indignantly, "How cruel to sell spirits to the poor Indians," and how, "if I could speak in their own tongue, I should be glad to converse with & endeavour to do them some good."

For thousands of argonauts like John Eagle, Lydia Burns, and Elias Ketcham, mining

SONORA

January, 1852.

Sonora, January, 1852, letter sheet
published by Pollard & Brittons.
(Huntington Library: RB 48052 #67)
Blessed with particular advantages
such as proximity to major mining
districts, wagon trails, or rivers, some
mining camps such as Marysville on
the Feather River or Sonora in the
southern mines developed into hubs of
commerce and social life.

camps and towns like Volcano had become the closest thing to home, in many cases for year after year. Very few, however, completely abandoned those hopes of eventually departing from El Dorado with a hefty share of its wealth in their pockets, for the parting from loved ones had involved too many hardships and tribulations. As forty-niner Charles Cochran of New York State noted in a diary entry of February 3, 1849, those sufferings could be borne only because of the compelling allure of the golden reward: "Old scenes, among which I had passed the most of my life, were to be parted with: friends with whom I had been acquainted from my earliest recollection were to be shaken by the hand for the last time for years, perhaps forever. Family ties, which we know not the strength of till the time to say the sad word farewell has arrived, were to be broken asunder: everything dear and familiar to be seen for the last time; and what was the object to be gained by all this sacrifice of feelings? I answer—*gold.*" Most argonauts remained deeply bound to friends and family left behind, sensing keenly the barriers erected by time and distance. One column of "The Sluice-Box" was devoted almost entirely to a poignant poetic plea entitled "Write" that urged, "Write to me very often, / Write to me very soon, / Letters to me are dearer / Than loveliest flowers in June" and concluded, "Write to me very often, / Letters are links that bind, / Truthful hearts to each other, / Fettering mind to mind." Many pledged their devotion and their sense of obligation to loved ones, as Mary Jane Megquier did in a May 22, 1849, letter to her children back in Maine: "You need not give yourself any uneasiness about our being injured in any way....There is a fair prospect of your father making money enough in a year or two so we can come home."

**The Miners' Ten Commandments,
letter sheet published by Sun Print.**

(Huntington Library: RB 48052 #78A)

In addition to depicting such sober matters as mining processes and the cities or towns of the gold country, many letter sheet publishers also poked fun at the way the miners lived. The best-known example, James M. Hutchings's celebrated *The Miners' Ten Commandments* (seen here in its original 1853 incarnation), sold thousands of copies.

**Receipt from Gregory's
California and New-York Package,
Parcel, and Message Express for
shipment of $1,000, July 1850.**

(Huntington Library: MQ 79)

**Adams & Co., sight draft for $125.00
payable to Margaret H. Eagle,
October 28, 1852.**

(Huntington Library:
John Eagle Collection)

For those emigrants who had begun to prosper, sending money home represented a tangible way to alleviate the pain of separation and to demonstrate their success. Although banking in the modern sense was still in its infancy, a network of express companies and commercial agents developed that would allow argonauts like Thomas L. Megquier and John Eagle to transfer funds securely.

Commandments to California Wives, **letter sheet published by W. C. Butler.**

(Huntington Library: RB 48052 #76)

Letter sheet publishers found inspiration for satire in nearly every subject, including the domestic affairs of California husbands and wives. This 1855 example, with its mockery of alleged wifely failings, reflected certain commonly held stereotypes about feminine extravagance and vanity.

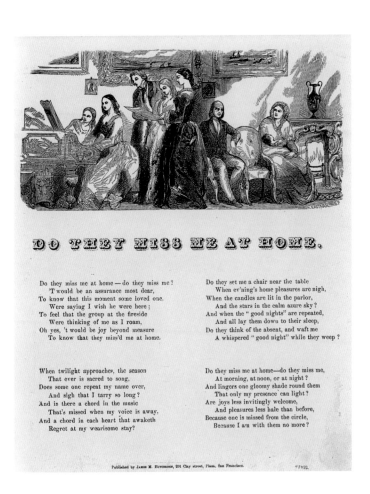

DO THEY MISS ME AT HOME.

Do they miss me at home — do they miss me?
  'T would be an assurance most dear,
To know that this moment some loved one.
  Were saying I wish he were here ;
To feel that the group at the fireside
  Were thinking of me as I roam,
Oh yes, 't would be joy beyond measure
  To know that they miss'd me at home.

When twilight approaches, the season
  That ever is sacred to song,
Does some one repeat my name over,
  And sigh that I tarry so long ?
And is there a chord in the music
  That's missed when my voice is away,
And a chord in each heart that awaketh
  Regret at my wearisome stay?

Do they set me a chair near the table
  When ev'ning's home pleasures are nigh,
When the candles are lit in the parlor,
  And the stars in the calm azure sky ?
And when the " good nights" are repeated,
  And all lay them down to their sleep,
Do they think of the absent, and waft me
  A whispered " good night" while they weep ?

Do they miss me at home — do they miss me,
  At morning, at noon, or at night ?
And lingers one gloomy shade round them
  That only my presence can light ?
Are joys less invitingly welcome,
  And pleasures less hale than before,
Because one is missed from the circle,
  Because I am with them no more ?

Published by JAMES M. HUTCHINGS, 291 Clay street, Plaza. San Francisco.

Scene at the San Francisco Post Office,
— SHOWING —
HOW WE GET OUR LETTERS.

The above illustration will be recognized as a correct Post-Office scene upon the arrival of the mails from the Atlantic. An interval of two weeks elapsing from the arrival of one mail to another, creates an anxiety to hear from home that can scarcely be comprehended by other than residents of California. At an early hour of the morning on which it is announced the mails will be ready for delivery, anxious faces commence forming in the lines leading to the different deliveries, and by 8 o'clock the whole interior of the spacious building is completely jammed with persons, as well as the streets adjoining. The letters are generally delivered with all possible dispatch, yet evening will often find the different lines but little shortened ; and the rush sometimes continues for three days.

Persons in the Atlantic States will readily understand the disappointment a friend here experiences at being told at the window, after undergoing for three or four hours the persecution of being jammed and jostled by an anxious crowd, exposed to a burning sun or the freezing and disagreeable winds which at seasons sweep round the corners of our streets carrying with them clouds of dust—yes, at being told by the clerk that there is nothing for him. The announcement falls harshly upon his ear, and with the speed of thought settles upon his countenance a shade of gloom and disappointment. On the other hand, should a letter be handed him, it is refreshing to note the gleam of joy that sparkles in his eyes, and the smile of thankfulness that beams upon his face, as he places the sacred epistle in his pocket, and walks hurriedly away. Friends in the Atlantic States, could they but for a moment witness the scene so perfectly represented by the artist in the sketch above, and watch the anxiety depicted in the features of each figure slowly working his way to the delivery, we think they would be more punctual in their correspondence, for it would be no pleasing sight to notice the disappointment of a husband, a father, a brother or a friend, caused perhaps, by their negligence.

Published by LELAND & McCOMBE, Post Office, Building, San Francisco. Engraved expressly for the Publishers, by ANTHONY & BAKER.

Do They Miss Me at Home,
**letter sheet published by
James M. Hutchings.**
(Huntington Library: RB 48052 #64)
Most argonauts feared that they eventually would be forgotten by
the people back home, especially as the length of their absences increased. Some of the letter sheets spoke to this anxiety, hoping that "a chord in each heart that awaketh / Regret at my wearisome stay."

*Scene at the San Francisco
Post Office, Showing How We Get Our
Letters,* **letter sheet published by
Leland & McCombe.**
(Huntington Library: RB 48052 #98A)
All argonauts attached great importance to their mail as seen in this letter sheet depiction of the crowds at the San Francisco Post Office. The accompanying text warned of the "shade of gloom and disappointment" that would fall upon those Californians turned away without letters from home.

Tangible expressions of this commitment from the more successful argonauts such as Mary Jane and Thomas Megquier usually consisted of shipments of gold dust or bills of exchange drawn on one of the different express companies that had sprung up for just such purposes. Frequent letters, however, filled with encouragement, consolation, and admonition sought to preserve the strongest possible links between separated family members. Just as the Megquiers gave their repeated promise of beginning the journey home after ensuring their family's financial future, they wrote urging their younger children to "be good boys so that your friends all around you will love & respect you,…be kind to each other & your mates & be obedient to those with whom you live."

While struggling to attend to their affairs in California, many argonauts also struggled to retain some part in the conduct of family affairs back home as the Megquiers did. Many, like Jonathan Heywood writing from Jackson Creek on March 8, 1851, could only sympathize with the difficulties spawned by their departures. Heywood, commiserating with his wife, Jane, wrote, "You must have had a hard task to manage the farm and take care of the children and built so much as you have." As months and years slipped by, with news of more and more changes communicated in every letter from home, some even grew concerned that they might have no place left for them, as Heywood suggested when he wrote that "I am almost afraid you are making more improvements and more money for the farm than I could if I were there. I don't expect," he continued wistfully, "to know the place when I return."

III | California Transformed:
Organizing a New Society, 1850–58

**Accommodating
Social Change**

EVEN AS THEY WISTFULLY REFLECTED upon the transformations taking place at home in their absence, many of the argonauts were struggling to cope with the precipitous pace of change in their adopted homeland as well. California's explosive population growth in the first few years after gold discovery (from approximately fifteen thousand in the summer of 1848 to more than one hundred thousand by the end of 1849, reaching nearly two hundred twenty-five thousand by 1852) set loose upon the land a restless and often combative multitude, impatient of any restraint upon their efforts to grasp the golden reward that had drawn them to California. Thrown together in the search for El Dorado from many different nations, they often found the peaceful reconciliation of conflicting cultures and beliefs difficult to achieve under the best of circumstances.

Exacerbated by the ferocious pressure many felt to succeed in their gold digging at all costs, confrontations between gold seekers from the United States and those from Latin America or Europe, between the argonauts and the Indian peoples who occupied the gold country, and between newly arrived emigrants and Californios who claimed large ranchos across Northern California frequently escalated into violent collisions. On other occasions, around the mining claims, in the gold camps, and in the flourishing cities, repeated instances of robbery, assault, and murder incited such widespread feelings of fear and anger that groups of outraged citizens sought their own remedies outside the scope of traditional courts and law enforcement. The resulting episodes of lynch mobs enacting vigilante justice convulsed entire communities in the name of forestalling further occurrences of crime and violence. For the vast majority of argonauts, however, daily life in Gold Rush California revolved around the struggle to fulfill their dreams of success in fortune hunting and to escape the moral and financial failures they saw ensnaring many of their peers.

With the great upsurge in the numbers of miners in 1849 and 1850, as the first large waves of emigration from the eastern United States began to arrive, fears arose among many that they might be crowded out by new mobs of competitors. For many American argonauts, this anxiety was compounded by a sense of their republic's proprietary rights to newly conquered California, acquired in their victorious conflict with their Mexican neighbor. Resentment of foreign intruders in the goldfields, as described by Hugo Reid in his letter of July 14, 1849, to Abel Stearns, also drew strength from the rampant hostility toward peoples of different races and religions rooted in many quarters of American society at a time of rising immigration from various European nations to the United States.

< Detail from "Chinese Camp in the Mines," lithograph in J. D. Borthwick, *Three Years in California*, Edinburgh, 1857.

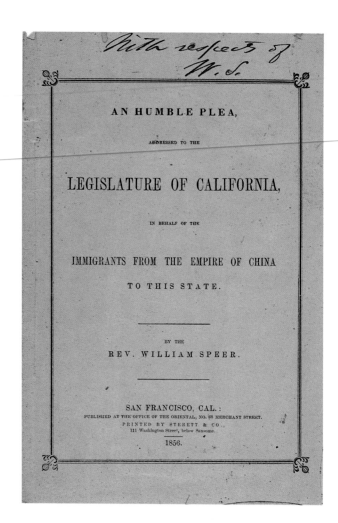

Jacob P. Leese, labor contract with Ai, Chinaman, Hong Kong, July 28, 1849.
(Huntington Library: VA 160)

Especially during the early years of the gold fever, most argonauts scorned low-paying menial jobs, and employers sought out new sources of labor. Jacob P. Leese, on a trading voyage to Hong Kong in 1849, recruited a small number of Chinese workers to fill certain trades.

William Speer, *An Humble Plea, Addressed to the Legislature of California, in Behalf of the Immigrants from the Empire of China to This State*, San Francisco, 1856.
(Huntington Library: RB 1688)

Anti-Chinese sentiment in California intensified as the number of Chinese immigrants rose during the early 1850s. Some individuals such as the Reverend William Speer, however, advocated just treatment for the Chinese, opposing what he described as "the temper of meanness, and spite, . . . and bigotry."

John Hovey, a gold seeker from Newburyport, Massachusetts, who had come to California by sea in the winter of 1849, depicted one occasion when such sentiments propelled some of the argonauts into action. In a short manuscript entitled "Historical Account of the Troubles between the Chilian & American Miners in the Calaveros Mining District," he described a confrontation between Chileans and Americans in December 1849 over the rights to mine a particular claim, which Hovey maintained had been provoked by the aggression of the Chileans. The initial incident soon faded into the background, however, as the American miners in that part of the southern mines assembled in fury to avenge this perceived insult offered by "these invaders of our territory." At a subsequent mass meeting of the "resident citizens" in the Calaveras district, the miners proposed various resolutions embodying rules to protect the rights of all American miners and to enforce a proposal that "no foreigners shall be permitted to work at these mines after the tenth day of December 1849." The sense of the meeting, in passing these resolutions, seemed to be echoed by its chair, an Iowan named Abraham Nash, who Hovey quoted as saying that "in his opinion, 'foreigners' and especially these d----d copper hides, every s-n of a b---h of 'em, should be driven from our diggings. They've got no business here in the first place, gentlemen, as we all know they've been drove from up North." Filled with righteous indignation, the miners formed a militia that mobilized against the detested foreigners and, according to Hovey's account, expelled them from the neighborhood. Similar episodes during 1849 and 1850 in other mining districts or camps drove some Chileans, Peruvians, Mexicans, and Frenchmen into the southern reaches of the gold country,

Henry Valentine,
***California; or, the Feast of Gold,* London, c. 1849.**

(Huntington Library: RB 471780)

The worldwide hysteria about California's riches inspired parody in many forms such as plays, novels, and cartoons. Composers of widely varying talents ground out music and lyrics about the "feast of gold" as seen in this 1849 English sheet music.

CALIFORNIA;

OR,

THE FEAST OF GOLD.

A New Comic Song,

Written by Henry Valentine,

AND

SUNG BY MESSRS. CARROL, WARDE, MARTIN, MILLS,

And all the Principal Comic Singers,

WITH THUNDERS OF APPLAUSE.

LONDON:

R. MACDONALD, 30, GREAT SUTTON STREET, CLERKENWELL.

Price One Shilling.

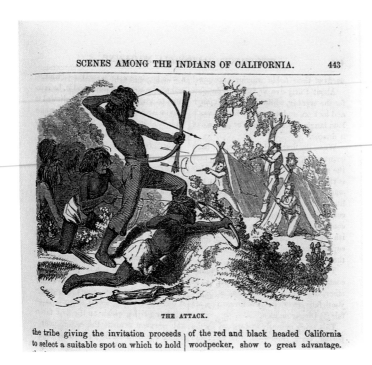

THE ATTACK.

the tribe giving the invitation proceeds | of the red and black headed California
to select a suitable spot on which to hold | woodpecker, show to great advantage.

"The Attack," engraving in *Hutchings Illustrated California Magazine* 3, no. 10 (April 1859).
(Huntington Library: RB 420)
With their very existence threatened during the 1850s, many California Indians resisted the encroachments of prospectors, miners, and settlers. The resulting warfare decimated many Indian communities and drove others to flight.

around the community of Sonora, and hastened the departure from California of many more.

If the influx of French- and Spanish-speaking gold seekers proved unsettling to many Anglo-American emigrants, raising in their minds the specter of a California occupied by racially inferior and religiously suspect peoples, the arrival of more and more Chinese laborers during the early 1850s stirred even greater concern. Although probably totaling less than one hundred in the first eighteen months of the rush, the number of Chinese emigrants grew into the thousands by 1852 and the tens of thousands soon thereafter. Completely outside the experience or understanding of nearly all Americans in the 1850s in terms of everything from food and clothing to language and spiritual beliefs, the Chinese wayfarers to what they termed "Gold Mountain" puzzled or disturbed most who came in contact with them. The fact that most came as laborers indentured to the Chinese merchants who paid for their transportation further alienated many Americans, who regarded the use of forced labor of any kind in the goldfields as grossly unfair competition with hardworking free white men. To many Americans, they represented a people fundamentally incompatible with all features of American society at that time.

To others in California during the Gold Rush era, however, the presence of these sojourners appeared in a less bleak light. Among the Protestant missionary societies of the era, for example, the Chinese in America represented an opportunity to make progress in their efforts to bring the Christian gospel to China's millions. Bodies such as the Presbyterian Board of Foreign Missions assigned clergymen like the Reverend William Speer to the task. Speer himself became an eloquent and ardent advocate for what he believed were the rights of the Chinese. In his 1856 pamphlet *An Humble Plea Addressed to the Legislature of California,* he argued forcefully that the true superiority of Christian America would be revealed if Californians would "put off the temper of meanness, and spite, and selfishness, and bigotry" and show the Chinese a people who live "in the truest refinement of human nature, and in the knowledge of a Heaven-descended charity and hope of salvation" worthy of emulation.

Other observers of the Chinese, less spiritually oriented, had noticed their exceptional capacity for hard work under adverse conditions with little or no visible protest. Speculating about how desirable such a labor force might be for many different tasks, various mining companies and agricultural enterprises began recruiting Chinese workers. As Speer himself noted in his *Humble Plea,* further Chinese immigration was already desired by "many in the agricultural districts, particularly in Southern California, and [those] interested in cultivating the swamp lands" by the use of Chinese labor. Even before the migration en masse had begun, a few American merchants had been involved in the hiring of Chinese workers. Jacob Leese, an early Anglo-American emigrant to California and brother-in-law of Mariano G. Vallejo, had been recruiting Chinese laborers in Hong Kong during a trading voyage to China in the summer of 1849, signing up individuals in such capacities as cook, tailor, or coolie under three-year contracts. Another entrepreneur, Leslie Bryson, sailed out of San Francisco in December 1851 and wrote to a friend back East on December 3 that he proposed to "return here in 5 or 6 months with some 300 Chinese under contract to serve 5 years in Cal[ifornia]." Already, Bryson noted, he had commitments in hand for nearly half that number, including an order from "one poor New Jersey Morman [who] gives me an order for 50 Chinese at $120.00 per capita." On Bryson's return voyage from Amoy in March 1852, his entrepreneurial vision

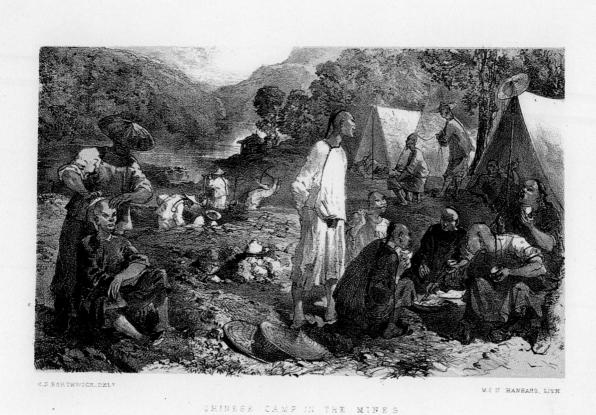

CHINESE CAMP IN THE MINES.

Although few Chinese arrived in California during 1849 or 1850, they were numbered in the thousands by 1852, as the enthusiasm for "Gold Mountain" took root. Some of the Caucasian argonauts appreciated Chinese energy and determination, but most found the Chinese way of life disturbingly alien.

went awry, for the 450 contract laborers revolted against the poor treatment they received, murdering Bryson and his officers and running the ship aground on the coast of Formosa, where they fled ashore. More successful contractors, however, continued to bring in contingents of laborers, expanding the already sizable Chinese population during the 1850s to the dismay of many Anglo-Californians.

Within a few years after gold discovery, California thus had become the arena in which the hopes of argonauts from many nations were thrown into contrast with the powerful nationalism of mid-century America as expressed in the spirit of "Manifest Destiny." In the same way that American merchants such as Thomas O. Larkin had worried before the Mexican-American War about British and French intrigues to acquire Alta California, many Americans in California after 1848 seemed to worry about the presence of foreigners who might interfere with the absorption of the Golden State into the Union. Securing the place of California in that scheme of Manifest Destiny, however, would be further complicated by the presence of other peoples who had a firmer, if still contested, claim to a part of that American future. Mid-nineteenth-century America had begun anew its struggles as a nation over the role that African-Americans and American Indians would play in the life of the nation.

Acrimonious debates over slavery's future had occupied much of the American public's attention during the 1840s, peaking at decade's end with a bitter controversy about the possibility of its extension into the territory recently conquered from Mexico. Although still consigned to the radical fringe of American politics, the movement to abolish human slavery

English language front page of _The Oriental_, San Francisco, May 1856.
(Huntington Library: RB 55030)

Chinese language front page of _The Oriental_, San Francisco, May 1856.
(Huntington Library: RB 55030)

The Reverend William T. Speer, sent to California by the Presbyterian Board of Foreign Missions, devoted himself to spreading Christianity to the Chinese in California. Through his pamphleteering and the newspaper he founded in San Francisco, _The Oriental_, he also defended the Chinese against the rampant prejudices of the era.

pursued its goal relentlessly, to the consternation of the slaveholding South. Even among many abolitionists, however, the immutable racial differences they saw between black and white made a society that regarded the two as equals an utter impossibility. Against such a backdrop, the free blacks residing in the North and Midwest, either freeborn citizens of those states or escapees from the slave states, lived a difficult existence, often carrying the burden of legal discrimination and social prejudice.

Like so many of their peers, some free blacks found in the news of the gold discovery in California sufficient inspiration to abandon their previous lives and set out in search of opportunities to improve their circumstances, start a fresh life, and escape the legacy of slavery. Though the number of blacks who came to California was not large (possibly six or seven hundred in the first eighteen months and fifteen hundred in the first three or four years), they provoked comment and concern. Their very presence incited much hostility, especially from argonauts who hailed from the slave states, and aroused discussion and debate in the framing of the California state constitution in 1849. The promise of California nonetheless proved as irresistible to some black Americans as it did to many others of every region, religion, or ethnicity. James Williams, a runaway bondsman who traveled the Underground Railroad and lived to tell about it in an 1873 memoir entitled _The Life and Adventures of James Williams, a Fugitive Slave,_ described his difficult trek to California in 1851 by ship and across the Isthmus of Panama despite the hostility of quite a few fellow travelers. As he wrote of the path he traveled, "I never made a cent for my time or labor, so you can see what a man that has made

Petition of Citizens of California to the U.S. Congress, February 21, 1859.

(Huntington Library: HM 514)

Even after the land commission passed out of existence in 1856, many of the cases it had begun dragged on for years thereafter. In this 1859 petition to the American Congress, a number of Californio landowners vehemently protested the "destruction of the rights of the old native Californians."

his escape from the blood-hounds hath to undergo to reach the shores of California, where he could be free and safe from all danger of being apprehended. Whilst in that country, I saw some that I had to run away from, yet I would have you to understand that I had no running away to do in California" (p. 29). Though he often suffered from the prejudice so commonly directed toward his race, he found in the goldfields many who would treat him like any other man in search of his golden reward.

Other black Americans came to California not of their own choosing but in the company of their masters, like Reuben Murrell, who arrived with George McKinley Murrell from their home in Bowling Green, Kentucky, in 1849 despite the legal risks of bringing a slave into free territory. Although even fewer slaves came than free black emigrants (perhaps two or three hundred), the very notion of competing with slave labor infuriated most argonauts more than the competition of Chinese contract workers. Once again, it seemed to offer an unfair advantage to the men who reaped the profit (in this case the slave owner) but who invested none of the labor required every day of most other argonauts. Such opposition, coupled with California's entrance into the Union in September 1850 as a free state, made it a relatively inhospitable environment for slavery. Nonetheless, those who did rely upon the peculiar institution did what they could to maintain it undisturbed even on free soil. In an October 4, 1849, letter home, allegedly composed by Reuben and written by "master George" for him, Reuben expressed the same cares and worries found in the letters of many other argonauts when he wrote that "I desire to hear from you all as soon as I can…every thing that has

Edward Lewis & G. Bohn, 15, Coleman St. London.

FARMING SCENE IN NAPA VALLEY

INDIAN RANCHERIE ON DRY CREEK.　　　[Published at the UNION OFFICE.

happened since I left," that "I have strong faith to believe that we are going to be lucky," and that "now we expect to go to work in a few days & make something & get back as soon as we possibly can." For his part, George noted in a November 8, 1850, letter that, despite exposure to the propaganda of the antislavery crusaders, "I do not think that their contaminating and poisoning principles has in the least weakened [Reuben's] fidelity and devotedness to me."

In the meantime, the steady upsurge of American emigration west to California during the 1850s brought more and more pressure to bear upon the native peoples of the Sierra Nevada foothills as gold seekers roamed further and further afield in search of rich diggings. Americans had been engaged for generations in the dispossession of Indian communities from one part of the landscape to another, culminating with the designation of large chunks of land west of the Missouri River as permanent reserves for various tribes relocated from the states east of the Mississippi. Now, engaged in the frenzied treasure hunt that followed gold discovery, they encountered indigenous peoples numbering in the tens of thousands who resisted efforts to push them aside so that more claim sites could be opened. Parties of prospectors blundered into bands of Indians as the former searched for gold and the latter for food; on occasion, despite their pervasive fear of the "savage" natives, some argonauts stepped back from the brink of violence. While on one prospecting expedition in the autumn of 1850, Augustin Hale, the mechanically inclined forty-niner from New Jersey, encountered two Indians, one of whom began to harangue him forcefully from a distance. "I was much pleased with his style & earnestness & would have given much could I have understood him," Hale wrote in a September 1, 1850, diary entry, but, fearing the likely reaction of his fellow prospectors, "I told them to 'vamoose' as I knew if they remained until our boys came up they would shoot them....I shall never forget his manner as he continued to address me in the most earnest manner & with a loud voice until he saw the approach of our party from the camp, then ran off at great speed. I was much blamed," he concluded, "for not shooting them, but under the circumstances I could not."

Reversing the reliance upon Indian labor (recruited from such Sierra Nevada tribes as the Miwoks) that had characterized the first months of the Gold Rush, the argonauts of 1849 and thereafter drove them out of the goldfields. Indian resistance only provoked more vigorous responses from the miners, initiating an increasingly violent cycle of skirmishes, ambushes, and massacres. Ad hoc militia companies, similar to the bodies of miners who gathered to discipline recalcitrant foreign miners, marched off into the mountains, tracking down Indians suspected of crimes ranging from stock theft to murder. In their haste to inflict punishment, many of these part-time soldiers swept away the innocent with the guilty, burning out rancherias and shooting down their inhabitants indiscriminately. By 1851, conflict had become so frequent that Governor Peter Burnett could write in his message to the state legislature that "our American experience has demonstrated the fact, that the two races cannot live in the same vicinity in peace" due to the chasm of social, cultural, and racial differences separating them. With relations between the races irretrievably poisoned by mutual incompatibility and perpetual hostility, Governor Burnett concluded any contact could have only one outcome: "That a war of extermination will continue to be waged between the races, until the Indian race becomes extinct, must be expected. While we cannot anticipate this result but with painful regret, the inevitable destiny of the race is beyond the power or wisdom of man to avert" (p. 7). Such a ready acceptance of the "inevitable" at the highest levels of the state's government only amplified the willingness of other Californians to bring that destiny to pass as quickly as possible. Through most of the 1850s, private and state-sponsored expeditions battled the Indians of California's interior again and again.

The proprietary regard with which American argonauts often viewed California's gold extended in the minds of many of those argonauts to California's land as well. Reconciling the rights of current landholders with the aspirations of land-hungry settlers involved sorting out bitter conflicts similar to those between American miners and their foreign counterparts over

< **"Farming Scene in Napa Valley,"** lithograph in Ernest Seyd, *California and Its Resources: A Work for the Merchant, the Capitalist, and the Emigrant*, London, 1858.

(Huntington Library: RB 27189)

Despite the attention focused on California's gold during the 1850s, more and more observers began to take note of California's significant agricultural potential. That growing awareness only heightened conflicts over some California land titles.

< *Indian Rancherie on Dry Creek,* letter sheet published at the Union Office.

(Huntington Library: RB 48052 #187)

The gnawing hunger for land felt by many newly arrived Californians only aggravated relations between them and the Indian peoples who occupied many parts of the state. Indian villages (often known as *rancherias*) were driven off land desired by whites for farming or mining.

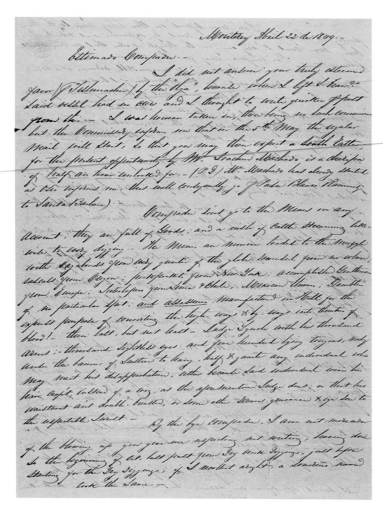

Hugo Reid, autograph letter to Abel Stearns, April 22, 1849.

(Huntington Library: SG Box 53)

The lure of gold attracted fortune seekers of widely varying moral character. By 1849, complaints could be heard on all sides about the rampant crime and violence that stalked the goldfields. Writing to Abel Stearns in April 1849, Hugo Reid denounced the scoundrels, rascals, thieves, and assassins that deluged the mines.

OPPOSITE >

Committee of Vigilance of San Francisco membership certificate for Sylvanus B. Marston, 1856.

(Huntington Library: HM 56797)

During the 1850s, widespread fears of crime provoked episodes of lynch law in most Gold Rush mining camps and towns, including San Francisco. The 1856 San Francisco committee enrolled its members in an elaborate, quasi-military body that proclaimed an unwavering devotion to justice under the all-seeing eye of heaven.

access to the goldfields, frequently to no one's ultimate satisfaction. For the American settlers who had crossed the continent to California in the early 1840s before the Mexican-American War, the remarkable potential of certain California landscapes such as the Sacramento Valley around John Sutter's New Helvetia had been the great attraction. Their ambitions to acquire land of their own, unencumbered by the need to become naturalized Mexican citizens, had played a part in the unrest leading up to the Bear Flag Revolt in the early phases of the American conquest of California.

Following gold discovery in 1848, the hordes of gold seekers who came in 1848, 1849, or 1850 at first seemed far less concerned with ownership of land than with access to its mineral wealth. Some of the gold seekers, however, soon began to see a brighter future in other pursuits than the endless search for El Dorado, while other pioneers came to California with every intention of finding some fertile plot of land to claim for themselves. In either case, the rules and regulations governing the acquisition of land in California grew to have a pressing importance for them. Unfortunately, like so much else in the wake of the Gold Rush, the control of land became a subject for continuing controversy.

Under the terms of the Treaty of Guadalupe Hidalgo at the conclusion of the Mexican-American War, Mexican nationals remaining in the conquered territories, whether they retained their citizenship or adopted that of the United States, were promised that "property of every kind…shall be inviolably respected" and that they would be "maintained in the free enjoyment of their liberty and property." In the ensuing effort to incorporate California into the Union, however, the encounter between Mexican and American systems of outlining and occupying property led to lengthy legal and political wrangling.

Unlike the mathematically precise surveys and formal deeds common under American land law, many of the Mexican land grants in Alta California rested upon indistinct boundaries and casual registration of the final documents. Grants of varying size issued under varying circumstances heightened the confusion about who held what property and who had what rights to dispose of it. Henry H. Haight, a Missouri lawyer who had come to California in 1850, in writing to his father on July 17 of that year enumerated eight separate classes of land titles in the city of San Francisco alone, created under Mexican and American civil and military administrations, and concluded in frustration that "it is confusion worse confounded," for which as a remedy, "almost any system would be preferable." Many other Americans bitterly resented the extensive terrain, sometimes running to thousands of acres, incorporated within some of the rancho grants. They shared the views of Dr. Israel S. P. Lord, an Illinois physician of strong opinions who had come overland in 1849. Writing in his journal on November 8, 1849, about the Sacramento Valley, he characterized it as land that would be "a delightful country for farming.…There is much, however, to oppose and finally prevent so desirable a consummation. I will only mention one now—The Spanish Grants.…If…the old claims are confirmed, the whole land will continue a wilderness of tangled briers and vines and shrubs and weeds and grass." Returning again and again to this topic of the iniquities of

THE FIRST TRIAL & EXECUTION IN S. FRANCISCO ON THE NIGHT OF 10ᵗʰ OF JUNE AT 2 O'CLOCK

del after the nature by W.C.K.

John Jenkins, a Sidney man, entered the store of M'V on long Wharf, in the evening of 10ᵗʰ of June & carried off a safe after he was captured he was brought to the corner of Sansome & Bush Sts. where he was tried by a jury of the highest respectability, and condemned to be hung. The execution took place on the Plaza on the same night at 2 o'clock Immediately after sentence of death was passed upon him, he was asked if he had anything to say, he replied. No, I have nothing to say, only I should wish to have a cigar & brandy & water, which was given him.

The First Trial & Execution in S. Francisco on the Night of 10th of June at 2 O'Clock, letter sheet published by Quirot & Co.

(Huntington Library: RB 48052 #23)

San Francisco's first vigilance committee in 1851 pursued various criminals, many of whom were associated with escaped convicts from Australia. Like those that would follow it, this committee operated outside the existing structure of courts and laws and carried out its own sentences, swiftly and without appeal.

California land law as he wrote of his travels through California, he concluded that "almost all the arable land in California is claimed by a very few lazy, idle, worthless individuals, not particularly friendly to the government, and held at prices out of reach of the tillers of the soil."

Determined to acquire part of California's landed bounty for themselves, many of those same "tillers of the soil" refused to wait for the settlement of these questions through the legal or political process. Instead, bands of "squatters" seized parcels of property for their own and forcibly resisted the efforts of landowners and civil authorities to remove them. Dismissing their defiance of the law, squatters and their supporters such as Dr. Lord appealed to a higher moral authority that justified such behavior. Writing indignantly on November 14, 1850, about a defeat of the squatter position in court, Dr. Lord asserted that "most assuredly the squatters were in the right. They had as much right to the land where Sacramento City stands as anybody (certainly more than the swindling minions of Sutter) and so took possession and built upon the lots. In fact, occupancy was the only title anybody could have.…The decision of the court was wrong in principle if not in fact, for the squatters only claimed what they could and did then and there occupy, i.e., one or two lots at most for each." Even some who opposed such outbreaks of violence sympathized with the situation of the squatters. Sacramento merchant Mark Hopkins, writing to his brother Moses about these events on August 29, 1850, noted that "the present officers of the country, from the Governor down, both *Executive & Judicial,* are land speculators whose interest is to maintain the claims of Sutter.…Thus wholesale land speculators, under color of a Quit Claim Deed from Sutter or

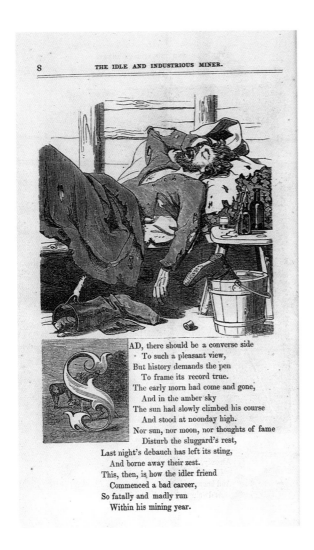

AD, there should be a converse side
  To such a pleasant view,
But history demands the pen
  To frame its record true.
The early morn had come and gone,
  And in the amber sky
The sun had slowly climbed his course
  And stood at noonday high.
Nor sun, nor moon, nor thoughts of fame
  Disturb the sluggard's rest,
Last night's debauch has left its sting,
  And borne away their zest.
This, then, is how the idler friend
  Commenced a bad career,
So fatally and madly run
  Within his mining year.

EQUITED toil! Eureka! Look!
  And read within those eyes
Their speaking luster, as they dwell
  Upon the glittering prize!
The vein is struck! ah, noble heart!
  A thrill of joy is thine!—
A purer and a better thrill
  Than that produced by wine.
A thousand thoughts of home, and bliss
  Reserved for coming years
Have swiftly flashed across thy soul!
  And melted thee to tears—
Tears—not of grief, or vain regrets,
  For thou art still a man—
But, thinking of thy poverty
  And gazing in the pan!

2

Alonzo Delano, two illustrations from *The Idle and Industrious Miner*, Sacramento, 1854.

(Huntington Library: RB 32382)

Despite increasing evidence to the contrary, many miners still clung to the belief that those who exhibited diligence and moral rectitude certainly would succeed in the hunt for wealth. Alonzo Delano's 1854 morality tale, with illustrations by well-known artist Charles Nahl, reiterated this point of view.

some other wholesale claimant…are monopolizing the possession of all the lands to the exclusion of emigrants who claim the right to settle…expecting a preemption in accordance with the established usage of the U.S. in the settlement of all the Western States." Hopkins went on, however, to add that "I regret, as every good citizen regrets, this resistance of our constituted authorities in the discharge of their duties—It is inexcusable." The resulting pro and antisquatter agitation spilled over into the courts and the legislature, generating lawsuits and riots throughout the 1850s.

In an effort to resolve this continuing turmoil, the federal government in 1849 commissioned reports to examine the legal procedures under which the Spanish and Mexican governments had granted land to private parties, thus laying the groundwork for determining the legitimacy of specific land grants. Unfortunately, the two principal surveys came to very different conclusions about the legality of many existing grants, leaving it up to the Congress to propose a course of action. After much debate, that body in turn adopted the plan submitted to it by William M. Gwin, one of California's first two senators following its admission to the Union in September 1850. Gwin's bill established in 1851 a three-member commission empowered to examine all private land claims issued under the authority of the Spanish or Mexican governments and pass upon their legitimacy, subject to appeal to the federal court system. Gwin, in his published address on behalf of the bill, declared that the commission would "put an end to doubt, …recognizing what is bona fide and valid, and denouncing what is fraudulent, thereby securing and indicating the rights of honest claimants on the one hand, and

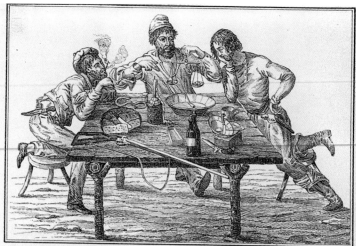

MINERS WEIGHING THEIR GOLD.

THE DREAM OF A PROSPECTING MINER.
Lith. & Published by Quirot & Cᵒ. corneʳ Montgomery & California Sᵗ S.Francisco.

Miners Weighing Their Gold/The Dream of a Prospecting Miner, **letter sheet published by Quirot & Co.**

(Huntington Library: RB 48052 #44)

This letter sheet, like many others, portrayed the dreams that gave miners the strength to carry on. The illustration at the top of the page, however, showed the dream taking a tangible form as three miners watch the weighing of their gold dust.

protecting on the other the great mass of honest settlers seeking titles from our Government in the public lands" (p. 12).

Though Gwin and his partisans assured all who would listen that such a commission would "in a plain and direct manner, …relieve the titles of the country from confusion," the end results proved far more troublesome. By requiring all holders of Spanish or Mexican land grants to prove a particular grant's legitimacy, the United States Land Commission's enabling legislation threw an aura of suspicion around such grants and their claimants from the beginning. Despite the stipulations of the Treaty of Guadalupe Hidalgo about the inviolability of the property of those Mexican citizens now under the authority of the United States, the commission's activities opened many titles to challenge. Moreover, the conduct of its proceedings under the rules of American jurisprudence forced many of the Californios to defend their claims in a legal system and a language completely foreign to them. Although the vast majority of the claims eventually were confirmed either through the commission's hearings or subsequent court cases, many landowners were financially ruined by the costs of lawyers, translators, and repeated litigation. One group of Southern California landowners, proposing in 1855 to band together for their mutual defense against "the falsehoods and calumnies circulated in the public press about the validity of our titles," denounced the "interminable litigation" and the "effort made against us to carry out a general confiscation of our properties" resulting from the land commission's work. Despite such criticism, however, the commission's endeavors ground on through nearly five years in reviewing more than eight hundred claims, until its hearings finally came to an end in 1856.

Even after the commission's disbanding, frequent court challenges to its decisions led to interminable litigation, prompting one group of Californio landholders to speak out in a February 1859 petition forwarded to the United States Congress. Invoking the promises made to them during the Mexican-American War by the occupying forces and reiterated in the Treaty of Guadalupe Hidalgo that their property *"shall be inviolably protected and insured,"* they argued that, on the contrary, their lands and their way of life had never been less secure. The procedures of the land commission, the hordes of law-defying land seekers brought by the Gold Rush, and the crushing burden of taxation imposed by the new state all acted to threaten many with financial ruin or dispossession. "The manifest injustice of such an act," the petition continued, "must be clearly apparent to those Honorable Bodies [the Senate and the House of Representatives] when they consider that the native Californians were an agricultural people and they have wished to continue so; but they have met the obstacle of the enterprising genius of the Americans, who have assumed possession of their lands, taken their cattle and destroyed their woods, while the Californians have been thrown among strangers to their language, customs, laws and habits." The American Congress, the petitioners argued, had a duty based upon "justice and equity" to "respect, protect and uphold the treaties of Guadalupe Hidalgo," which in turn would preserve the honor "of the general Government of the United States." For the Californios, the tumultuous Gold Rush era had brought disappointment and, in many cases, disaster, transforming dreams into nightmares.

As the decade following gold discovery unfolded, many people in California thus demonstrated their willingness to resort to violence, or at least the threat of violence, in order to advance a particular purpose. With a weak and impoverished government that spent its first few years in search of a permanent seat of residence and local administrations little better off, resolute individuals often did not hesitate to pursue their own ends through other means than the formal channels of law and order. Many argonauts, on the other hand, having no interest in setting down roots in California, ignored government and civic life as much as possible, devoting themselves only to fulfilling their dreams of finding El Dorado. In such an environment, the unscrupulous and the wicked, attracted to California by their own particular vision of a golden reward, found significant scope for their activities. Hugo Reid, writing to his friend Abel Stearns from Monterey on April 22, 1849, encapsulated what became a common view of the gold country as the rush accelerated. "Compadre, don't go to the Mines on any account," he warned Stearns, "The Mines are…loaded to the muzzle with vagabonds from every quarter of the globe: scoundrels from no where, rascals from Oregon: pickpockets from New York: accomplished Gentlemen from Europe: Interlopers from Lima & Chile: Mexican thieves: Gamblers of no particular spot: *and assassins* manufactured in Hell for the express purpose of converting the high-ways & by-ways into theatres of blood!" Throughout the 1850s, the letters and diaries of many argonauts offered (though usually in less florid language) similar indictments and repeated stories of lawlessness occurring on all sides, both in the mining camps and in the cities.

With courts, prisons, and peace officers frequently lacking in the mining country, the perception of rampant crime and violence drove many argonauts toward vigilante justice as the only remedy left to them. In some instances adopting the forms of civil authority by organizing vigilance committees and constituting their own courts, vigilantes were often a specific group of men coalescing in response to a particular outrage in a particular community. Dispensing with the structures of judge and jury, they might settle guilt or innocence and then impose punishment by popular consensus, brushing aside anyone, whether public official or private citizen, who dared to oppose them. At the El Dorado County jail in April 1852, for instance, as described in the county sheriff's daybook, one crowd of vigilantes marched upon the jail in the absence of the sheriff and forced the surrender in sequence of two men being held under indictment for grand larceny. After hanging both, the vigilantes demanded that a third man then being tried be handed over to them, and only the return of the county sheriff and the conclusion of the third man's trial deflected the mob from carrying out a third execution. Prior to the sheriff's return, neither what the keeper of the daybook described as the "eloquent and stirring appeal in support of law and order" made by a local judge nor the delaying tactics of the jailer could forestall the operation of lynch law.

Like the vigilantes who ran the Chileans out of the Calaveras mining district or rounded up Mexicans suspected of murder in Sonora, an armed and boisterous mob could be irresistible as Edward G. Buffum discovered when he attempted to stand against one at Dry Diggings (later known as Hangtown and eventually Placerville) in January 1849. Two Frenchmen and one Chilean, being charged with attempted robbery and murder, "were tried in the open air by a crowd of some two hundred men, who had organized themselves into a jury and appointed a *pro tempore* judge." After a universal verdict of guilty, the crowd proposed to hang them for their punishment. Appalled by such a plan, Buffum protested "in the name of God, humanity and law" to no avail, for "the crowd, excited by frequent and deep potations of liquor from a neighboring groggery, would hear nothing contrary to their brutal desires, and even threatened to hang me if I did not immediately desist from any further remarks" (*Six Months in the Gold Mines*, p. 109). Buffum abandoned his protest, and the mob carried out its triple execution, despite the fact that none of the victims could speak or understand English. To

Augusto Ferran lo Litografió.   Litogª de I. Marquer Cª de Lamparilla, nº 95

Realizacion.   Selling off.

Augusto Ferran lo Litografió.   Litogª de I. Marquer Cª de Lamparilla, nº 95

Posiciones cómodas.   Comfort.

"Selling Off," lithograph in Augusto Ferran and José Baturone, *Album Californiano*, Havana, c. 1850.
(Huntington Library: RB 31800)

"Comfort," lithograph in Augusto Ferran and José Baturone, *Album Californiano*, Havana, c. 1850.
(Huntington Library: RB 31800)

In these 1850 lithographs by two Cuban artists, one group of miners takes a first step toward realizing the dreams that brought them to the goldfields by cashing in their "pile" while others enjoy some "comfort" in the confines of a saloon as a respite from their labors.

Hugo Reid, as he urged his compadre Abel Stearns to avoid the mines at all costs, the other great evil lurking in the mining country was the presence of "Judge Lynch with his thousand arms: thousand Sightless eyes and five hundred lying tongues, ready under the banner of Justice to hang, half & quarter any individual who may meet his disapprobation."

In the Gold Rush cities generally and in San Francisco particularly, vigilantes also would be active as agents for suppressing crime and violence. First in 1851 and then again in 1856, large and well-organized vigilance committees would actually supplant the municipal government of San Francisco for weeks at a time, resolved to usurp the police and the courts in apprehending, convicting, and punishing criminals. Hundreds of men, especially from the merchant classes of the city's population, enrolled each time in paramilitary bodies. Committee detachments drilled under arms and, in 1856, gathered at a fortified headquarters known variously as "Fort Vigilant" or "Fort Gunnybags" (the latter title because of the number of sandbags surrounding the building). Also in 1856, with many merchants and other members of the middle classes concerned about political and social corruption, the murder of newspaper editor James King of William by local politician James Casey not only brought the second vigilance committee into being but pushed it into pursuing electoral fraud and deceit.

Of its composition and activities, one observer, the merchant Thomas O. Larkin, wrote to Abel Stearns on May 31, 1856, that "there never was in an association of 3000 men more inteligence, respectabiluty & wealth than in this one," while, he scornfully continued, "I suppose most of the small lawyers & the Pol[it]cians and all the loafers & gamblers are against [it]." To others, however, such activities presented a less-benign face, as Mary Jane Megquier wrote to her daughter Angeline on June 19, 1856: "We look upon tomorrow as big with the fate of this unfortunate city. I cannot be frightened but many can neither eat, nor sleep, they say the law and order people will plunder and burn the city….I assure you it looks very like war, to go through our streets in the evening and see thousands [of] bayonets glimmering in the moonlight….Never was such a state of things known to exist in any country, …I shall be glad when it is decided for such a state of things suspends all business and makes it decidedly bad for me." No such desperate battle in the end transpired, and the city returned after much excitement to the rule of the elected government. Never again in the Gold Rush period would vigilante activity reach such a peak.

Shocked as she was by the menacing atmosphere that seemed to permeate the city of San Francisco in the summer of 1856, Mrs. Megquier also expressed her dismay at the obstacles this turmoil threw in the way of transacting business in the city. Eager to wind up certain long-standing business affairs, she chafed at the delays imposed by these events. Like many of her peers in the Gold Rush era, Megquier focused first and foremost on achieving the financial success that she had promised her family would justify their sacrifices. For nearly all the argonauts, painfully aware of the financial, emotional, and psychological costs inflicted upon their loved ones by these expeditions to El Dorado, the burden of realizing their dreams under the looming shadow of failure wore them down with its weight.

Mrs. Megquier, a fond if irregular inhabitant of San Francisco since her first arrival in the summer of 1849 with her physician husband, obviously felt that she understood this painful dilemma. As early as November 11, 1849, after observing the progress of the great excitement through the autumn, she had written to Milton Benjamin in Maine that "some will get into business the moment they put foot on land, in three months will find themselves with fifty thousand, while others whose prospects are much brighter, will in the same short space of time be breathing their last in some miserable tent…they are tumbled into a rough box with their clothes on, in which they died, this has been the fate of thousands since I have been here." The glistening confidence felt by many, and expressed by J. Goldsborough Bruff before leaving home that "as regards the gold, with God's blessing I am sure of that," had been dulled by the tarnish of experience. Luther Fitch, writing home to his father from San Francisco on August 27, 1850, reflected the diminished aspirations of many argonauts when he described the difficulties of establishing his medical practice upon a firm footing: "I have a few calls but have done nothing since the third day. I took an office, but the rent is so high that it together with my board will soon consume all I have." Determined to reverse these setbacks, he announced his intention to relocate to Stockton and then pledged that "if I can do nothing at S[tockton], I shall go to the mines. I cannot bear the idea of returning," he continued gloomily, "without at least making myself whole and Shall make every effort to do so."

Among the women who had joined the rush to El Dorado, most became involved in the same struggle between success and failure in pursuit of a golden reward as their male counterparts had. While some braved it only vicariously, through the careers of their husbands, many of them were pulled into the fray directly. Lucy Stoddard Wakefield, writing to "Lucius and Rebecca" from Placerville on September 18, 1851, proclaimed that "I love California and probably now shall make my home and final resting place here," but continued, "I have been toiling hard for the last two and a half years and am still doing an almost incredible amount of work." That would be the lot of any of her sex who came, she added, for "there is no way for a woman to make money except by hard work of some sort," requiring "years of toil, hardship, and in some respects severe privation, [though] if it is a husband she would be after she could find them with any amount of fortune as thick as toads after a rain, pardon the vulgarity of my comparison." Echoing many other women and men after lengthy exposure to the hard labor of making money, she concluded that she expected to stop working in a few months since "I am tired of work and though I have not a very big pile, yet I am not ambitious of wealth. A competency is all I look for, for myself." Writing to her friend Alfred Grey about her San Francisco boardinghouse on July 29, 1852, Maria F. Noatts sounded a similar note, remarking that "my health is good but I never worked so hard in all my life as now....I have had one Man to work for me but he is gone to the mines[.] I paid him 35 per month[.] [G]ood help is scarce. I could pay 45 for good help and not save a dollar for my self." Strictly limited by the moral standards of the Victorian era as to the occupations that might be considered "proper" for their sex, women like Megquier, Wakefield, and Noatts found their options few. In Gold Rush era California, with its emphasis upon manual labor in the goldfields and commerce in the cities and towns, respectable women were relegated to a few roles that mirrored their culturally prescribed responsibilities within the family as homemaker. Wakefield baked pies, averaging as many as twenty dozen a week on her own, while Megquier and Noatts kept house for others in boarding establishments.

The unremitting toil and drudgery so many men and women found in El Dorado and wrote of so frequently in their diaries and journals, whether as prospector or miner, cook or charwoman, convinced some that California was nothing more than a snare and a delusion. Hinton Helper, an acid-tongued North Carolinian who came out in 1854 to explore its possibilities, quickly concluded that nothing it offered could possess the slightest value, an opinion he shared freely in his relentlessly critical 1855 publication *The Land of Gold: Fiction versus Reality.* Casting a baleful eye around the city of San Francisco, for instance, he wrote that "while in this vicinity, we may observe men, who in the Atlantic States bore unblemished reputations for probity and honor, sinking into the lowest depths of shame and degradation. Others, whose moral characters are unobjectionable, have been pecuniarily unfortunate, and are driven to the necessity of engaging in the most menial and humiliating employments....They could not help themselves; they were out of friends, and were compelled to take advantage of the first opportunity of earning their daily bread. Half the lowest and most servile situations or offices in this and other cities in the State are filled, often without any other remuneration, than board and lodging, by these unlucky and depressed adventurers" (pp. 60–1).

For many of the argonauts, such complaints would have struck a sympathetic chord, for they found themselves struggling against the same challenges, sometimes with the same lack of success. The majority, however, putting on the bravest front possible, wrote home of their undiminished resolution to pursue their golden dreams, even as the months and years flew by. Alonzo Delano, one of the overlanders in 1849, captured this sense of the argonaut's world vividly in an 1854 pamphlet, *The Idle and Industrious Miner.* Delano, an accomplished writer, had become a sort of poet laureate for the gold seekers, producing many humorous sketches of the miner's life. This pamphlet, illustrated with a wonderfully satirical series of drawings, told the tale of "Two school-boy friends, with buoyant hearts, / and grown to man's estate, / Repaired to California's shores, / To fill their cup of fate." Following the two through their adventures, it pointed out the contrast between the idle miner, already suffering from the effects of dissipation, "Nor sun, nor moon, nor thoughts of fame / Disturb the sluggard's rest, / Last night's debauch has left its sting, / And borne away their zest," and his industrious colleague, whose devotion to duty has borne fruit: "Requited toil! Eureka! Look! / And read within those eyes / Their speaking luster, as they dwell / Upon the glittering prize!" (pp. 8–9).

Other argonauts, struggling with various frustrations, made their peace with the circumstances of separation and disappointment. Writing to his sister and brother-in-law in Farmington Falls, Maine, on December 17, 1857, William Farnsworth outlined his travels in the previous few months before coming to rest on a claim two hundred yards from the mining town of Columbia, "where I have remained ever since as busy as a bee trying to catch some of the shining specks." His health, he reported, had remained excellent over the last three years but, he wistfully admitted, "it would be more agreable for me to live whare I would see my friends a little oftener without being to so much expense of traveling." Nonetheless, he asserted, if he was going to be a

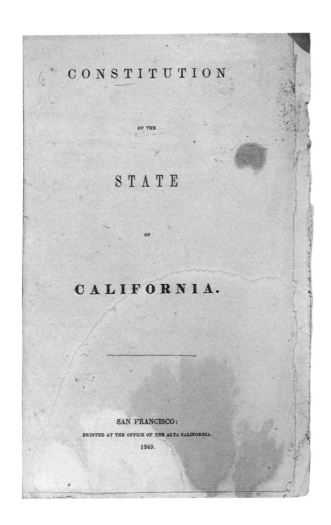

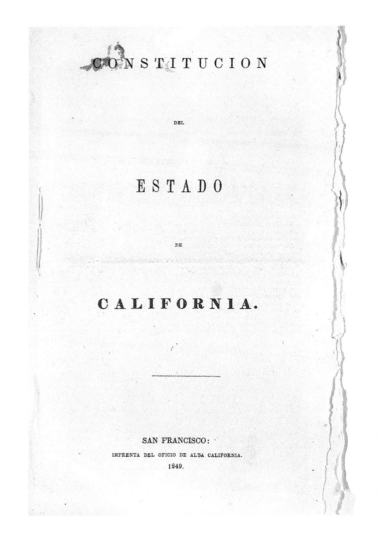

westerner, California was the place for him: "You will not catch me to go to Kansas or any of those new countries to beat the bush and let somebody [else] catch the bird." He would move out of the mountains, he thought, to one of the coastal valleys: "It is some of the finest climates in the world and cant be beat by your Nebraska nor no other wild land." In so saying, Farnsworth reflected yet another transformation he and like-minded argonauts had worked upon California during its golden age: they had begun to turn it into home.

Defining a New California: The Constitution of 1849 and Political Life

Other than Marshall's discovery of gold itself, perhaps the most important event in the transformation of California during the Gold Rush era occurred on February 2, 1848, when the Mexican and American commissioners initialed the Treaty of Guadalupe Hidalgo, bringing the Mexican-American War to a conclusion. At that point, as hostilities between the two North American republics ended, California's metamorphosis from Mexican province to American state began. The process unfolded awkwardly at first, since the federal government had made no provision for the administration of its new possession after the end of hostilities. Lacking any detailed guidance, the successive United States military commanders in California improvised. They sustained such Mexican institutions as the alcalde (a figure whose closest American counterpart might be the mayor of a town or city) to govern on the local level, while retaining for the senior American army officer the effective position of military governor.

The perpetuation of military government in California, even when amalgamated with some elements of civil authority, soon excited suspicion and hostility in some quarters. Although

William Rich Hutton, watercolor drawing entitled *View of Monterey*, 1849.

(Huntington Library: HM 43214 #46) Monterey occupied center stage in California politics briefly during the fall of 1849 when it hosted the convention that drafted a constitution for the as-yet-unborn state of California.

many of the gold seekers had no immediate interest in the finer intricacies of California's governance, some of those Americans who had come before the Gold Rush grew restless quickly under what they regarded as the "arbitrary" rule of the army. These "old settlers" (as they sometimes referred to themselves) had wished for American rule to be extended over California as early as the mid-1840s. Now, with the fulfillment of that goal near at hand, they found their fate absorbed in the great national convulsion over the question of allowing slavery in the nation's new western territories.

Unwilling to wait upon the resolution of such questions, Californians in various places, including the city of San Francisco, launched local governments of their own design in opposition to military rule. More and more Americans, disenchanted with military control, supported such movements. A perception that anarchy was rampant in the land increasingly took hold, as one New York argonaut, lawyer and California constitutional convention delegate Elisha Crosby, remembered in his 1885 handwritten memoir: "Every man carried his code of laws on his hip and administered it according to his own pleasure. There was no safety of life or property so far as the intervention of law was concerned there was no police.…We were in a state of chaos, society was entirely unorganized, and the recognition of our status as a state with a state government seemed to be the one essential thing to give us a foundation to start upon" (p. 44). Soon after his arrival in April 1849, General Bennett Riley, the new military governor, decided that, before the situation escaped his control completely, he would issue a call for a constitutional convention in return for the dissolution of the various ad hoc local

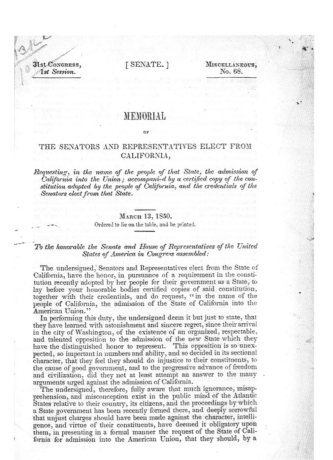

MEMORIAL

OF

THE SENATORS AND REPRESENTATIVES ELECT FROM CALIFORNIA,

Requesting, in the name of the people of that State, the admission of California into the Union; accompanied by a certified copy of the constitution adopted by the people of California, and the credentials of the Senators elect from that State.

MARCH 13, 1850.

Ordered to lie on the table, and be printed.

To the honorable the Senate and House of Representatives of the United States of America in Congress assembled:

The undersigned, Senators and Representatives elect from the State of California, have the honor, in pursuance of a requirement in the constitution recently adopted by her people for their government as a State, to lay before your honorable bodies certified copies of said constitution, together with their credentials, and do request, "in the name of the people of California, the admission of the State of California into the American Union."

In performing this duty, the undersigned deem it but just to state, that they have learned with astonishment and sincere regret, since their arrival in the city of Washington, of the existence of an organized, respectable, and talented opposition to the admission of the new State which they have the distinguished honor to represent. This opposition is so unexpected, so important in numbers and ability, and so decided in its sectional character, that they feel they should do injustice to their constituents, to the cause of good government, and to the progressive advance of freedom and civilization, did they not at least attempt an answer to the many arguments urged against the admission of California.

The undersigned, therefore, fully aware that much ignorance, misapprehension, and misconception exist in the public mind of the Atlantic States relative to their country, its citizens, and the proceedings by which a State government has been recently formed there, and deeply sorrowful that unjust charges should have been made against the character, intelligence, and virtue of their constituents, have deemed it obligatory upon them, in presenting in a formal manner the request of the State of California for admission into the American Union, that they should, by a

Memorial of the Senators and Representatives Elect from California, Requesting… the Admission of California into the Union…, Washington, D.C., 1850.

(Huntington Library: RB 275323)

Following the adoption of its constitution and the election of potential members of Congress, California's new government applied to the United States Congress early in 1850 for admission as a state.

What We Want in California from New York Direct, letter sheet published by Britton & Rey.

(Huntington Library: RB 48052 #66)

After California's admission to the Union, many Californians began to agitate for a direct link to the eastern United States by rail. As this letter sheet suggests, the railroad represented progress in bringing to life a vision of a civilized and thoroughly domesticated society in the Golden State.

governments. Although Riley's authority to take such action seemed uncertain at best, his proclamation of June 3, 1849, met with a generally favorable reaction and led, in turn, to elections of delegates from various districts around California.

The forty-eight men chosen to devise a written charter for the state-to-be arrived in Monterey to begin their work on September 3, 1849. Californios, Anglo-American "old settlers," veterans from the American army of occupation who had settled in California after their release from the service, and argonauts from various parts of the United States, they possessed a formidable array of backgrounds, occupations, and interests. Included among them were men who had stood on opposite sides of the Mexican-American War, men whose ties to California reached back decades, and men who had only just arrived from the United States. Drawn heavily from the ranks of merchants, lawyers, farmers, and ranchers, the membership of the convention represented segments of the population who all desired the establishment of stable, orderly government, although the degree and scope of its power could be debated.

In trying to give the new government shape and form, the delegates relied heavily upon preexisting models such as the constitutions of Iowa and New York State as well as consulting those of several other states. The constitution's provisions, therefore, represented the sort of institutions familiar to most of the participants and to thousands of the argonauts who had come to El Dorado from those states. The document touched upon various issues of surpassing significance to many Americans in the middle of the nineteenth century, such as the suspicion with which the general public regarded the power exercised by banks and corporations. Efforts to ban the former and greatly restrict the latter were among the results of the debates. In most instances, however, as the memoirs of Elisha Crosby make clear, the routine work of draftsmanship continued "by discussions in Committees and interviews outside the public sittings and debates." The convention as a whole would then proceed with its consideration of the drafts prepared for it.

No matter how routine the process or familiar the end results might seem to the Anglo-American delegates, for the Californios the convention's efforts constituted a fundamental redrawing of their political landscape according to the vision of others. Nonetheless, they did manage to secure certain measures to protect matters of importance to their constituents, such as ensuring that the new government's public documents would have to be published in Spanish as well as English. Though not a solidly unified voting bloc, they and their Anglo-American allies such as Abel Stearns and Stephen Foster represented a quarter of the convention's strength. Crosby, writing more than three decades after the convention, still remembered his colleagues from the "Spanish delegation" with respect, if not affection, in all instances. "The Spaniards," he recollected, "served in the convention because they saw the necessity for so doing: recognizing the fact that American occupation was inevitable, and they submitted with what grace they could" (p. 38).

Reshaping the political world of California, however, did pull Anglo-Americans and Californios into fractious debate on more than one occasion during the convention. When the convention began to lay out the standards for who could exercise the right to vote, for example, it followed the standard American practice of the time and limited suffrage to white male citizens over the age of twenty-one. Some members of the convention pointed out, however, that under the stipulations of the Treaty of Guadalupe Hidalgo citizens of the Mexican republic who accepted American citizenship had to be accorded the full rights and privileges of any other citizen. Moreover, while the notion of granting the right to vote generally to members of what one delegate described as those "objectionable races," African-Americans and Indians, received no strong support, other delegates noted that to limit the franchise only to *white* males might well act to bar some of the Californios of mixed ancestry and dark complexion. As a compromise, the final version of the suffrage article included a provision that the legislature, at a later date, could choose to grant Indians the right to vote, though such a measure would need the support of two-thirds of the legislature. Furthermore, it specifically recognized the right of citizens of Mexico to vote after they had become citizens of the United States, as long as they were white.

The same sense of racial prejudice concerning people of color drove forward a proposal that the first legislature be instructed to prohibit free blacks from moving to the new state. Although the convention had accepted a provision that outlawed slavery in California, such an action hardly represented an acceptance of racial equality or even, on the part of some delegates, a belief in racial tolerance. Even those who believed that slavery was an unmitigated evil often accepted the notion of black inferiority and felt that putting the races in proximity would drag down the superior white race. In the end, only a fear of the impact that such a measure might have upon Congress and the opposition that it might arouse there to California's admission as a state forestalled such a restriction. In both instances, the convention's debates became embroiled in the question of defining who might participate and how in certain aspects of California's public life and, by extension, who might even be defined as a Californian and who might be excluded. Thus, as the constitutional convention struggled to lay out the blueprint of a successful government, it also influenced whose dreams might be part of California's future and whose might be excluded.

Completion of the convention's work on October 12, 1849, only five weeks after it had begun, provided that blueprint. Building a government from that plan began almost immediately, with military governor Riley calling an election for November 13 of that year to ratify the constitution and to elect the first civilian officials to such posts as governor and the two houses of

Republican and People's Reform Ticket...for Presidential Electors (and reverse side), California, 1856?
(Huntington Library: Eph. F28-C1856/2)
In the 1856 presidential election, Californians could vote for a candidate, John C. Frémont, with long-standing ties to the Golden State who associated himself and his party with the long-sought transcontinental railroad (as demonstrated by the Frémont advertising on the reverse of the ballot).

the legislature. With its approval by a margin of more than twelve to one at that election, the constitution came into force and the first legislature to meet under its authority began on December 15, 1849, to grapple with all the mundane details of organizing local governments, courts, and executive departments to conduct the people's business. As Elisha Crosby, a member of the first state senate, described it, "All the laws then prevailing were superceded by the laws we enacted when we organized the State Government….We organized courts and enacted laws and just as fast as we did so the officers under the Spanish laws went out and their laws became obsolete" (p. 55). The legislature also took up the cause of statehood for California, with the selection of William M. Gwin and John C. Frémont as United States senators-designate to present a petition to the United States Congress urging California's admission. Once again, however, the hopes of statehood's advocates became enmeshed in the ongoing national debate over the extension of slavery. Another eight months would pass after the arrival of California's free-state constitution before the Congress would finally pass an act in September 1850 to admit the Golden State as part of the elaborate program of legislative measures known as the Compromise of 1850.

Even before formal admission to the Union, of course, political life in California according to the rites and customs of the United States had been in full swing. Following Bennett Riley's October 1849 proclamation scheduling the election that would ratify the California constitution, local public officials scrambled to organize an election in less than a month's time. Bayard Taylor, who observed the conduct of it at Lower Bar on the Mokelumne River, wryly captured its unconventional flavor in his 1850 account *El Dorado, or, Adventures in the Path of Empire:* "The election day dawned wet and cheerlessly….The election was held in the largest tent in the place, the inspectors being seated behind the counter, in close proximity to the glasses and bottles, the calls for which were quite as frequent as the votes….As there were two or three candidates for State office in the place, the drumming up of voters gave one a refreshing reminiscence of home….Names in many instances were made to stand for principles; accordingly, a Mr. Fair got many votes….Some went no further than to vote for those they actually knew" (vol. 2, pp. 6–7). Soon enough, though, some of the argonauts had begun to throw themselves into the political affairs of the newly hatched state.

In Gold Rush California, as in most other parts of the Union, party politics held a great and continuing fascination for many Americans. Although far away from their familiar surroundings, they still carried with them their political allegiances and

sentiments, just as they carried with them memories of home and family. Some, of course, hoped for a share of the spoils to be distributed by successful candidates for elective office; others shared a commitment to the principles espoused by one party or another. Various ambitious individuals such as Gwin, T. Butler King, or Lansford Hastings saw politics in California as their quickest path to advancement on the state and even national level. Similarly, many Californians ambitious for the development of the state saw the political parties as the mechanisms to achieve such results as the creation of a transcontinental railroad. Moreover, as the debates in the constitutional convention over the exclusion of slavery and the proposed exclusion of free blacks demonstrated, many argonauts were drawn into politics because of their devotion to one side or the other in the great slavery controversy.

For many Americans, political life involved not merely the contest of issues but the grand pageantry sponsored by the opposing sides. These political rituals soon appeared in California, especially during the first presidential election, that of 1852, in which Californians were eligible to participate. George M. Turner, writing to his brother Larkin on October 31 of that year, described an excursion he had taken to Sacramento early in the month with the Young Whigs and the Chapultepec Clubs, groups affiliated with the Whig Party and their candidate, General Winfield Scott. Arriving at 3 a.m., Turner and his fellows spent hours engaged in marches, songfests, and rallies, culminating that evening at 7 p.m. with "a tip top torchlight procession, nearly a mile long, had some more speeches, burnt some tarbarrels, &c., and then adjourned." Although a disappointed candidate for the Whig nomination for county surveyor, he still had great enthusiasm for the party ("It is a good political movement.") and hoped that its final push ("Tomorrow evening we are to have a grand torchlight procession....It will be the last chance and I am in hopes it will be nice.") would carry the day ("I think the state will just go for Scott, but the city is real whig."). To Turner, an ascendant Whig Party represented opportunity for his own success as well as the blessings it would bring to California and to the Union in the wake of a Scott victory.

As the decade of the 1850s passed and the currents of national politics continued to influence the ebb and flow of affairs in California, the ever-deepening sectional division within the country caused by the slavery issue dominated the agenda even within the Golden State. Billington C. Whiting, writing to his wife on May 19, 1858, while she visited family members back east, described the ferocious infighting inside the Democratic Party, California's dominant political organization by that point, between the adherents of Senator Gwin, the pro-Southern wing known as the "chivalry democracy," and those of California's other serving senator, David C. Broderick (formerly of New York State), whose pro-Northern, working-class wing of the party had acquired the derisive name of the "shovelry democracy" in its battles with Gwin's followers. Whiting, apparently a strong opponent of the "chivalry," also commented scathingly about Gwin's dereliction of his duty to California, noting that "Gwin had better stay where he is unless he can satisfy the people of California that his absences from his seat when the Rail Road Bill lost its place on the calendar was unintentional." The escalating tone of these conflicts would lead, in the end, to the death of Broderick a year later in a duel with one of Gwin's partisans, State Supreme Court Justice David Terry, and shortly afterward to the collapse of the Democratic Party's power in California as the country entered the Civil War.

The continued agitation of the slavery question in national politics, embroiling most issues of public life by the end of the 1850s, was mirrored in California by other divisive controversies revolving around matters of race and ethnicity. Although these questions arose from peculiarly Californian circumstances, they exemplified many of the same issues embedded within the debate over slavery. In trying to resolve them during the decade, various Californians quarreled about who would be included and who would be excluded from full participation in the economic, political, or social life of the Golden State.

For many of California's Indian peoples, the struggle in the 1850s only intensified be-

HONEST VOTERS TRYING TO ELECT THEIR OFFICERS
in front of the house

BALLOT BOX STUFFERS, ELECTING THEIR MEN
behind the house.

NOISY CARRIERS 64. & 66. Long Wharf
48052(68)

GRAND ADMISSION CELEBRATION.

PORTSMOUTH SQUARE OCTR 29TH 1850

Grand Admission Celebration.
Portsmouth Square Octr. 29, 1850,
letter sheet published by C. J. Pollard.
(Huntington Library: RB 48052 #137)
Congress's acceptance of California's petition for admission in September 1850 occasioned much celebrating in the Golden State when the news finally reached the West Coast.

tween them and the enormous influx of gold-seeking outsiders that had begun after James Marshall's discovery. In many parts of the Sierra Nevada and especially in the far northern forests and mountains that comprised Shasta, Trinity, Klamath, and Siskiyou counties, hostile encounters between Euro-American prospectors and Yuroks, Klamaths, Karoks, and other tribal communities escalated into bloody warfare with little quarter shown. With the meager allotment of federal troops for California stretched thin across the state, militia expeditions authorized by various governors and independent bands of Indian fighters took up the cause of suppressing Indian resistance. Federal Indian agents such as Redick McKee in Northern California protested the near-automatic resort of local settlers to violence, no matter how slight the justification, as seen in the 1852 volume *Official Correspondence between the Governor of California, the U.S. Indian Agents, and the Commander of U.S. Troops Now in California.* Writing to California Governor John Bigler in April 1852 about two massacres of Indians in the northern counties, McKee encouraged him to issue a proclamation "calling upon all who have the true interests of California at heart, to frown upon such attempts to imbrue the frontier in blood, by exciting in the Indian the spirit of revenge and retaliation [and] urging the great importance of preserving good faith with the tribes" (p. 22). Like many other Americans in the age of Manifest Destiny, however, Bigler shared a conviction that national expansion remained of paramount significance. Responding to McKee, he wrote that, while he too might "deplore the unsettled conditions" in the counties where Indians and Euro-Americans collided, "the settlement of new countries, and the progress of civilization have always been attended by perils." "The career of civilization, under the auspices of the American people," he continued

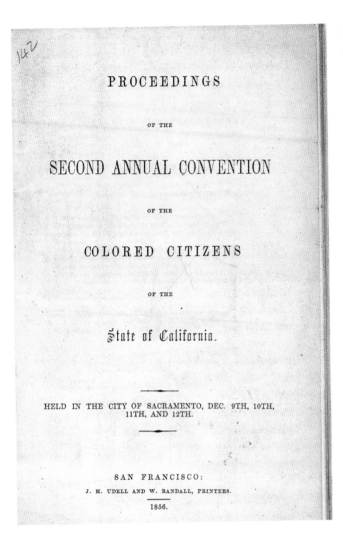

PROCEEDINGS

OF THE

SECOND ANNUAL CONVENTION

OF THE

COLORED CITIZENS

OF THE

State of California.

HELD IN THE CITY OF SACRAMENTO, DEC. 9TH, 10TH,
11TH, AND 12TH.

SAN FRANCISCO:
J. H. UDELL AND W. RANDALL, PRINTERS.
1856.

Proceedings of the Second Annual Convention of the Colored Citizens of the State of California, San Francisco, 1856.

(Huntington Library: RB 42781)

Although the California Constitution of 1849 outlawed slavery, state law forbade African-Americans from testifying or serving on juries in any court cases that involved white people. The Colored Citizens Conventions of 1855 and 1856 agitated against this and other social and legal barriers faced by black Californians.

proudly, "has been an ovation, steady, august and resistless." In demanding the support of federal troops, Bigler asserted that "whites and Indians cannot live in close proximity in peace" and that, to ensure peace, "an ultimate evacuation of the northern counties by the whites or the Indians will be unavoidable" (p. 23). Such resolute antipathy, echoing the sentiments expressed by Bigler's predecessor, Governor Peter Burnett, foretold the destructive warfare that unfolded through the 1850s. That warfare, combined with the effects of disease and starvation as many of California's Indians were exposed to new illnesses and crowded off their traditional habitats, led to a catastrophic population collapse among California Indians that may have cut down their numbers from one hundred and fifty thousand in 1848 to thirty thousand by 1860.

The unrelenting hostility commonly felt toward California's Indians, as stated so baldly by men like Bigler and Burnett, reflected the understanding shared among most Californians that the Indians could have no place in the evolving society of the 1850s. Described routinely by politicians and editorialists as the "savage enemies" of Americans, their resistance to the onward sweep of settlement made them fair game for conquest. Of course, as we have already seen, some of the argonauts themselves also felt such hostility directed toward them from white American emigrants, though usually not to such a vitriolic degree. Peoples of color, however, rarely escaped discrimination of one form or another; Chileans, Peruvians, and Mexicans, for instance, all suffered under bitter waves of prejudice and even mob violence.

Black Californians, among Californians of color, had been the target of a particularly virulent animosity, for their very presence in the state had been an object of controversy during the constitutional convention. Furthermore, even after the exclusion of free blacks had been defeated, few public schools were open to them, and the legislature in 1850 passed an act specifying that "no black or mulatto person or Indian shall be permitted to give evidence in favor of or against any white person." With such *de facto* and *de jure* disabilities imposed upon them, black Californians were thus consciously assigned a status of permanent inequality despite the increasing success of various black entrepreneurs. Refusing to accept such a status, however, leaders of the black community mobilized in subsequent years, especially against the prohibition on giving testimony in cases where white people were involved. Having absorbed many of the precepts of American democracy in the struggle for the liberation of their people, they hammered away eloquently at the fundamental injustice of the law. Petitions from black and white Californians alike arrived in the legislature year after year, despite that body's steadfast refusal to consider the issue until during the Civil War, nearly fifteen years after the first enactment of the prohibition.

To further galvanize support for such efforts on behalf of black equality, various prominent black Californians concluded that a statewide organization was necessary. To that end, leading figures in the black community gathered in Sacramento during the fall of 1855 and then again a year later. At the Second Colored Citizens' Convention in December 1856, E. A. Booth of Nevada County proclaimed, "It is with pride I say it, we are showing to our white fellow-citizens that we have some natural abilities; we are resolved to let them see that all we want is an equal chance, an open field, and a fair fight.…We intend to disprove the allegation

WAY-SIDE SCENES IN CALIFORNIA.

The stranger, as he ascends the mountains towards the mining towns, or passes from one mining district to another, notices the contrast in the scenes around him to anything he ever saw before. The hills are covered with pines and oaks, and shrubs, and flowers of every color and variety. Indians are met in groups, and in every stage of filth and pitch, carrying their "papoose" or baskets of "chemuck" (food) upon their backs, or with pan and tin cup are looking out for "prospects" in the tailings of the miners. Strings of Chinamen pass, and greet you in broken English with "how you do, John?"—are are all Johns to them, and they to us —their faces, tails and dress, their bamboo canes and heavy loads, are strangely singular to us. Next comes a Negro, with polite "good morning, sar"; or Chileno, Mexican, or Kanaka, with his boney horse and heavy load; then come horse teams, mule teams, ox teams, or mules laden with provisions, tools and clothing for the mines. Now a stage whirls past, or ladies and gents ride by in buggies or on horseback, to look at whom the miner drops his pick and wipes his brow. Here comes the Expressman, he who links the vallies with the mountains, brings gladdening words of love from home, of tidings from the absent ones, of friendly hopes and cheering thoughts; he is always welcome; through rain or snow, or danger, dust and mud, onward he rides, and brings the latest news. Did our friends afar but know how dearly prized their favors are, how eagerly we watch for the Expressman, or besiege the office window as every mail arrives; or did they know how their kind epistles take our thoughts back to live in pleasant memories of the happy past, no mail would leave the shores of the Atlantic without a letter to the absent ones in California.

Below is represented a Chinese Battle, that was fought on "Five Cent Gulch," Weaverville, Trinity County, California. It originated in sectional hatred and clannish differences, brought from their native land, which gradually increased, so that all endeavors by their leaders or Americans to settle them amicably, were in vain. Preparations were progressing, weapons the most singular were made, such as double handed swords seven feet long; lances with large hooks near the head; fork handles ten feet long, having three-tined forks, about fifteen inches across the points; shields two feet six inches long, and about twenty inches wide, made of inch pine covered with tin; hand swords, dirks, etc.; all very rude, and made at the blacksmith shops in town, at considerable expense. On the afternoon of July 15th, 1854, the two factions assembled,—one called the "small party" and numbering about one hundred and thirty, the other called the "large party," numbering nearly four hundred,—their banners were flying, and the parties were ranged on opposite sides of the gulch. Much defiant language was used, and some slight manœuvres were made. At length the small party charged upon the large one, and amid shouts and cheers from many hundreds of Americans, who stood upon the hill side to witness the battle, the small party put the others to flight, capturing their flag as a trophy of war, and killing eight of their opponents, losing but two on their own side. An excited Swede firing at random among the combatants was shot down by some one behind. On Sunday, the large party collected their dead together and burned them, as do the Indians, then burying the ashes. The small party buried theirs with all the imposing ceremonies of war, walking in funeral procession with music and banners to the grave.

Published by J. M. HUTCHINGS, San Francisco.

exhibiting extraordinary virtues." Instead, he observed, they had encountered a mounting tide of "insults and ridicule" offered by "the little and the mean." "Look at the mines. There openly they have planned, and in secret they have wrought us injury. They have destroyed life, and plundered property. Wagoners have extorted from us; boatmen vexed and done us violence. To these barbarities we dared not reply; we must submit to the degradation" (p. 4).

For a substantial number of Californians during the 1850s, however, neither appeals to California's economic well-being nor to the principle of the Golden Rule could overcome the essential feature of their encounter with the immigrant Chinese, that of the chasm separating one race from the other. As State Senator Wilson Flint argued in 1856 during debate over legislation to increase the Foreign Miner's Tax, far more was at stake than merely increasing the commercial prospects or material wealth of Californians: "It cannot have come to this, that the philanthropist will make no remonstrance when he sees the God endowed white man forced into degrading equality with races who can never share with him the duties and burdens of self-government, the responsibility and glory of a free citizen!" For Senator Flint, the future of California rested upon the foundation of a purely Anglo-Saxon population: "Banish, then, from this gold land the races who can never share the equalities and the responsibilities of citizenship, and there will spring up, as by magic, in every mountain dell, the cottage and hamlet, the 'home sweet, sweet HOME, fireside,' and…will…be heard the merry church going bell, the laughter of childish glee, the sweet voice of woman, and the glad songs of miners' hearts from miners' homes." To Senator Flint and those who shared his conception of California's unfolding destiny in the 1850s, the Chinese represented an intrusion of barbarism from the shores of Asia that could only retard California's march to greatness.

< *Way-Side Scenes in California,* **letter sheet published by J. M. Hutchings.**
(Huntington Library: RB 48052 #36)
Arriving in Gold Rush California, argonauts from the United States found that the world had indeed rushed to El Dorado. As this letter sheet suggests, their reactions to the peoples and cultures they encountered ran the gamut from wonder to revulsion.

IV | The Legacies of El Dorado

Building the Commonwealth: Gold Discovery and California's Development

However bitterly Californians might debate who would be included in the brilliant future of the Golden State, many seemed to accept without question that greatness did lay ahead in the 1850s. To thousands of argonauts, of course, the boom had long since collapsed and would never be resurrected, either due to the obstacles of race or nationality or due to persistent bad luck in the hunt for treasure. Other observers, like the morose Hinton Helper, simply rejected the notion that any good could arise out of the endemic iniquity and sinfulness that characterized life in the Gold Rush era. Even among many of the argonauts who failed to pick up a pocketful of nuggets, however, there were many who found California's possibilities intriguing.

Before the great rush reached its second anniversary, it was clear that the wealth of El Dorado would galvanize economic enterprises of all kinds. As gold production vaulted upward from two hundred and fifty thousand dollars in 1848 to more than ten million dollars in 1849 to beyond forty million dollars in 1850 and the number of miners increased tenfold in the same period, many astute men and women saw endless opportunities for profit from the combination of vast amounts of ready money and enormous demand for nearly every commodity and service imaginable. Many entrepreneurs gravitated to the mining camps and towns to meet the demands of the miners themselves for shirts and blankets, flour and beans, shovels, and long toms, not to mention the perennial threesome of wine, women, and song. Frank Marryat, commenting upon the mining business in his account *Mountains and Molehills,* noted that "the diggings will be replenished by new comers, and high prices, whether for potatoes or trowsers, will still…be maintained in a fair proportion to the yield of gold;…for it is an extraordinary fact that, let the diggings fall off as they will, the miners will still require *bread* and *breeches*, and will find the money to pay for them" (p. 376). Other business people, though, found that flush times in California meant good prospects in many other undertakings as well.

California's booming cities, for instance, contained fast-growing populations that comprised large markets in themselves as well as way stations for supplies and equipment funneled on to the mining country. Merchants like Collis Huntington, his eventual partner Mark Hopkins, or their contemporary Albion Sweetser, in their struggle for success, cultivated a detailed appreciation of the possibilities for any merchandise. In a November 27, 1850, letter to business acquaintances Alvah Littlefield and A. Blood back east, Sweetser appraised the market for various goods from leather purses to razor strops and offered to handle shipments

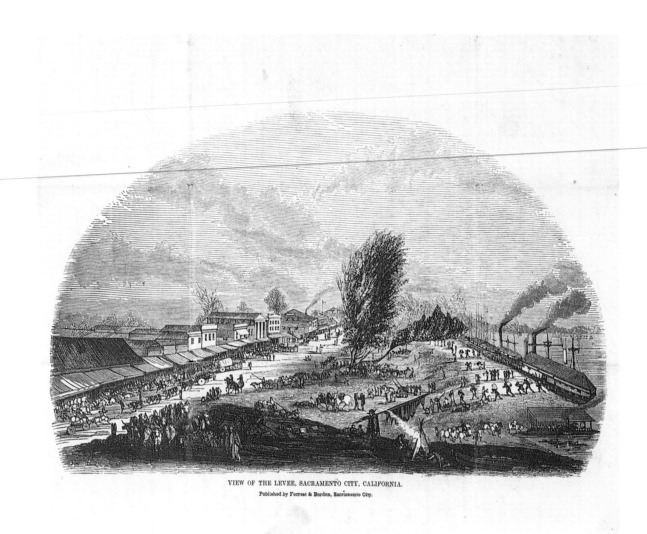

VIEW OF THE LEVEE, SACRAMENTO CITY, CALIFORNIA.

Published by Forrest & Borden, Sacramento City.

View of the Levee, Sacramento City, California, letter sheet published by Forrest & Borden.

(Huntington Library: HM 50515)

Accessible by shallow-draft vessels sailing upriver from San Francisco Bay, Sacramento became the marketplace for the mining country, with goods of every description flowing through its port, as shown in this early letter sheet view of its levee on the Sacramento River.

for his friends as long as they did not include "Mofat pills,…hair Brushes and cheap jewelry. I have not been able to sell any of those yet and them that have them say that they have no call for them." Despite the vagaries of the California market, however, he also wrote that "you say you wish me to inform you If I intend to stay in California, I will now say that I do; If I have my health I expect to remain here a number of years." Mark Hopkins, writing home to his brother Moses in New York on July 30, 1850, found the market even livelier than Sweetser, reporting that "in New York the great trouble is to find sale for goods—Here it is the reverse, our greatest trouble is in buying goods. They sell themselves and there is hardly any goods that are wanted in this country, but that pay a *large* advance to the shipper if sent to a house having a country trade to dispose of them.…You would be astonished to see the loaded waggons that daily go out of this town bound for all parts of the country."

Other business ventures responded to other needs common at a time of explosive population growth. While her husband pursued his medical practice, Mary Jane Megquier had set up her boardinghouse only months after her June 1849 arrival in San Francisco. By the summer of 1850, with the boardinghouse running full tilt, she found herself swamped by the chores it demanded, as she described them in a June 30 letter to her daughter Angeline in Maine: "I should like to give you an account of my work if I could do it justice.…I get up and make the coffee then I make the biscuit, then I fry the potatoes then broil three pounds of steak, and as much liver, while the woman is sweeping, and setting the table, at eight the bell

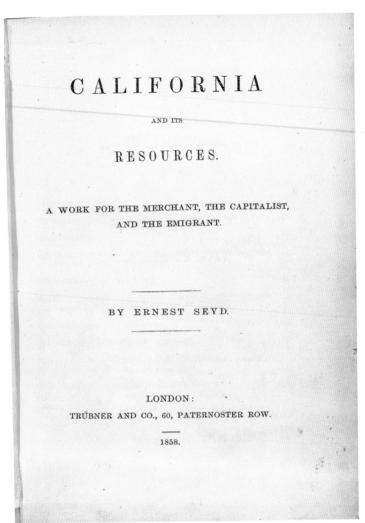

CALIFORNIA

AND ITS

RESOURCES.

A WORK FOR THE MERCHANT, THE CAPITALIST,
AND THE EMIGRANT.

BY ERNEST SEYD.

LONDON:
TRÜBNER AND CO., 60, PATERNOSTER ROW.

1858.

Ernest Seyd, *California and Its Resources: A Work for the Merchant, the Capitalist, and the Emigrant,* London, 1858. (Huntington Library: RB 27189) After studying the development of its economy in the 1850s, English author Ernest Seyd concluded that California offered exceptional opportunities for profitable investments.

rings and they are eating until nine. I do not sit until they are nearly all done.…I bake six loaves of bread (not very big) then four pies, or a pudding, then we have lamb…beef and pork, baked, turnips, beets, potatoes, radishes, sallad, and that everlasting soup, every day, dine at two…and I have cooked every mouthful that has been eaten.…I make six beds every day and do the washing and ironing…and when I dance all night I am obliged to trot all day and if I had not the constitution of six horses I should [have] been dead long ago." The cost of Megquier's success, in terms of the exhausting physical toil it required, demonstrated that, even at the height of the gold fever, few could win a golden reward in California without great effort. Outside of the cities, the possibilities of exploiting California's fertile landscapes to feed the state's booming population attracted the attention of newcomers and longtime residents alike. Jesse Smart, a farmer and nurseryman from Maine who emigrated to California in 1852, found its climate and its rich soils exceptionally promising. Convinced that the Golden State offered opportunities far surpassing those of home, he wrote confidently to his son on October 31, 1852, urging him to "sell the Frye lot for what you can get in ready pay you had better sell your own for my word for it you will never work on it after you see California, its beauties, its health, its productions, I have seen its winter, its summer, its autumn, I know its capacities for acquiring property and the purity of its air water & health which is not surpassed by any country.…The nursery business on a large scale will occupy all our efforts for the future 10,000 a year may be done at it."

With precisely such a calculation in mind, many of the Californios in the 1850s found that the cattle they had once raised for hides and tallow now held far greater value as groceries on the hoof to nourish hungry miners. As early as the summer of 1849, rancheros like Hugo Reid were contemplating the market for their stock in the northern counties. Within another year, Abel Stearns, Cave Couts, and many others were running cattle drives north to the gold country, fifteen years before the more celebrated trail drives from Texas to the Kansas rail towns. The cattle trade became the major industry of the southern half of the state, providing a welcome financial infusion for the rancheros in their battles before the federal government's land commission. It proved so attractive that Sam Brannan, the San Francisco tycoon who made his first fortune supplying shovels to miners in the early days of the gold fever, wanted to take a hand in it. Offering Abel Stearns the use of his rancho on the Feather River, "the finest range…in the upper country," he suggested a partnership involving his land and Stearns's cattle. No doubt aware of Stearns's great herds as well as his reputation as a very savvy businessman, Brannan proposed in a letter of December 5, 1856, to take a herd of five hundred heifers from Stearns, holding out the inducement that "Stear Calves can be sold there at an average of $15 per head Six months old." Furthermore, if Stearns wanted to place one thousand head of beef cattle annually on the same rancho, Brannan offered to manage them and arrange for their sale for half the profits over twenty dollars per head. Unfortunately, like so

"Street in San Francisco," watercolor drawing in Joseph Warren Revere, manuscript autobiography, 1849.

(Huntington Library: HM 56913)

In the early months of the Gold Rush, San Francisco's population expanded so rapidly that builders could never keep pace with the demand for shelter. Many new arrivals settled for temporary quarters under canvas, giving the city the appearance, one observer wrote, of a great "Camp Meeting."

With substantial and growing populations of well-to-do city dwellers came cravings for concerts, plays, balls, and dinner parties. Theaters and auditoriums appeared during the 1850s to meet the demand, hosting itinerant theatrical companies, minstrel troupes, orchestras, and a host of other entertainers from acrobats to aerialists. At San Francisco's Adelphi Theatre on May 26, 1852, for instance, "The Alleghanians" in their "Second Grand Concert in California" offered the public a "Grand Musical Soiree" consisting of duets, quartets, and solos with chorus. The Sacramento Theatre on May 23, 1855, could advertise the "Immense Attraction" of the "Chinese Dramatic Company" who would present "the Truly Wonderful Tragedy Of 'The Mountain Wizard'" followed by "The Great Rebellion" (while offering the public an assurance that "there shall be nothing of a vulgar nature in the performances, so that all may witness them with interest"). Sacramento's Forrest Theater could entice the public that same year with "the Great and Unrivalled Pantomimist Gabriel Ravel, The Martinetti Family, And their Numerous and Talented Troupe, Comprising Over Twenty Superior Artists!" performing "the laughable and interesting Pantomime entitled the Milliners, Or, The Hungarian Rendezvous!" followed by tightrope walking and "the Comic Fairy Pantomime entitled the Red Gnome, Or, the Famous Warrior!" In 1856, it could offer the "Grand Complimentary Testimonial to Mr. Jas. Stark" playing the role of Sir John Falstaff in Shakespeare's *The Merry Wives of Windsor* accompanied by a "sailor's hornpipe" and a "Fancy Dance" performed by Miss Louisa Graves and "La Petite Susan Robinson," respectively, with the play *The Iron Chest or, the Mysterious Murder* to open the evening's festivities.

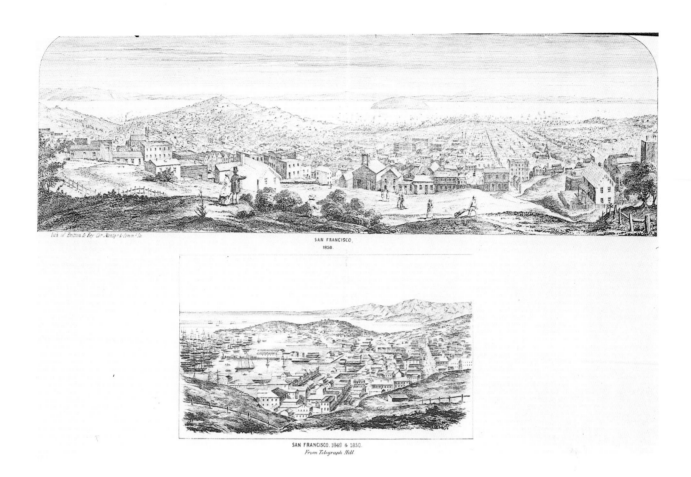

SAN FRANCISCO.
1858.

SAN FRANCISCO. 1849 & 1850.
From Telegraph Hill.

San Francisco, 1858, **letter sheet published by Britton & Rey.**
(Huntington Library: RB 48052 #113)
Gold seekers who had watched San Francisco's phenomenal growth created a market for letter sheets portraying the same topic. By combining a panoramic view of the city in the late 1850s with an insert depicting it at the beginning of the Gold Rush, this 1858 letter sheet produced an especially striking depiction of the changes over time.

While many residents of San Francisco or Sacramento might applaud such performances as symbols of the increasing sophistication and cultivation present in their communities, no Gold Rush city or town could afford to jettison the more rough-and-tumble entertainments wanted by other argonauts. Forty-niner physician Charles Ross Parke, during a visit to Sacramento in the fall of 1850, wrote disparagingly in his diary on September 6 that "if the good old saintly people of the States could only look in on these gambling dens for a minute or two, I know they would feel like calling home all *foreign* missionaries and turning them loose on this God-forsaken people....At every table, there is a man dealing Monte and surrounded by a crowd, some betting and some looking on. At the far end of the hall is a bar, where all fashionable drinks are dealt out for *one dollar* a drink. There is also a good band of music to enliven the crowd....At times those little tables are literally covered with buckskin bags filled with gold dust. Thousands and thousands of dollars changing hands every hour from morning until late in the night." Bayard Taylor, visiting Sacramento at nearly the same time, recalled in his book *El Dorado* a vision of the city's nightlife little better than that of Dr. Parke: "The door of many a gambling-hell on the levee, and in J and K Streets, standing invitingly open; the wail of torture from innumerable musical instruments peals from all quarters through the fog and darkness. Full bands, each playing different tunes discordantly, are stationed in front of the principal establishments, and as these happen to be near together, the mingling of the sounds in one horrid, ear-splitting, brazen chaos would drive frantic a man of delicate

SACRAMENTO in Californien.

Druck v. J Hesse in Berlin

DES AUSWANDERERS HOFFNUNG

Lithograph entitled *Sacramento in Californien*, Berlin, 1849?

(Huntington Library: Pr. Box 582/73)

The general fascination with most things Californian extended well beyond the first outbreaks of gold fever. This German edition of a bird's-eye view of Sacramento represented only one of more than fifty versions of this same image, including other foreign printings.

nerve" (vol. 2, p. 28). Frank Marryat, writing of his encounter in San Francisco with this world of morally lax but financially successful enterprise, noted that "no expense is spared to attract custom, the bar-keepers are 'artists' in their profession; rich soft velvet sofas and rocking-chairs invite the lounger; but popular feeling runs strongest in favour of the saloon that contains a pretty woman to attend the bar. Women are rarities here; and the population flock in crowds and receive drinks from the fair hands of the female dispenser, while the fortunate proprietor of the saloon realized a fortune in a week—and only has that time to do it in, for at the end of that period the charmer is married!" (p. 32).

Although never rivaling the remarkable development of San Francisco, the biggest boomtowns such as Sacramento and Stockton certainly followed most of the patterns set by their coastal cousin during the 1850s. Upon his first acquaintance with Sacramento, the caustic Dr. Israel Lord portrayed its combination of thriving business activity and moral disintegration caused by the boomtown mentality, writing in his diary on November 26, 1850, that "when business is lively, and three or four steamers and twice as many other vessels are unloading every day, the levee is a tangled mass of men and rogues and Mexicans and Chinese and Chileans and Kanakas and horses and mules and asses and oxen and drays and lumber and flour and potatoes and molasses and brandy and pickles and oysters and yams and cabbages and books and furniture and almost everything that one could think of—except honesty and religion. These articles not being in demand here are not thrown into market." Depicting

LOS ANGELES,

LOS ANGELES COUNTY, CAL. 1857.

Engraving entitled *Los Angeles, Los Angeles County, Cal., 1857*, **San Francisco, 1857.**

(Huntington Library: B-V/M-8)

Although sheltered by distance from the brunt of the changes brought about by the Gold Rush, Los Angeles and its surrounding counties did feel its impact. By 1857, when this view of the pueblo was published, Southern California had become the center of a very prosperous trade supplying beef cattle to the gold country.

events in Sacramento in a September 30, 1850, letter to his brother, Mark Hopkins wrote, with more restraint than Dr. Lord, that "the population of the town continues to increase, and buildings are going up in every direction more rapidly than ever—J street running at right angles with the river is the most extensive business street running through the center of the town—It is completely built up a mile in length....I should think there are no less than fifteen thousand & perhaps twenty thousand....The principal business streets are perfectly thronged with teams & the side walks like Broadway, but not with so elegantly draped people—You would be quite surprised to see the activity of business here....The roads in every direction are traversed with heavily laden teams." Especially at the height of the great excitement during the early 1850s, similar accounts were written about Stockton or Marysville or any one of several dozen mining camps scattered throughout the mining districts.

Instant cities, the products of uncontrolled and uncontrollable growth, often paid a disastrous price for the unrestrained gusto with which they grew. Among any aggregation of people, from the smallest mining camps all the way to San Francisco itself, flimsy construction, shoddy building materials, and a dismaying tendency to be careless with open flames condemned communities large and small to fiery obliteration. San Francisco itself repeatedly suffered from devastating blazes in 1849, 1850, and 1851, setting loose forces of destruction that Frank Marryat in *Mountains and Molehills* captured in agonizing detail after one conflagration: "No conception can be formed of the grandeur of the scene: for at one time the

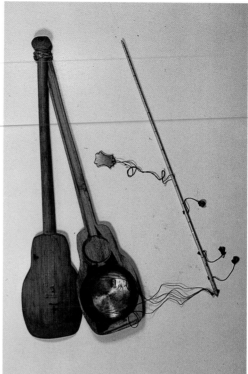

Wells Fargo treasure box and lock.

(Wells Fargo)

Express companies such as Wells Fargo operated in the gold country and accumulated large amounts of gold from individuals and businesses alike. They in turn supplied the essential service of transporting it securely, using devices such as this sturdy treasure box with its imposing padlock.

Chinese scales (*dotchen*).

(Wells Fargo)

Chinese argonauts, like their European and American counterparts, needed reliable devices with which to measure the value of each day's golden harvest. This version, unlike the balance scale that operates like a child's seesaw, relies upon a weight that slides along the single arm until it matches the weight of the substance in the attached pan.

burning district was covered by one vast sheet of flame that extended half a mile in length.…the shouts of the excited populace—the crash of falling timbers—the yells of the burnt and injured…maddened horses released from burning livery-stables plunging through the streets…as the swaying crowd, forced back by the flames, tramples all before it" (p. 188).

Other towns and cities, particularly low-lying Sacramento and Stockton, fell prey to the overwhelming power of swollen streams and rivers, fed by winter rainfalls or spring snow-melts in the mountains. Merchant Stephen Davis, arriving in Stockton on December 19, 1852, described in his diary the wilderness of water all around him: "Several bridges were swept away. A few buildings also were carried off by the flood, which was rising every hour.…Ferrys were established across the principal streets which were now foaming cataracts, and unsafe to cross, or traverse with carriages.…For miles around a vast sheet of water presents itself to view, with a fleet of houses, some apparently at anchor and some in motion, while boats are out in every direction steming the flood, rescuing families from their aquatic situations, and also picking up goods that are floating in [every] direction."

Sacramento too, located as it was at the convergence of the Sacramento and American Rivers, found itself under constant threat of inundation. Recording his impressions of Sacramento in his diary on September 8, 1850, Dr. Parke wrote about its drowning in the previous spring: "The water broke over the levee or artificial bank of the American river, and covered the face of the whole valley from Sutter's Fort down. The citizens who were so fortunate as to have two-story houses were compelled to move upstairs, going out the upper

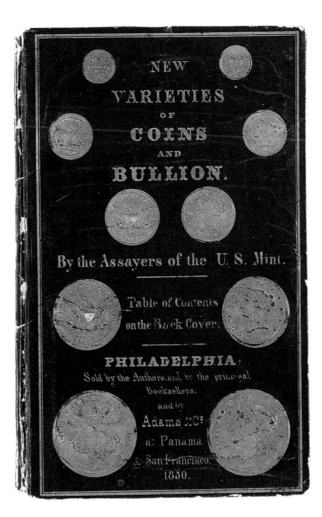

Jacob Eckfeldt and William DuBois, *New Varieties of Coins and Bullion,* **Philadelphia, 1850.**

(Huntington Library: RB 33004)

In this informative little pamphlet for gold seekers and merchants, the assayers at the United States Mint in Philadelphia discussed the standards of purity and value by which raw gold would be measured, the values and denominations of coins from around the world, and the various means of packing and moving gold in bulk.

windows and about in skiffs, while those dwelling in tents and sheds had to flee back toward the base of the mountains for protection. Here on these mounds all were collected, all sorts of living creatures." Mrs. Megquier, writing home about the floods on February 26, 1850, reported that "Sacramento has been entirely under water, those that had two story buildings could still transact business in the second story, those that had not, fled to the shipping, and the highlands, but an immense number of cattle and horses were drowned, they intend to levy the city at an expense of five million, quite a sum for the states but nothing for Cal." Commenting further upon the imperishable optimism of California city pioneers in pursuing their vision no matter what the cost, she added that "every spot that is not overflown, they are now building cities upon, lots two or three hundred miles up the river have in [a] week gone from nothing, to thousands, every one of them at the head of steamboat navigation, steamboats are running now where in two months time they cannot get a canoe but they do not stay one moment to consider."

Making Sense of It All: Interpreting the Gold Rush Experience

Mary Jane Megquier's slightly bemused description of such fervent optimism aptly reflected the seductive appeal to so many Californians of a belief in the Golden State's great possibilities. Although the vast majority of those who attempted to earn their golden reward from the mines had failed to do more than pay their expenses, many of the argonauts still found aspects of life in California too tempting to abandon easily. Some, like Maine nurseryman Jesse Smart, who still saw golden visions of California's future, remained. Absolutely overcome by California's possibilities, Smart could write again to his son, this time from Jacksonville in Tuolumne County on January 19, 1853, with unimpaired enthusiasm: "I advise you to rent the farm and make your arrangements to come to California by Oct. next if practicable....This is a country where an industrious man can earn money. You can make yourself...independent in five years." "The miners," he noted wryly, "will not farm and they must eat." As in Smart's case, such visions often grew out of endeavors far removed from the life of the gold miner.

Intoxicated by the wonders of its climate, the beauties of its landscapes, or the richness of

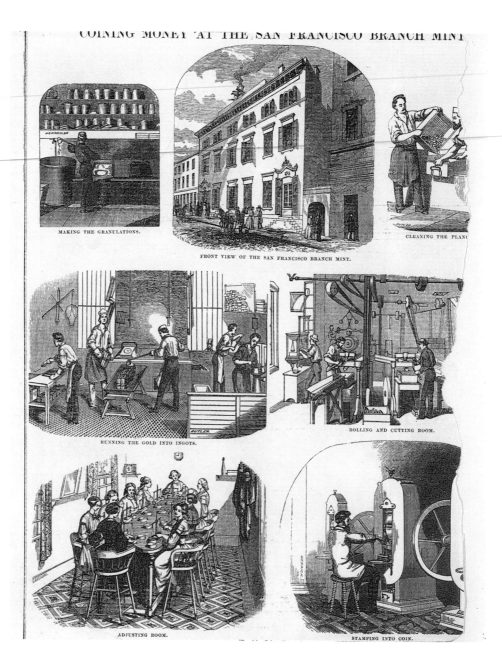

COINING MONEY AT THE SAN FRANCISCO BRANCH MINT

MAKING THE GRANULATIONS.

FRONT VIEW OF THE SAN FRANCISCO BRANCH MINT.

CLEANING THE PLANC

RUNNING THE GOLD INTO INGOTS.

ROLLING AND CUTTING ROOM.

ADJUSTING ROOM.

STAMPING INTO COIN.

Coining Money at the San Francisco Branch Mint, **letter sheet published by Hutchings & Rosenfield.**

(Huntington Library: RB 48052 #156)

After much urging, the United States Treasury Department in 1854 established a branch of the United States Mint in San Francisco. Thereafter, anyone could exchange raw gold for gold currency at the officially established rate of sixteen dollars per ounce. The mint, in turn, would melt down the gold received and convert it into coinage.

its natural resources, various argonauts found new employment for their talents and their energies. John S. Hittell, writing in the preface to the 1874 edition of his detailed analysis *The Resources of California*, admitted freely that "I am so much attached to California, that I could not live contentedly elsewhere; and I imagine that neither the earth, the sky, nor the people of any other country, equal that of this State" (p. v). In an 1869 address to the Society of California Pioneers on the anniversary of Admission Day, he recounted his vision of what California had offered and would offer to the argonauts who had put aside their restless ways to stay on the Pacific Coast: "She gave to all a cherished home, a sunny and genial sky, a fertile soil, a delightful landscape, a clime suited to the development of every energy, the companionship of the most intelligent and enterprising people, and a site suited for the great city and for the concentration of the commerce of a wealthy coast....Much we have seen, more we shall see....The highest civilization will make one of its chief centers here....[It] will be the favorite place of residence for many thousands from abroad. They will fill the land with wealth, luxury, and art. California will occupy in the hemisphere of the Pacific, as a focus of intellec-

173. EAST SIDE MONTGOMERY STREET—Looking
North from California Street.

148. Montgomery street, from California, North,
instantaneous.

"East Side Montgomery Street Looking North from California Street," photograph in Thomas Houseworth & Co., *Pacific Coast Scenery,* San Francisco, 1872.
(Huntington Library: RB 296133, #173)

"Montgomery Street, from California, North...," photograph in Thomas Houseworth & Co., *Pacific Coast Scenery,* San Francisco, 1872.
(Huntington Library: RB 296133, #148)

These two photographs, reproduced from a Houseworth & Co. stereograph catalog of 1872, attest to the ongoing popular interest in San Francisco, still the commercial, financial, and industrial heart of the Far West.

tual culture, a position similar to that long held by Attica in the basin of the Mediterranean....Let us be proud that we have taken part in a work which has contributed much and will contribute more to stimulate commerce and to extend civilization; and as a consequence, to enrich and benefit mankind: a work which will be forever prominent in the history of mankind" (pp. 16, 20–21).

Other writers, echoing some of Hittell's sentiments, put the matter in more concrete terms, appealing with specific details to those in the growing American middle class who had an interest in relocating permanently to better their circumstance or in traveling for recreation and leisure. Charles Nordhoff stated plainly his purpose in writing the 1872 guidebook *California for Travelers and Settlers:* "I would like to induce Americans, when they contemplate a journey for health, pleasure, or instruction, or all three, to think . . . particularly of California, which has so many delights in store for the tourist and so many attractions for the farmer or settler looking for a mild and healthful climate and a productive country" (p. 11). Discussing the wonders of its agriculture in greater detail, he affirmed that "very few suspect that the Californians have the best of us, and that, so far from living in a kind of rude exile, they enjoy, in fact, the finest climate, the most fertile soil, the loveliest skies, the mildest winters, the most healthful region, in the whole United States. California has long passed with us in the east as a good-enough sort of country for over-adventurous young men; it is, in fact, the best part of the American continent, either for health or for profitable and pleasant living in any industrious pursuit" (pp. 118–19). During the same years, through the late 1860s and early 1870s, similar

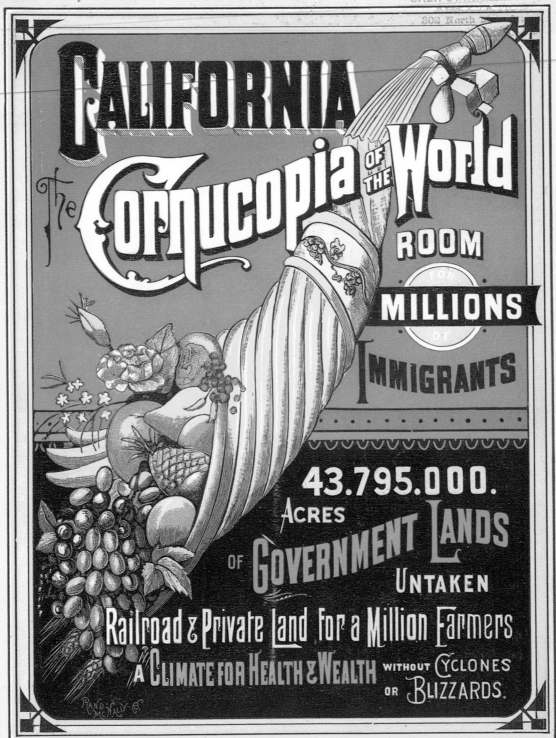

Rand, McNally & Co., Printers and Engravers, Chicago.

Union Pacific and Central Pacific Railroads, broadside entitled *Union and Central Pacific Route to Southern California...,* **Omaha, 1877.**
(Huntington Library: RB 475611)

California Immigration Commission, *California, the Cornucopia of the World...,* **Chicago, 1883.**
(Huntington Library: RB 248676)

Despite gold mining's continued importance to California's economy through the 1860s and 1870s, California's agricultural possibilities took on greater significance. During the 1870s and 1880s, broadsides and brochures describing the marvelous opportunities available for farmers proclaimed that a new golden age was at hand for the Golden State.

assertions in such guidebooks as *California for Travelers and Settlers* were only bolstered by the rapidly evolving art of photography. As photographic processes became more sophisticated and more portable, photographers were able to venture further afield from the studio to produce images which in turn could be more easily reproduced and distributed to a wider audience. Thus, greater numbers of people were exposed to a greater variety of California views. Stereographs, a pair of photographs taken of the same subject by a special double-lensed camera and mounted side by side upon stiff board stock, became all the rage. Placed a precise distance apart, these bipolar images created a remarkably vivid three-dimensional effect when seen through a viewer equipped with two lenses and an adjustable holder for the stereograph that allowed the user to move the image closer or further depending upon one's eyesight. Publishers such as Houseworth and Company collected tens of thousands of stereographs and reproduced them as quickly as possible for a fast-growing market. The images thus distributed could inform, entertain, or intrigue the user, much as the California letter sheets had done a generation earlier and postcards would do throughout the twentieth century. Now, however, although exotic subjects such as Chinese residents in full traditional regalia would appear because of their continuing sales appeal, many other, more mundane images would commonly fill the catalogs and sample books. These photographs would highlight the continued development of San Francisco into a great city, as marked by three- and four-story stone office buildings, grand wide boulevards, and majestic civic structures. They would also stress the ease and comfort in which one could make the journey to California from points east on the luxuriously equipped trains of the Central Pacific and the Union Pacific railroads on their linked transcontinental route, during which the passenger could enjoy the use of sleeping compartments, dining rooms, and parlors.

By the 1880s, forty years after gold discovery, California's advantages were the stuff of legend, promoted around the world to attract tourists, investors, and especially immigrants. The railroads that served the western United States collaborated with local authorities and the state government to produce pamphlets and brochures to champion the proposition that California could be "Cornucopia of the World," a veritable paradise whose staggering natural abundance was matched only by the equally staggering amounts of land available for the taking. California possessed, in the words of one 1883 pamphlet, "Room for Millions of Immigrants," including more than forty-three million acres of unoccupied government land, "railroad & private land for a million farmers," and, not least important for many of the eastern and midwestern farmers who would read such brochures, "a climate for health & wealth, without Cyclones or Blizzards." Here, the boosters of California argued, was opportunity on an unparalleled scale "for immigrants desiring to secure lands at cheap rates, on which to make happy and prosperous homes." For the immigrants of the 1880s, like the argonauts of 1849, here was El Dorado in all its glory, where they might reach for dreams once thought permanently out of their grasp.

Many of the argonauts who had stayed on in the Golden State joined the cheering for California's glorious future, celebrating the remarkable transformation that had already taken place in the land they had once known. Alonzo Delano, in an 1868 pamphlet entitled *The Central Pacific Railroad or, '49 and '69,* wrote wonderingly about the comparison be-

tween California past and present: "Six months upon the Plains, nineteen years ago, and California only a wilderness. What is it now? The Californian has only to cast his eye over our land,
and see its growing cities, its beautiful towns, its immense commerce with the whole world, its
magnificent homes, its manufactories, its railroads, and its overflowing abundance of the comforts and luxuries of life, the produce of its rich soil through the energies of our people. To an
old pioneer, whose memory of his early trials is still fresh, these changes seem like the enchant-
ment of the magician's wand" (p. 4).

As vigorously as they might applaud such spectacular progress, however, many of the gold
seekers also shared a desire to ensure that their contributions to California's history would be
remembered. With the passage of the years and the natural thinning of their ranks due to the
deaths of fellow pioneers, former argonauts began to organize celebrations of the monumental
events in which they had participated. The model for them all was the Society of California
Pioneers, founded in 1850 with the express intent "to collect and preserve information con-
nected with the early settlement and conquest of the country, and to perpetuate the memory of
those whose sagacity, enterprise, and love of independence induced them to settle in the wilderness and become the germ of a new state." Later, in the 1870s and 1880s, came other, more
narrowly focused groups such as the Society of First Steamship Pioneers, the Territorial Pioneers
of California, the Associated Pioneers of the Territorial Days of California, the New England
Associated California Pioneers, the Society of California Pioneers of New England, and the Western Association of California Pioneers. Women's organizations also took shape, either as auxiliaries

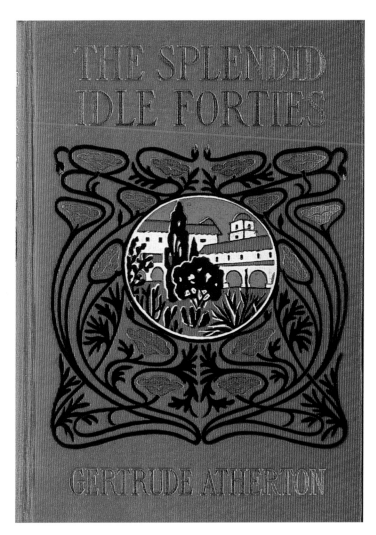

Gertrude Atherton,
*The Splendid Idle Forties:
Stories of Old California,*
New York, 1902.

(Huntington Library: RB 988)

Atherton, contemplating California's history at the end of the nineteenth century, chronicled many of its events in her fiction. *The Splendid Idle Forties,* a collection of short stories, presented a romantic portrait of Californio society and its sad but inevitable decline after the arrival of the Americans.

within existing groups, such as the Society of California Pioneers, or as independent entities, such as the Association of Pioneer Women of California, incorporated in 1901 "to collect and preserve the history and reminiscences of pioneer women of California" and to solicit the membership of all "eligible" (defined as "moral" and "white") "pioneer women and their female descendants who arrived in California prior to and including the thirty-first day of December, 1853." In their meetings and their memorials, they would commemorate the particular roles their members played in helping (in the words of one publication from the Associated Pioneers of the Territorial Days) "to *lick*…our splendid territory into shape, and soon after, …erecting her into a vast and sovereign State" and would reminisce about the many challenges and hardships they endured while involved in what they only later realized was "the grand work of civilization." An 1894 invitation to a reunion dinner for the Western Association of California Pioneers asked "Why not, as we may, come together and recall the days of the pick, shovel and rocker; the days of tramping and of sleeping on the ground, the joy of success and the sadness of disappointment; the long journey over the plains, the storms of Cape Horn, the tramp through Mexico or the fevers of the Isthmus? The memories of those stirring and exciting days renews our youth and invigorates us for the days ahead."

Their reminiscences of times past grew more important to many of these pioneers as the years since "the days of '49" passed by, leaving fewer and fewer behind who had lived through those extraordinary circumstances. At the fortieth anniversary of gold discovery in 1888, former gold seekers organized both the New England Associated California Pioneers and the Society of California Pioneers of New England, impelled by the desire of the survivors of those times, in the words of one of them, to preserve the "noble history" of that era with its "poetic fancy, and…thrilling adventures." Describing preparations for the First Grand Annual Reunion of the Society of California Pioneers of New England, the society's secretary wrote in its bulletin, "These scenes [of Gold Rush days] come back to us laden with the tender recollections of departed days, which linger around and about us, like half forgotten dreams. In our declining dreams, they fill a space, that no other theme can reach.…Around this alter which has been built to awaken anew the reminiscences of bygone days, let us gather once a year and revive scenes long since forgotten, and keep green the memories of our departed dead" (p. 8). To John S. Ellis, presiding over the thirteenth annual meeting and dinner of the Associated Pioneers of the Territorial Days of California in New York City on January 9, 1888, these reunions had a special meaning. In his published remarks, he asserted that such gatherings allowed each argonaut, "after ascending the ladder of life, and getting more than half way down the other side," to look back "upon passages of his life, wherein he has a fair reason to be satisfied with his motives, his achievements, and the commendation of his friends and fellow citizens, if he has done anything worthy of such notice" and to gather around him "those who participated at the same period with him in stirring times" (p. 6). In an effort to renew their acquaintance with the land of gold (probably in most cases for one last time), nearly one hundred aging pioneers as well as wives,

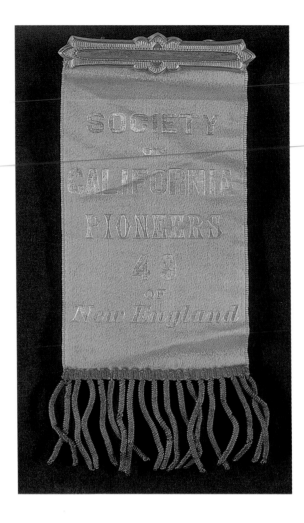

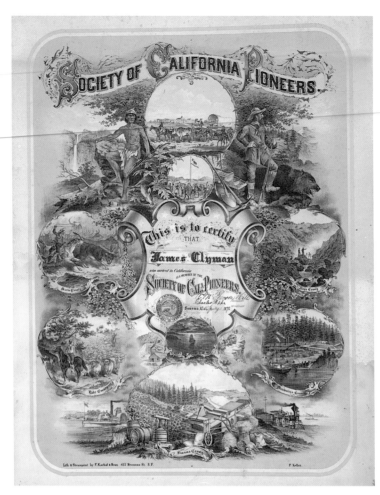

Badge from Society of California Pioneers of New England meeting.

(Huntington Library: Norton Collection)

By the fortieth anniversary of Marshall's discovery, groups like the Society of California Pioneers of New England had begun holding regular reunions. At those gatherings, the members would celebrate the great events in which they took part and commemorate their colleagues who had passed from the scene.

Society of California Pioneers membership certificate for James Clyman, San Francisco, 1876.

(Huntington Library: RB 70775)

The Society of California Pioneers, founded in 1850, had set the pattern for all subsequent associations. In preserving and honoring the record of the pioneers drawn to California by the Gold Rush, it also celebrated their triumph over California's native peoples and over nature itself, as illustrated by this 1876 membership certificate.

children, and friends even ventured forth to California from Boston by train in April 1890 under the auspices of the Society of California Pioneers of New England. Arriving in Southern California, they traversed the state, stopping for ceremonial welcomes at many communities, before reaching the gold country where they retraced some of their experiences as argonauts. Awash in the sentiment of the moment, the society's secretary composed an ode that, to the tune of "Home, Sweet Home," sent them back to Boston singing "With joy shall we remember, / In days of new lang syne, / The friends and dear companions / Of the men of '49."

Even among those who venerated the memory of the "days of '49," some of the celebrations possessed a certain tinge of regret as some argonauts or their heirs considered the costs of what most Californians regarded as unalloyed progress. As John Ellis in 1888 reflected upon the Gold Rush experience, he paid homage to the Californios ("a fine, healthy, brave, and courteous race") and observed with remorse that "some of my countrymen are far from being free from the charge of doing great injustice" to them. He went on to acknowledge that "their lands were greedily seized, and partitioned among the host of invaders by fair means or foul." Such were the "wrongs perpetrated by individuals upon the former possessors of [California's] soil" for which he asked that divine forgiveness be sought. Put into the balance against those injustices, however, was the fact that "the outcome of it all is Beautiful California, sung by the poet and the bard, imaged by the sculptor, loved and admired by all, but by none so much as by the faithful few who helped to start her in her glorious existence" (p. 5). Clearly, Ellis implied, the end results justified at least the price paid, if not the means used.

Of course, assessing what had been gained and what had been lost in the transforma-

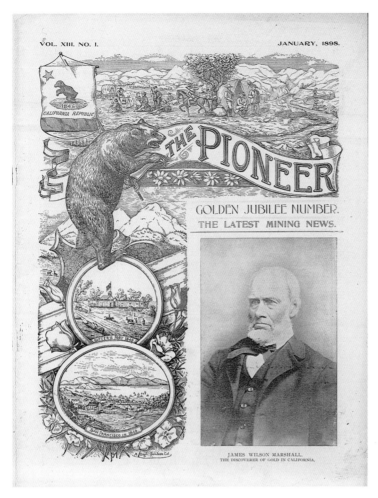

The Pioneer (**Golden Jubilee Number**) **13, no. 1 (January 1898).**

(Huntington Library: RB 81765)

At the end of the first half-century since gold discovery, the imagery of the Gold Rush had become irretrievably fixed in the popular consciousness. Hardy emigrants, the ferocious grizzly bear and the Bear Flag, San Francisco and Sutter's Fort, and the first gold seeker, James W. Marshall, supplied the props against which the great pageant of the Gold Rush would unfold.

tion of California during the Gold Rush began only a few years after the dramatic discovery of January 24, 1848. The argonauts themselves had worried about the impact of the frenzied pursuit of riches upon their health, their morals, and even their chances for salvation in the next life, as an endless parade of sermons, letters, and diary entries testified. Many of the letter sheets produced during the Gold Rush years offered moral instruction, reminding the argonaut who might stray from the path of righteousness about the lonely grave or, at the very least, the broken life of the wastrel that awaited him if he did not resist such temptation. Conversely, the gold seeker's own moral code and that of his society, as seen through the letter sheets, guaranteed an appropriate reward for those who stayed the course despite the many paths to sin at hand.

For many of the argonauts, such a straightforward conception of the Gold Rush period, in which both virtue and iniquity received their just desserts, summed up the salient points of the experience. With the passing of the years, however, writers and scholars began to probe more deeply. In the 1860s and 1870s, authors Bret Harte and Mark Twain found that the mining camps revealed much about the men and women who inhabited them. Both discovered in their primitive conditions and backwoods characters rich sources of humor about the miner and the life he led. Twain, in particular, discovered innumerable opportunities to satirize the pretensions and the ambitions of the get-rich-quick miner of Nevada's Comstock Lode in his celebrated 1872 travelogue *Roughing It.* At the same time, writing of his travels in the California gold country more than twenty years after its boom times, he conveyed a sense of the fascinating allure already exercised by that receding era: "They were rough in those times! They fairly reveled in gold, whisky, fights and fandangoes, and were unspeakably happy....It was a wild, free, disorderly, grotesque society! *Men*—only swarming hosts of stalwart men—nothing juvenile, nothing feminine, visible anywhere!" (p. 391). Harte, by contrast, in such stories as "The Luck of Roaring Camp" or "The Outcasts of Poker Flats," portrayed a world that might be filled with boisterous adventure but that usually possessed a rough-hewn sentimentality as well, tinged with nobility and pathos. Harte's Gold Rush characters often demonstrated that unexpected strengths and weaknesses might be found in the search for gold.

While Harte and Twain, like the argonauts themselves, might concentrate upon the fate of the individuals caught up in the mining mania, the society that sprung up in response to the Gold Rush provoked considerable study as well. Other novelists writing in the 1880s and 1890s found the events of the era from the American conquest through the frenzy of the Gold Rush of compelling interest. Gertrude Atherton, granddaughter of an Anglo-American pioneer, wrote extensively about California's past, publishing short stories and historical novels. In her most celebrated collection of short stories, *The Splendid Idle Forties*, she looked back upon the years before, during, and after the Mexican-American War. In portraying the people and the places of those years, she created a romantic vision of the lives of the Californios, in tune with many other writers of her time such as Helen Hunt Jackson and Charles F.

INNOCENT DREAMS.

CALIFORNIA'S JUBILEE NUMBER

THE OVERLAND 10 CENT

Edited by JAMES HOWARD BRIDGE

FEBRUARY

◆ CONTENTS ◆

The Discovery of Gold . . . .
The Golden Jubilee . . . . .
Outfitting for Klondike . . . .
A Klondike Story . . . . .
Fresh View of Manifest Destiny
                By the Editor
Douglas Tilden, the Mute Sculptor
A Prize Story . . . . . .
The Holy Grail . . . . .
Can We Build Steel Ships? . .

OVERLAND MONTHLY PUBLISHING COMPANY
SAN FRANCISCO, CAL.

"Innocent Dreams," engraving in Mark Twain (Samuel Langhorne Clemens), *Roughing It,* **Chicago, 1872.**
(Huntington Library: RB 47363)
The legacy of gold fever persisted long after the Gold Rush wore out. In his 1872 account of traveling to Nevada Territory, Mark Twain captured the powerful allure exerted by the prospect of finding sudden wealth in a mining rush, in this case at the silver fields of the Comstock Lode.

Cover illustration of the *Overland Monthly* **(California's Jubilee Number), 2nd ser., 31 (February 1898).**
(Huntington Library: AP 2 O9)
When the *Overland Monthly* published its commemorative issue for the fiftieth anniversary of gold discovery, its union of the California grizzly, the exuberant forty-niner, and the forty-niner's golden reward rang a note of triumph. Surely, this powerful image implied, even better things would lie ahead.

Lummis, to serve as a reminder of what had been lost in the transformation of Mexican California following the Gold Rush. María Amparo Ruiz de Burton, by contrast, the child of a well-established Baja California landowning family, took a more complicated view of these events, reflecting her own personal circumstances. Linked by blood to various important Californio families, she also possessed connections to the new Yankee society through her husband, Colonel Henry S. Burton, an American army officer she had married after the Mexican-American War. Sharply critical of the premises on which the Land Commission Act of 1851 had been established and of the commission's operations, her 1885 novel *The Squatter and the Don* offered a stinging indictment of the resulting impoverishment and dispossession of many Californios. She also decried the ongoing concentration of wealth and power in California that she saw during the decades after the Civil War.

In this appraisal of California society, Ruiz de Burton echoed other critics, most particularly the San Francisco newspaperman Henry George. George's writings, especially his most prominent work, *Progress and Poverty,* approached the unfolding nature of the American economy from a similarly critical perspective. For George, events in California particularly influenced his perspective as seen in the case of California's land titles. In his 1871 pamphlet *Our Land and Land Policy, National and State,* he concurred with the Californios who had so vocally if futilely opposed the proceedings of the land commission and decried the extravagant concentration of land ownership in a few hands. Had the Mexican land grants been confirmed and then incorporated by government purchase into the public domain, a realm of successful

"Worked Out Claims," photograph by Thomas Houseworth & Co.
(Huntington Library: Placer Mining Series #152)
The frenzied search for gold across a broad swath of California's landscape left less triumphant legacies. Especially after more intensive techniques such as hydraulic mining were introduced, large portions of the landscape in the mining regions were thoroughly despoiled.

yeoman farmers would have brought California even greater prosperity and success, rather than instituting what George considered a regime of land monopolists, creating "the blight that has fallen upon California, stunting her growth and mocking her golden promise."

Two other interpreters of California's transformation in this decade, Charles Howard Shinn and Josiah Royce, also found the Gold Rush experience instructive for pondering the nature of contemporary American society. Shinn, another California newspaperman, had spent much time during the 1870s in the old mining camps talking with surviving pioneers. From these encounters, he became fascinated with the ways and means by which the miners had conducted their affairs, even in the absence of other forms of government. Evaluating their successes and failures in an 1885 volume entitled *Mining Camps: A Study in American Frontier Government* (begun as a thesis at Johns Hopkins University), Shinn regarded the experience of the miners as indicative of certain common American traits, reaching back even beyond the colonization of North America to the roots of democracy that could be found in English and German folk cultures. Shinn noted when the miners' experiments with self-government fell short, especially in dealing with outsiders: "Sometimes, however, the Americans were unjust and overbearing, or were at least careless and indifferent to the rights of others" (p. 212). On the whole, however, Shinn concluded that "when youth and energy from older communities of the Atlantic States, and adventurers from every land under the sun, joined in the famous gold-rush of 1849,—the marvel of marvels is, that mob-law and failure of justice were so infrequent, that society was so well and so swiftly organized" (p. 231).

"Boating Party on Donner Lake," photograph by Alfred A. Hart.
(Huntington Library: Album 184, #128)
As time passed, Californians began to look at the state's many landscapes as more than a storehouse of mineral treasures. Some found great pleasure in the enjoyment of the state's natural beauties for leisure and recreation, as did this party of boaters on Donner Lake in the late 1860s.

Royce, a California-born professor of philosophy at Harvard University, published his work *California, from the Conquest in 1846 to the Second Vigilance Committee in San Francisco* in 1886, a year after Shinn's book had appeared. Intrigued, like Shinn, by what the events in California meant for his country as a whole, Royce had chosen to describe his work with the subtitle "A Study in American Character." Unlike Shinn, Royce discovered within the era far more deeply entwined roots of violence and disorder. In the wholesale abandonment of their duties to help maintain civil society, Royce found, the best men among the forty-niners and their peers aggravated the tensions that had begun to fracture what little social order existed in this frenzied era. Thus empowered by the dereliction of the best, the worst in any community could seize the day, especially in deal-ing with the foreigners who had come to the mines. Toward them, Royce wrote, "ours were the crime of a community, consisting largely of honest but cruelly bigoted men, who encour-aged the ruffians of their own nation to ill-treat the wonders of another, to the frequent destruc-tion of peace and good order. We were favored of heaven with the instinct of organization; and so here we organized brutality and, so to speak, asked God's blessing upon it" (p. 363). With this conclusion, it would be hard, even one hundred years later, to disagree, at least with the notion of exonerating the Americans who dominated the mining country.

Upon reviewing the entire experience, Royce was not prepared, however, to condemn without exception the argonauts and the other American emigrants or the California in which he had lived. He concluded instead that Americans in California "exhibited a novel degree of carelessness and overhastiness, an extravagant trust in luck, a previously unknown blindness to our social duties, and an indifference to the rights of foreigners, whereof we cannot be proud. But we also showed our best national traits—traits that went far to atone for our faults. As a body, our pioneer community in California was persistently cheerful, energetic, courageous, and teachable. In a few years, …it was ready to begin with fresh devotion the work whose true importance it had now at length learned—the work of building a well-organized, permanent, and progressive state on the Pacific coast" (p. 2). As we reflect upon the extraordinary events of the Gold Rush decade and upon the ordinary people who lived through them, Royce's measured appraisal of the era still has much to commend it to our attention a century and a half later.

Checklist of the Exhibition

Certain items, because of their age and fragility, will be replaced during the course of the exhibition; this checklist, therefore, includes only those items displayed in the inaugural phase of the exhibition.

Gallery One:
The Adventure Begins

Case 1: Gold Discovery

Henry W. Bigler, manuscript autobiography, 1898.
(Huntington Library: HM 57034)

Capt. Sutter's Account of the First Discovery of the Gold, letter sheet published by Britton & Rey.
(Huntington Library: RB 48052 #94)

Piece of wood from the original sawmill of John A. Sutter.
(Wells Fargo Bank)

William Rich Hutton, pencil and watercolor drawing entitled *Sutter's Saw Mill,* April 16, 1849.
(Huntington Library: HM 43214 #90)

"Upper Mines" and "Lower Mines or Mormon Diggings," in Colonel Richard B. Mason's report on gold in California to the War Department published in *Message from the President of the United States to the Two Houses of Congress...Dec. 5, 1848,* Washington, D.C., 1848.
(Huntington Library: RB 248140)

The California Indians, letter sheet published by Anthony & Baker.
(Huntington Library: RB 48052 #103)

"Indian Woman Panning Out Gold," engraving in *Hutchings Illustrated California Magazine* 3, no. 10 (April 1859).
(Huntington Library: RB 420)

"Gold Mine Found," in the *Californian,* San Francisco, March 15, 1848.
(Huntington Library: RB 140552-3)

John Sutter, autograph letter to William A. Leidesdorff, March 15, 1848.
(Huntington Library: LE 413)

Walter Colton, *Three Years in California,* New York, 1851.
(Huntington Library: RB 12508)

Case 2: Mexican California

Alexander Forbes, *California: A History of Upper and Lower California... ,* London, 1839.
(Huntington Library: RB 357803)

William A. Leidesdorff, autograph petition for use of a specific brand and earmark (with illustrations), July 12, 1844.
(Huntington Library: LE 21)

Abel Stearns, autograph letter to "Messrs. Pierce and Brewer," April 25, 1842.
(Huntington Library: SG Box 61)

"Californian Mode of Catching Cattle, with a Distant View of the Mission of St. Joseph," engraving in Alexander Forbes, *California: A History of Upper and Lower California...,* London, 1839.
(Huntington Library: RB 401667)

William Rich Hutton, pencil and watercolor drawing entitled *Trying Out Tallow, Monterey,* c. 1848.
(Huntington Library: HM 43214 #61)

California Vaqueros, Returned from the Chase, letter sheet published by Anthony & Baker.
(Huntington Library: RB 48052 #188)

Case 3: Mexican California

Richard Henry Dana, *Two Years before the Mast,* New York, 1840.
(Huntington Library: RB 13877)

Thomas O. Larkin, autograph letter to Abel Stearns, April 18, 1843.
(Huntington Library: SG Box 39)

John A. Sutter, autograph letter to William Leidesdorff, May 11, 1846.
(Huntington Library: LE 129)

"Map of Upper California. . .1841," in Charles Wilkes, *Narrative of the United States Exploring Expedition,* vol. 5, Philadelphia, 1845.
(Huntington Library: RB16211)

"Monterey—Capitol of California," engraving in Joseph Warren Revere, *A Tour of Duty in California; Including a Description of the Gold Regions,* New York, 1849.
(Huntington Library: RB 662)

William Rich Hutton, pencil and watercolor drawing entitled *Santa Barbara Mission from the Hill,* 1852.
(Huntington Library: HM 43214 #35)

Case 4: Mexican California

W. D. M. Howard, autograph letter to Abel Stearns, April 21, 1846.
(Huntington Library: SG Box 35)

Lansford W. Hastings, *The Emigrants' Guide to Oregon and California. . . ,* Cincinnati, 1845.
(Huntington Library: RB 1782)

Sir George Simpson, *Narrative of a Voyage round the World,* London, 1847.
(Huntington Library: RB 1970)

Alfred Robinson, *Life in California before the Conquest,* New York, 1846.
(Huntington Library: RB 401662)

William Rich Hutton, pencil drawing entitled *San Francisco (from the Hill Back),* 1847.
(Huntington Library: HM 43214 #81)

Case 5: Mexican-American War

William B. Ide, autograph manuscript, "Proclamation" [of the Bear Flag Revolt], June 15, 1846.
(Huntington Library: HM 4116)

Pio Pico, autograph letter to Thomas O. Larkin, June 29, 1846.
(Huntington Library: HM 37548)

U.S. Army Corps of Topographical Engineers, *Notes of a Military Reconnaissance from Fort Leavenworth. . . to San Diego*, Washington, D.C., 1848.
(Huntington Library: RB 195294)

Richard Barnes Mason, broadside entitled *Proclamation. To the People of Upper California*, Monterey? 1848.
(Huntington Library: RB 35682)

"Sutter's Fort—New Helvetia," engraving in Joseph Warren Revere, *Tour of Duty in California; Including a Description of the Gold Regions*, New York, 1849.
(Huntington Library: RB 662)

L. Scherer, lithograph entitled *Travail en Californie*, Paris, 185-?
(Huntington Library: RB 183903)

Case 6: Gold Fever
Kimball Hale Dimmick, diary entry beginning May 25, 1848.
(Huntington Library: HM 4014)

William P. Reynolds, autograph letter to his brother John Reynolds, December 27, 1848.
(Huntington Library: HM 4157)

R. V. Sankey, *The Good Time's Come at Last, or the Race to California. A Comic Song Written to a Golden Measure and Dedicated to the Master of the Mint by One of the Golden Fleece*, London, 1849.
(Huntington Library: RB 1221)

Cave Johnson Couts, diary entry dated November 28, 1848.
(Huntington Library: CT 2541, vol. 1)

Message from the President of the United States to the Two Houses of Congress. . .Dec. 5, 1848, Washington, D.C., 1848.
(Huntington Library: RB 248140)

"California," in the *Sandwich Island News*, Honolulu, June 22, 1848.
(Huntington Library: RB 226131)

N. Currier, lithograph entitled *California Gold*, New York, c. 1850.
(Huntington Library: RB 10285)

"California. Medicines Suitable for California," in the *Boston Shipping List*, May 2, 1849.
(Huntington Library: RB 54472)

"California! Mexican Saddles" and "Blunt's New Chart of California," in the *Boston Shipping List*, May 2, 1849.
(Huntington Library: RB 54472)

"California Outfits," in the *California Bulletin*, Boston, April 5, 1849.
(Huntington Library: RB 54464)

"Smith's California Gold Washer," in the *California Bulletin*, Boston, April 5, 1849.
(Huntington Library: RB 54464)

"Important to Those Going to California," in the *National Intelligencer*, Washington, D.C., January 2, 1849.
(Huntington Library: RB 111337)

Case 7: Gold Fever—To Go or to Stay Home
Elisha L. Cleaveland, *Hasting to Be Rich: A Sermon, Occasioned by the Present Excitement Respecting the Gold of California. . .*, New Haven, 1849.
(Huntington Library: RB 55506)

The Reverend Samuel M. Worcester, *California: Outlines of an Address*, Salem, 1849.
(Huntington Library: RB 1130)

Dr. Thomas L. Megquier, autograph letter to Milton Benjamin, February 21, 1849.
(Huntington Library: MQ 55)

Henry Mellus, autograph letter to Abel Stearns, June 27, 1849.
(Huntington Library: SG Box 43)

"For California," in the *National Intelligencer*, Washington, D.C., January 13, 1849.
(Huntington Library: RB 111337)

"Incidents in California," in the *National Intelligencer*, Washington, D.C., February 20, 1849.
(Huntington Library: RB 111337)

"Interesting from California," in the *National Intelligencer*, Washington, D.C., March 8, 1849.
(Huntington Library: RB 111337)

Gallery Two:
Days of '49

Case 8: Planning the Trek
Henry I. Simpson, *The Emigrant's Guide to the Gold Mines*, New York, 1848.
(Huntington Library: RB 2598)

G. K. Blok, *A Short Geographical and Statistical Survey of California*, Saint Petersburg, 1850.
(Huntington Library: RB 880)

Colección de artículos, noticias I capitulos de carta con respecto a California. . ., Santiago, 1849.
(Huntington Library: RB35621)

Carl Meyer, *Nach dem Sacramento*, Aarau, Switzerland, 1855.
(Huntington Library: RB 931)

Edwin Bryant, *What I Saw in California. . .*, New York, 1848.
(Huntington Library: RB 32838)

Joseph Ware, *The Emigrant's Guide to California*, Saint Louis, 1849.
(Huntington Library: RB 43743)

Californien en Skildring, Stockholm, 1850.
(Huntington Library: RB 29115)

G. A. Fleming, *California: Its Past History, Its Present Position, Its Future Prospects*, London, 1850.
(Huntington Library: RB 2606)

Case 9: Sea Voyages to California
John E. Grambart, journal of a voyage on the brig *Cordelia*, May 2, 1849.
(Huntington Library: HM 17013)

"The Shark," a handwritten newspaper produced aboard the ship *Duxbury*, August 4, 1849.
(Huntington Library: HM 234)

Illustrated trade cards from various businesses in Rio de Janeiro, Brazil, c. 1849.
(Huntington Library: Augustin Hale Collection)

Celebration of the Seventy-Third Anniversary of the Declaration of Independence . . . on Board the Barque "Hannah Sprague," at Sea, New York, 1849.
(Huntington Library: RB 19900)

Clark Oliver, painting of the ship *Argonaut* off Cape Horn, January 1850.
(Huntington Library: Manuscripts Department, William Norton Collection)

California Emigration Society, broadside entitled *Emigration to California!* Boston, 1849?
(Huntington Library: RB 82892)

Case 10: The Isthmus of Panama
Mary Jane Megquier, autograph letter to Milton Benjamin, May 14, 1849.
(Huntington Library: MQ 10)

Luther Fitch, autograph letter to "dear sisters," July 12, 1850.
(Huntington Library: HM 49740)

Ticket for Jerry Stevens signed by J. B. Farand for steerage passage on the steamer *Humbolt* to San Francisco from Panama, April 20, 1849.
(Huntington Library: HM 52580)

John A. Lloyd, *The Isthmus of Panama, with Portovelo, Chagres, & Panama*, New York, 1849.
(Huntington Library: RB 34999)

"Through the Woods to Panama," watercolor drawing in Joseph Warren Revere, manuscript autobiography, 1849.
(Huntington Library: HM 56913)

"Chagres River," lithograph in Frank Marryat, *Mountains and Molehills, or, Recollections of a Burnt Journal*, London, 1855.
(Huntington Library: RB 32560)

Case 11: Overland Crossings

Alonzo Delano, *Life on the Plains and at the Diggings,* Auburn, New York, 1854.
(Huntington Library: RB 908)

Sarah Nichols, autograph letter to Samuel Nichols, April 7, 1849.
(Huntington Library: HM 48291)

Samuel Nichols, autograph letter to Sarah Nichols, May 6, 1849.
(Huntington Library: HM 48272)

A New Map of Texas, Oregon, and California. . . , Philadelphia, 1849.
(Huntington Library: RB 560)

J. Goldsborough Bruff, pencil drawing entitled *Tremendous Hailstorm,* 1849.
(Huntington Library: HM 8044 #18)

J. Goldsborough Bruff, pencil and pastels drawing entitled *View from the Summit of Independence Rock,* 1849.
(Huntington Library: HM 8044 #60)

Case 12: Gold Mining—The Early Stages

J. Goldsborough Bruff, pencil drawing entitled *Indians of N. Valley of Feather River,* 1849.
(Huntington Library: HM 8044 #192)

John Hovey, "Historical Account of the Troubles between the Chilian and American Miners in the Calevaros Mining District," January 1850.
(Huntington Library: HM 4384)

Henry P. Richardson, autograph letter to Abel Stearns, July 9, 1848.
(Huntington Library: SG Box 51)

Daniel B. Woods, *Sixteen Months at the Gold Diggings,* New York, 1851.
(Huntington Library: RB 772)

Daguerreotype of gold miners at Gold Rush diggings, c. 1850.
(Huntington Library: Dag. 55)

The Mining Business in Four Pictures, letter sheet published by Britton & Rey.
(Huntington Library: RB 48052 #9)

The Miners, letter sheet published by Britton & Rey.
(Huntington Library: RB 48052 #15A)

Case 13: Gold Mining—The Artifacts

David T. Ansted, *The Gold Seeker's Manual, Being a Practical Guide,* New York, 1849.
(Huntington Library: RB 536)

Gold nuggets.
(Wells Fargo)

William Rich Hutton, pencil drawing entitled *Mormon Island,* April 1849.
(Huntington Library: HM 43214 #95)

Gold nugget and quartz sample.
(Huntington Library: Rare Books Department)

Leather gold pouch.
(Wells Fargo)

Gold-washing pan.
(Wells Fargo)

Bowie knife.
(Wells Fargo)

Pickaxes.
(Wells Fargo)

James Jackson Jarves, *A Correct Map of the Bay of San Francisco and the Gold Region. . . ,* Boston, c. 1849.
(Huntington Library: RB 35684)

Case 14: Gold Mining—The Unfolding Process

James McMurphy, autograph letter to "Dear Relatives," April 3, 1850.
(Huntington Library: HM 52736)

James C. Riggin, autograph letter to his wife, Rebecca, May 8, 1851.
(Huntington Library: HM 27961)

Hutchings' California Scenes—Methods of Mining, letter sheet published by J. M. Hutchings.
(Huntington Library: RB 48052 #81)

Frank Marryat, *Mountains and Molehills, or, Recollections of a Burnt Journal,* London, 1855.
(Huntington Library: RB 32560)

"Mining by Hydraulic Power" and "Suspension Flume across Brandy-Gulch," lithographs in Ernest Seyd, *California and Its Resources: A Work for the Merchant, the Capitalist, and the Emigrant,* London, 1858.
(Huntington Library: RB 27189)

James Wyld, *World on Mercator's Projection, Shewing the Distribution of Gold throughout the World,* London, c. 1852.
(Huntington Library: RB 35008)

Case 15: Life in the Mining Camps

Charles R. Parke, diary entry for April 25, 1850.
(Huntington Library: HM 16996)

The Honest Miner's Songs, letter sheet published by Geo. H. Baker.
(Huntington Library: RB 48052 #102)

Elias Ketcham, diary entry for February 17, 1853.
(Huntington Library: HM 58269)

John Eagle, autograph letter to his wife, Margaret, December 25, 1852.
(Huntington Library: EGL 12)

"The Sluice-Box," a handwritten newspaper from Orleans, California, October 6, 1856.
(Huntington Library: Uncataloged manuscript)

"The Winter of 1849," lithograph in Frank Marryat, *Mountains and Molehills, or, Recollections of a Burnt Journal,* London, 1855.
(Huntington Library: RB 32560)

"The Bar of a Gambling Saloon," lithograph in Frank Marryat, *Mountains and Molehills, or, Recollections of a Burnt Journal,* London, 1855.
(Huntington Library: RB 32560)

J. Goldsborough Bruff, pencil drawing entitled *Indian Lodge in Lassin's Rancheria. . . ,* 1849.
(Huntington Library: HM 8044 #155)

Case 16: The Ties that Bind—Argonauts and Their Families

Charles Cochran, diary entry for February 3, 1849.
(Huntington Library: HM 58071)

Mary Jane Megquier, autograph letter to her children, May 22, 1849.
(Huntington Library: MQ 11)

The Miners' Ten Commandments, letter sheet published by Sun Print.
(Huntington Library: RB 48052 #78A)

Receipt from Gregory's California and New York Package, Parcel, and Message Express for shipment of $1,000, July 1850.
(Huntington Library: MQ 79)

Scene at the San Francisco Post Office, Showing How We Get Our Letters, letter sheet published by Leland & McCombe.
(Huntington Library: RB 48052 #98A)

Do They Miss Me at Home, letter sheet published by James M. Hutchings.
(Huntington Library: RB 48052 #64)

Commandments to California Wives, letter sheet published by W. C. Butler.
(Huntington Library: RB 48052 #76)

Platform 1: The '49er at Home

José de Alvear, *The Gold Seeker's Guide. . . ,* New York, c. 1850.
(Huntington Library: RB 442564)

John H. Magruder, autograph letter to Thomas Magruder, September 17, 1849.
(Huntington Library: HM 16727)

William T. Reynolds, autograph letter to wife, August 31, 1851.
(Huntington Library: HM 56914)

Lucy Stoddard Wakefield, autograph letter to "Lucius and Rebecca," September 18–25, 1851.
(Huntington Library: HM 16386)

John Eagle, autograph letter to Margaret Eagle, March 12, 1853.
(Huntington Library: EGL 18)

Placerville, letter sheet published by Quirot & Co.
(Huntington Library: RB 48052 #41)

Sonora, January, 1852, letter sheet published by
Pollard & Brittons.
(Huntington Library: RB 48052 #67)

Gallery Three:
California Transformed, 1850–58

Case 17: Racial Confrontations and Accommodations
Annual Message of the Governor of California. . . , San
Jose, 1851.
(Huntington Library: RB 42368)

Henry Valentine, *California; or, the Feast of Gold,*
London, c. 1849.
(Huntington Library: RB 471780)

"The Attack," engraving in *Hutchings Illustrated
California Magazine* 3, no. 10 (April 1859).
(Huntington Library: RB 420)

*The Life and Adventures of James Williams, a Fugitive
Slave,* San Francisco, 1873.
(Huntington Library: RB 14406)

Augustin Hale, diary entry for September 1, 1850.
(Huntington Library: Augustin Hale Collection)

Jacob P. Leese, labor contract with Ai, Chinaman,
Hong Kong, July 28, 1849.
(Huntington Library: VA 160)

"Chinese Camp in the Mines," engraving in J. D.
Borthwick, *Three Years in California,* Edinburgh, 1857.
(Huntington Library: RB 257]

Lithograph entitled *The Defence of the California
Bank,* New York, c. -1849.
(Huntington Library: Rare Books Department,
Prints Collection)

Case 18: Struggles over Land
Dr. Israel S. P. Lord, diary entry for November 14,
1850.
(Huntington Library: HM 19408)

William M. Gwin, *Land Titles in California . . . in
Reply to Mr. Benton,* Washington, 1851.
(Huntington Library: RB 1666)

Petition of Citizens of California to the U.S.
Congress, February 21, 1859.
(Huntington Library: HM 514)

Mr. Gringo's Experience as a Ranchero, letter sheet
published by Anthony & Baker.
(Huntington Library: RB 48052 #77)

Colt Dragoon Pistol.
(Wells Fargo)

"Farming Scene in Napa Valley," lithograph in Ernest
Seyd, *California and Its Resources: A Work for the
Merchant, the Capitalist, and the Emigrant,* London, 1858.
(Huntington Library: RB 27189)

Indian Rancherie on Dry Creek, letter sheet published
at the Union Office.
(Huntington Library: RB 48052 #187)

Committee of Vigilance of San Francisco membership certificate for Sylvanus B. Marston, 1856.
(Huntington Library: HM 56797)

Case 19: Crime and Violence
Hugo Reid, autograph letter to Abel Stearns, April
22, 1849.
(Huntington Library: SG Box 53)

Thomas Larkin, autograph letter to Abel Stearns,
May 31, 1856.
(Huntington Library: SG Box 40)

Colt single-shot derringer.
(Wells Fargo)

Edward Gould Buffum, *Six Months in the Gold
Mines,* London, 1850.
(Huntington Library: RB 33604)

Tremendous Excitement! letter sheet published by
Justh, Quirot & Co.
(Huntington Library: RB 48052 #16)

*The First Trial & Execution in S. Francisco on the
Night of 10ᵗʰ of June at 2 O'Clock,* letter sheet
published by Quirot & Co.
(Huntington Library: RB 48052 #23)

Case 20: Dreams of Success, Fears of Failure
Luther Fitch, autograph letter to his father, August
27, 1850.
(Huntington Library: HM 49710)

Lucy Stoddard Wakefield, autograph letter to
"Lucius and Rebecca," September 18–25, 1851.
(Huntington Library: HM 16386)

Alonzo Delano, two illustrations from *The Idle and
Industrious Miner,* Sacramento, 1854.
(Huntington Library: RB 32382)

Hinton Helper, *The Land of Gold: Reality versus
Fiction,* Baltimore, 1855.
(Huntington Library: RB 957)

The Dream of a Prospecting Miner, letter sheet
published by Quirot & Co.
(Huntington Library: RB 48052 #44)

"Selling Off," lithograph in Augusto Ferran and José
Baturone, *Album Californiano,* Havana, c. 1850.
(Huntington Library: RB 31800)

"Comfort," lithograph in Augusto Ferran and José
Baturone, *Album Californiano,* Havana, c. 1850.
(Huntington Library: RB 31800)

William Rich Hutton, watercolor drawing entitled
View of Monterey, 1849.
(Huntington Library: HM 43214 #46)

Case 21: Constitution of 1849
People's Ticket and Republican Ticket, election
ballots, c. 1849.
(Huntington Library: Augustin Hale Collection)

Constitutional Convention, autograph manuscript,
"Article II, Rights of Suffrage," with corrections, 1849.
(Huntington Library: HM 40405)

Elisha Crosby, autograph manuscript, "Memoirs
and Reminiscences," c. 1885.
(Huntington Library: HM 284)

Constitution of the State of California, San Francisco,
1849.
(Huntington Library: RB 124)

Constitución del estado de California, San Francisco,
1849.
(Huntington Library: RB 235208)

Wood and metal pen, c. 1849.
(Ellen Ellis Collection)

Governor Bennett Riley, broadside entitled *Proclamation to the People of California,* Monterey, June 3, 1849.
(Huntington Library: RB 43698)

Governor Bennett Riley, broadside entitled
Proclamation, Monterey, June 3, 1849.
(Huntington Library: RB 35683)

Lithograph entitled *Sacramento in Californien,*
Berlin, 1849?
(Huntington Library: Pr. Box 582/73)

Case 22: Politics in the New State
Bayard Taylor, *El Dorado, or, Adventures in the Path
of Empire,* New York, 1850.
(Huntington Library: RB 75832)

*Memorial of the Senators and Representatives Elect from
California, Requesting. . .the Admission of California
into the Union. . .* , Washington, D.C., 1850.
(Huntington Library: RB 275323)

What We Want in California from New York Direct,
letter sheet published by Britton & Rey.
(Huntington Library: RB 48052 #66)

Billington C. Whiting, autograph letter to Susan
Whiting, May 19, 1858.
(Huntington Library: HM 54493)

Republican and People's Reform Ticket. . .for
Presidential Electors, California, 1856?
(Huntington Library: Eph. F28-C1856/2)

*Honest Voters Trying to Elect Their Officers in Front of
the House,* letter sheet published by Noisy Carriers.
(Huntington Library: RB 48052 #68)

Grand Admission Celebration. Portsmouth Square Octr. 29, 1850, letter sheet published by C. J. Pollard.
(Huntington Library: RB 48052 #137)

Case 23: Politics of Race and Justice
Official Correspondence between the Governor of California, the U.S. Indian Agents, and the Commander of U.S. Troops Now in California, Sacramento, 1852.
(Huntington Library: RB 35372)

Proceedings of the Second Annual Convention of the Colored Citizens of the State of California, San Francisco, 1856.
(Huntington Library: RB 42781)

Wilson Flint, *Speech. . .in the Senate of California, March 21, 1856, on the Bill to Reduce the Chinese Mining License Tax,* Sacramento, 1856.
(Huntington Library: RB 254899)

Lai Chun-Chen, *Remarks of the Chinese Merchants of San Francisco upon Governor Bigler's Message,* San Francisco, 1855.
(Huntington Library: RB 191675)

Foreign miner's license, 1855.
(Wells Fargo)

Way-Side Scenes in California, letter sheet published by J. M. Hutchings.
(Huntington Library: RB 48052 #36)

Gallery Four:
The Legacies of El Dorado

Platform 2: J. Goldsborough Bruff, '49er Artist
J. Goldsborough Bruff, pencil and pastel drawing entitled *On the Plains Preparing to Feed,* 1849.
(Huntington Library: HM 8044 #16)

J. Goldsborough Bruff, pencil drawing entitled *A Camp-Scene, on the Platte,* 1849.
(Huntington Library: HM 8044 #20)

J. Goldsborough Bruff, pencil drawing entitled *Death of Charles Bishop from Cholera,* 1849.
(Huntington Library: HM 8044 #37)

J. Goldsborough Bruff, pencil and pastel drawing entitled *Presence of Mind, or Preventing a Horn Too Much,* 1849.
(Huntington Library: HM 8044 #70)

J. Goldsborough Bruff, pencil drawing entitled *Indian Drawings on a Sand-Stone Cliff,* 1849.
(Huntington Library: HM 8044 #76)

J. Goldsborough Bruff, pencil and pastel drawing entitled *W. End of Lodge, before the Snow-storm,* 1850.
(Huntington Library: HM 8044 #129)

J. Goldsborough Bruff, pencil drawing entitled *Cone of the Pinon,* no date.
(Huntington Library: HM 8044 #203)

Case 24: Galvanizing Economic Enterprise in California
Mary Jane Megquier, autograph letter to Angeline (Megquier) Gilson, June 30, 1850.
(Huntington Library: MQ 22)

Wells Fargo and Company, autograph document, receipt for treasure, September 17, 1856.
(Wells Fargo)

Samuel Brannan, autograph letter to Abel Stearns, December 5, 1856.
(Huntington Library: SG Box 11)

View of the Levee, Sacramento City, California, letter sheet published by Forrest & Borden.
(Huntington Library: RB 48052 #183/HM 50516)

Ernest Seyd, *California and Its Resources: A Work for the Merchant, the Capitalist, and the Emigrant,* London, 1858.
(Huntington Library: RB 27189)

"High and Dry," lithograph in Frank Marryat, *Mountains and Molehills, or, Recollections of a Burnt Journal,* London, 1855.
(Huntington Library: RB 32560)

San Francisco, letter sheet published by Marvin & Hitchcock Pioneer Book Store.
(Huntington Library: RB 48052 #175/HM 36395)

Case 25: Economic Enterprises Reaching Beyond California
T. Butler King, *California, the Wonder of the Age,* New York, 1850.
(Huntington Library: RB 1154)

William Van Voorhies, *Oration before the Society of California Pioneers. . . ,* San Francisco, 1853.
(Huntington Library: RB 68280)

United States Customs House (San Francisco), ledger, page 60, 1854–55.
(Huntington Library: HM 35253)

Wells Fargo and Company, check made payable to Huntington and Hopkins, July 12, 1863.
(Wells Fargo)

Augustin Hale, autograph letter to his mother and sisters, April 28, 1861.
(Huntington Library: Augustin Hale Collection)

Frazer River Thermometer, letter sheet published by Sterett & Butler.
(Huntington Library: RB 318379)

Long Wharf, letter sheet published by Charles P. Kimball, Noisy Carriers Publishing Hall.
(Huntington Library: RB 48052 #21)

Case 26: California's Urban Development
Mary Jane Megquier, autograph letter to "My Dear Children," April 8, 1853.
(Huntington Library: MQ 39)

Lewis Granger, autograph letter to his father, April 8, 1850.
(Huntington Library: HM 58073)

Assorted trade cards from various businesses in San Francisco, c. 1850s.
(Wells Fargo)

Citizen's Line, passenger list for stagecoach, "Way Bill," October 12, 1854.
(Wells Fargo)

"Street in San Francisco," watercolor drawing in Joseph Warren Revere, manuscript autobiography, 1849.
(Huntington Library: HM 56913)

"The Winter of 1849," lithograph in Frank Marryat, *Mountains and Molehills, or, Recollections of a Burnt Journal,* London, 1855.
(Huntington Library: RB 32560)

Engraving entitled *Los Angeles, Los Angeles County, Cal., 1857,* San Francisco, 1857.
(Huntington Library: B-V/M-8)

Case 27: Treasure in El Dorado
Wells Fargo treasure box, lock, and canvas moneybags.
(Wells Fargo)

Two assayer's crucibles.
(Wells Fargo)

Chinese scales (*dotchen*).
(Wells Fargo)

E. Justh, "Memorandum of Gold Bullion Deposited," August 19, 1859.
(Wells Fargo)

Jacob Eckfeldt and William DuBois, *New Varieties of Coins and Bullion,* Philadelphia, 1850.
(Huntington Library: RB 33004)

Coining Money at the San Francisco Branch Mint, letter sheet published by Hutchings & Rosenfield.
(Huntington Library: RB 48052 #156)

Two and one-half dollar United States gold coin, 1858.
(Huntington Library: Rare Books Department)

Platform 3: Gold Rush Cities
"North Side of Montgomery Street, from California to Sacramento," in G. R. Fardon, *San Francisco Album: Photographs of the Most Beautiful Views and Public Buildings of San Francisco,* San Francisco, 1856.
(Huntington Library: RB 1735, #17)

"Kearny Street," in G. R. Fardon, *San Francisco Album: Photographs of the Most Beautiful Views and Public Buildings of San Francisco,* San Francisco, 1856.
(Huntington Library: RB 1735, #19)

Broadside entitled *Second Grand Concert in California! The Alleghanians*, San Francisco, May 26, 1852.
(Huntington Library: RB 496505)

Broadside entitled *One Night Only! Immense Attraction! The Chinese Dramatic Company!* Sacramento, c. 1855.
(Huntington Library: RB 496506)

San Francisco, 1858, lettersheet published by Britton & Rey.
(Huntington Library: RB 48052 #113)

Broadside entitled *Rates of Labor in San Francisco*, San Francisco, 1856.
(Huntington Library: RB 497902)

Union Pacific and Central Pacific Railroads, broadside entitled *Union and Central Pacific Route to Southern California. . .*, Omaha, 1877.
(Huntington Library: RB 475611)

Case 28: Golden Prospects for the Golden State

Jesse Smart, autograph letter to his son, January 19, 1853.
(Huntington Library: Jesse Smart Papers)

John S. Hittell, *The Resources of California, Comprising Agriculture, Mining, Geography, Climate, Commerce, . . .and the Past and Future Development of the State*, San Francisco, 1863.
(Huntington Library: RB 32994)

Charles Nordhoff, *California for Health, Pleasure, and Residence*, San Francisco, 1872.
(Huntington Library: RB 253989)

California Immigration Commission, *California, the Cornucopia of the World. . .*, Chicago, 1883.
(Huntington Library: RB 248676)

Cover illustration of the *Overland Monthly* (California's Jubilee Number), 2nd ser., 31 (February 1898).
(Huntington Library: AP 2 O9)

"East Side Montgomery Street Looking North from California Street," photograph in Thomas Houseworth & Co., *Pacific Coast Scenery*, San Francisco, 1872.
(Huntington Library: RB 296133, #173)

"Montgomery Street, from California, North. . .," photograph in Thomas Houseworth & Co., *Pacific Coast Scenery*, San Francisco, 1872.
(Huntington Library: RB 296133, #148)

English language and Chinese language front pages of *The Oriental*, San Francisco, May 1856.
(Huntington Library: RB 55030)

Case 29: Golden Memories of the Gold Rush Era

Alonzo Delano, *The Central Pacific Railroad, or '49 and '69*, San Francisco, 1868.
(Huntington Library: RB 35617)

Bret Harte, *The Luck of Roaring Camp and Other Sketches*, Boston, 1872.
(Huntington Library: RB 481669)

Society of California Pioneers of New England, *The Fortieth Anniversary of the Discovery of Gold in California. . .*, Boston, 1888.
(Huntington Library: RB 253334)

Gertrude Atherton, *The Splendid Idle Forties: Stories of Old California*, New York, 1902.
(Huntington Library: RB 988)

Association of Pioneer Women of California, *Constitution, By-laws. . .*, San Francisco, 1908.
(Huntington Library: RB 251642)

Badge from Society of California Pioneers of New England meeting.
(Huntington Library: Norton Collection)

Society of California Pioneers membership certificate for James Clyman, San Francisco, 1876.
(Huntington Library: RB 70775)

Case 30: Gains and Losses from the Gold Rush Experience

J. Ross Browne, *Crusoe's Island: A Ramble in the Footsteps of Alexander Selkirk, with Sketches of Adventure in California and Washoe*, New York, 1864.
(Huntington Library: RB 2320)

Mark Twain (Samuel Langhorne Clemens), *Roughing It*, Chicago, 1872.
(Huntington Library: RB 47363)

María Amparo Ruiz de Burton, *The Squatter and the Don*, San Francisco, 1885.
(Huntington Library: RB 96314)

Charles Howard Shinn, *Mining Camps: A Study in American Frontier Government*, New York, 1885.
(Huntington Library: RB 1966)

Josiah Royce, *California, from the Conquest in 1846 to the Second Vigilance Committee in San Francisco*, Boston, 1886.
(Huntington Library: RB 1697)

"Worked Out Claims," photograph by Thomas Houseworth & Co.
(Huntington Library: Placer Mining Series #152)

"Boating Party on Donner Lake," photograph by Alfred A. Hart.
(Huntington Library: Album 184, #128)

The Pioneer (Golden Jubilee Number) 13, no. 1 (January 1898).
(Huntington Library: RB 81765)

Index

Page numbers in italics refer to illustrations.

A

advertisements, 37, *39, 41*
African-Americans, 83–85, 87, 100, 105–6
agriculture, 12, 17, 86, 87, 88, 90–91, 113, 127, 129, 131
Alaska, 24
Alta California (newspaper), 54, 73
Alta California (see Mexican California)
Alvarado, Juan Bautista, 12
American River, 11, 12, 17, 28, 58
Anglo-Americans in Mexican California, 21–22, 25–26; conflict with Californios, 100; xenophobia of, 79–80, 82–83
Argonaut, 44
Associated Pioneers of the Territorial Days of California, 132, 133
Association of Pioneer Women of California, 133
Atherton, Gertrude, 133, 135–36
Australia, 29, 36, 39, 54, 90

B

Baker, Geo. H., 68, *69*
Barber & Baker, *64,* 65
Baturone, José, *94*
Bear Flag Revolt, 27, 88
Beecher, The Reverend Edward, 33
Belgium, 36
Benjamin, Milton, 46, 95
Big Bar, 63
Bigler, Governor John, 104–5, 106
Bishop, Charles, 51
Blok, G. K., 36, *37*
Blood, A., 111
Booth, E. A., 105–6
Borthwick, J. D., *78,* 79, *83*
Bouchacourt, Charles, 36
Brannan, Sam, 113
Brazil, 43
Britton & Rey, 12, *13, 65, 99, 123*
Broderick, David C., 102
Brownsville, Texas, 50
Bruff, J. Goldsborough, 49, *51–52, 55–56, 72,* 95
Bryant, Edwin, 35–36, *38,* 49
Bryson, Leslie, 82
Buffum, Edward Gould, 33, 93
Burnett, Governor Peter, 87, 105
Burns, Lydia, 72, 73
Burton, Colonel Henry S., 136
Butler, W. C., *76*

C

Calaveras County, 72, 80, 93
California, admission to union, 83, 99, 101, *104;* argonauts settlement in, 95–97; businesses in, 111–21; emigration to, 11–25; entertainment in, 121–22; first elections, 101–2, *103;* guidebooks to, 35–39; lawlessness in, 93–95; links to international trade, 117, 120; population growth, 79, 111; social change, 79–96; tourism, 129; traveling to, 35–54; women in, 71, 95–96
California Bulletin (Boston newspaper), *40*
California Emigration Society, *45*
California Immigration Commission, *130,* 131

California Indians, *16,* 54, *56,* 58, 73, *86,* 100; conflict with prospectors, *82,* 87, 102, 104–5; as laborers, 14, *17, 19,* 22–23
California Trail, 50, 52, 54
Californian (newspaper), 28
Californios (original Spanish-Mexican settlers of California), 17, 22, 24, 27, 79, 85, 92, 99, 113, 133; conflict with Anglo-Americans, 100; romanticized, 134–36
Cape Horn, 40–41, *44,* 45, 56
Casey, James, 94
Castro, José, 27
Catholic Church, 17
cattle ranching and trade, 12, 17, *18,* 22, 113, 115, 120
Central Pacific Railroad, *110,* 111, 119–20, *131*
Central Valley, 12
Chagres, Panama, 46
Chagres River, *34,* 35, 46, *47*
Chapultepec Club, 102
Chihuahua, Mexico, 50
Chile, gold seekers from, 29, 37, 39, 54, 57, 80, 93, 105
China, gold seekers from, 28, 39, 73, *78,* 82–83, 106–7, 109; anti-Chinese sentiment, 80, 82, 106
Chinese Dramatic Company, *121,* 122
Chinese scales (*dotchen*), *126*
chivalry democracy, 102
cholera, 51, 53
Christman, Enos, 71
Cisco, California, *110,* 111, *120*
Civil War, 102
Clark, Dr. Francis, 33
Cleaveland, Elisha L., *30,* 32
Cochran, Charles, 74
Coloma, California, 17, 28, 68
Colored Citizens' Conventions, 105–6
Colton, Walter, 17, 30
Columbia, California, 68
Comstock Lode, 119, 135
Comstock, Orval, 121
Constitution of 1849, 97–101
Constitutional convention, 98–101
Cordelia, 42, 44, 45
Council Bluffs, Iowa, 50
Couts, Lieutenant Cave J., 29–30, 113
cowboys, 18
cowhides, 17, 18
Crawford, Ronald, 58, 60
crime, 93–95
Crocker, Charles, 119
Crosby, Elisha, 98, 100, 101
Currier, N., *31*

D

Dalton, Henry, 21
Dana, Richard Henry, 20
Davis, Stephen C., 46, 126
Death Valley, 120
Delano, Alonzo, 49–50, 91, 96, 131–32
Democratic Party, 102
Detter, T., 106
Dimmick, Kimball Hale, *27*
Donner Lake, *138*

dotchen (Chinese scales), *126*
Dry Diggings, 93
DuBois, William, 127
Duxbury, 42, 44

E

Eagle, John, *70, 72, 73, 75*
Eckfeldt, Jacob, 127
El Dorado County, 63
Ellis, John S., *133, 134*
emigration, 11–25, 35–54, *55*
Emory, William H., 35
England, gold seekers from, 25, 36
entrepreneurs, 111–12

F

Farnham, Thomas J., 35
Farnsworth, William, 96–97
Feather River, 58, 68
Ferran, Augusto, *94*
fires, 125
Fitch, Luther, 46, 95
Fleming, G. A., 60, *61*
Flint, Senator Wilson, 109
floods, 126
Forbes, Alexander, *18*
foreign miner's license, *107*
Foreign Miner's Tax, 107
Fort Smith, Arkansas, 50
Foster, George, 35
Foster, Stephen, 100
France, gold seekers from, 36, 39, 71, 73, 80, 93
Frémont, John C., 25, 35, 36, 100, *101*

G

gambling, 70, 123
George, Henry, 136–37
Gillespie, Archibald, 30
gold, discovery of, 11, 12, *13*; deposits, 55; mining, equipment and methods, 54–58, *59*, 60, *61*, 62–63, *64–65, 66–67*; production, 111; world distribution of, *66*
gold miners, 54–77; conflicts between, 79–80, 82; life of, 54–77; numbers of, 54, 57, 111
Gold Mountain, 82
gold nuggets, *62*
Gold Rush, beginning, 11, 17, 28–33; legacies of, 111–38; life during, 54–77
Gorgas, Solomon, 54
Gorgona, Panama, 46
Grambart, John E., 42, 44
Granger, Lewis, 120–21
Great Britain, 17; settlers from, 17, 21, 22
Grey, Alfred, 96
guidebooks, 22, 35–39, *41*, 131
Gwin, Senator William M., 91–92, 101–2

H

Haight, Henry H., 88
Hale, Augustin, 43, 62–63, 87, 119
Hart, Alfred A., *111*, 138

Harte, Bret, 135
Hastings, Lansford W., *22*, 25, 49, 102
Hawaiians, 54
Helper, Hinton, 96, 111
Heywood, Jonathan, 77
Hill, James O., 53
Hittell, John S., 128–29
Holland, gold seekers from, 36
Hong Kong, 28
Hopkins, Mark, 90, 111, 112, 119, 125
Houseworth and Company, 129, 131, 137
Hovey, John, *57, 80*
Hudson's Bay Company, 14, 20
Humbolt, 46
Huntington, Collis P., 68, 70, 111, 119
Huntington, Solon, 70
Hutchings, James M., *67, 75*
Hutton, William Rich, *14, 19, 22, 23, 63, 68, 98*
hydraulic mining, 62, *66*

I

Ide, William B., 27
Independence Rock, Wyoming, 52
Independence, Missouri, 50
Indian wars, 105
Isthmus of Panama, route through, 45–48

J

Jackson, Helen Hunt, 135
Jarves, James Jackson, 59
joint-stock companies, 49

K

Karok Indians, 104
Kearny, General Stephen W., 24, 50
Ketcham, Elias, 73
Kimball, Charles P., *118*
King, James, 94
King, T. Butler, 102, 116
Kinkade, John, 66
Klamath County, 104
Klamath Indians, 104

L

Lai Chun-Cheun, 107
land claims, 90–91
Land Commission Act of 1851, 136
land ownership, 88
Larkin, Thomas O., 21, 24, 30, 35, 36, 83, 94
Latin America, gold seekers from, 54, 79, 107
Leese, Jacob P., 80, 82
Leidesdorff, William A., 22, 23
Leonore, 44
Littlefield, Alvah, 111
Lloyd, John A., *46*
long toms, 57, 60, 62, 111
Lord, Dr. Israel S. P., 88, 90, 124
Los Angeles, 21, *23, 27*, 120–21, *125*
Lummis, Charles F., 136
lynchings, 79, 88, 93

M

Magruder, John, 58
Manifest Destiny, 83, 104
maps, *15, 20, 50, 59, 66*
Mariposa, California, 58
maritime routes, 39–48; cost of, 41; entertainments, 44; length of, 40; numbers using, 41
Marryat, Frank, 35, 46, 63, 70–71, 73, 111, 124, 125–26; illustrations from his book *Mountains and Molehills, 34, 47, 71, 72, 115*
Marshall, James W., 11, 12, 17, 28, 135
Marston, Sylvanus B., 88
Marysville, California, 68
Mason, Colonel Richard B., *15, 24*, 28, 35
McKee, Redick, 104
McMurphy, James, 62
Megquier, Mary Jane, 46, 74, 77, 95, 96, 112, 121, 127
Megquier, Dr. Thomas L., 33, 77, 121
mercury mines, 62, *68*
Mexican-American War, 24, 27, 88, 97
Mexican California, 17–28
Mexican land grants, 12, 22, 88, 90–92, 136
Mexicans, miners, 54, 71, 80, 93, 105, 107; right to vote, 100
Mexico, 18, 24–26, 29, 45, 50
Meyer, Carl, 38
military government, 97–98
militias, 80, 87, 104
Miners' Ten Commandments, 75
mining camps, 68, 70–75
Mission San Jose, *18*
Missouri River, 50
Miwok Indians, 14, 87
Monterey, California, 17, *21*, 28, *98, 99*
Mormon Island, *63*
Mount Shasta, 58
Murrell, George McKinley, 53, 85, 87
Murrell, Reuben, 85, 87

N

Nahl, Charles, *91*
Nash, Abraham, 80
National Intelligencer (newspaper), *32, 33, 41,* 49
Nevada, 119, 135
Nevada City, California, 68
New England Associated California Pioneers, 132, 133
New Helvetia, 12, 14, 25, 26, 88
newspapers, 29, *32, 33,* 36–37, *39, 40, 41,* 70, 73, *84*; shipboard, *42,* 44–45
Nicaragua, 45
Nichols, Samuel, *48,* 53
Nichols, Sarah, *48,* 53
Nisenan Indians, 14, 28
Noatts, Maria F., 96
Nordhoff, Charles, 129

O

Oliver, Clark, *44*
Oregon, *22,* 25, 29, 49, *50,* 58
Oriental, The (newspaper), *84*
Orleans Bar, 72–73

Overland Monthly, 136
overland routes, 48–54; mortality on, 54

P

Pacific Mail Steamship Company, 45, 46
Panama, 45–48
Parke, Dr. Charles Ross, 123, 126–27
party politics, 101–2
Peru, miners from, 29, 37, 54, 80, 105
Petrel, The (handwritten, shipboard newspaper), 42, 44
photography, 131
Pico, Andrés, 24
Pico, Pio, *24*, 27
Pioneer, The, 135
placer deposits, 58–62
Placerville, 68, 73
Platte River, 50, 51, 52
Plummer, Charles, 44, 45, 73
Polk, President James, 30, 35
Pollard, C. J., *104*
Presbyterian Board of Foreign Missions, 82
Protestant missionary societies, 82

Q

Quirot & Co., *73, 90, 92*

R

racism, 79–80, 82–85, 87; in California constitution, 100
railroad, transcontinental, *99, 100, 101,* 102, 119, *131*
ranching, cattle, 14, 17, *18,* 22, 113–14, 120
Reid, Hugo, 21, 54, 79, *88,* 93, 113
Revere, Joseph Warren, *21, 25,* 46, *47, 59, 122*
Reynolds, John, *26,* 30
Reynolds, William P., *26,* 30
Richardson, Henry, 54
Riley, General Bennett, 98–99, 100, 101
Rio de Janeiro, Brazil, 43
Robinson, Alfred, 21, 26
Robinson, Daniel, 33, 52, 53
rockers, *59*
Rocky Mountains, 50
Royce, Josiah, 137, 138
Ruiz de Burton, María Amparo, 136
Russia, 17, 24
Russian-American Company, 14

S

Sacramento, *38,* 68, 90, *112,* 117, 120, 123, *124, 125–26*
Sacramento Daily Union (newspaper), 73
Sacramento River, 12, 68
Sacramento Valley, 12, 88
Saint Joseph, Missouri, 50
Salt Lake City, 52
San Diego, 17
San Francisco, 68, 88, *90,* 94–95, 98, 102, 120, 121–24; views of, *22, 115, 116, 117, 118, 122, 123, 129*
San Francisco Post Office, *77*
San Joaquin River, 68

San Jose, 27
San Pasqual, Battle of, 24, 27
Sanger, Lewis, 42
Sankey, R. V., *26*
Santa Barbara, 17
Santa Barbara Mission, *19*
Santa Fe, New Mexico, 52
Scherer, L., *10,* 11, *29*
Schmölder, Bruno, 36
Scott, General Winfield, *60,* 102
Seyd, Ernest, *66, 86,* 87, *113, 114,* 115–16, 117
Shark, The (handwritten, shipboard newspaper), *42,* 44
Shasta County, 104
Sherwood, Ely, 35
Shinn, Charles Howard, 137–38
shovelry democracy, 102
silver boom, 119
Simpson, Henry I., 35, *36*
Simpson, Sir George, 20, 25
Siskiyou County, 104
slavery, 83–85, 87, 100–102
Sloat, Commodore John, 26–27
sluice boxes, 57, 62
Sluice-Box, The (handwritten newspaper), *70,* 72–73, 74
Smart, Jesse, 113, 127
Society of California Pioneers, 128, 132, 133, *134*
Society of California Pioneers of New England, *132,* 133, *134*
Society of First Steamship Pioneers, 132
Sonoma, California, 24
Sonora, California, 68, 70, 74, 82, 93
Sonora, Mexico, 50
South Pass, 50
Spain, 17
Spanish language, 100
Speer, William, *80,* 82, 84, 107
stamp mills, 62
Stanford, Leland, 119
state charter, 99–100
Stearns, Abel, 21, 22, 30, 54, 79, 88, 93, 94, 100, 113
stereographs, 131
Stevens, Jerry, *46*
Stevenson, Colonel Jonathan D., 33
Stockton, California, 68, 95, 117, 120, 124, 125, 126
Stockton, Commodore Robert F., 27
suffrage, 100
Sutter, John Augustus, 11–14, 23, 24, 26, 28, 88, 90
Sutter's Fort, *25*
Sutter's Mill, 11, *12, 14*
Sweetser, Albion, 111–12

T

tallow, 17, 18, *19,* 22, 113
taxes, customs, 116–17, *119;* foreign miner, 107, 109
Taylor, Bayard, 101, 118, 121, 123
Taylor, President Zachary, *60*
Territorial Pioneers of California, 132
Terry, David, 102
theaters, 122
trade cards, *43*

Treaty of Guadalupe Hidalgo, 24, 27, 88, 92, 97, 100
Trinity County, 104
Tuolumne Water Company, 62
Turner, George M., 102
Twain, Mark, 135, 136

U

Union Pacific Railroad, *131*
United States Mail Steamship Company, 45
Upper California (see Alta California)
U.S. Army, desertions, 27
U.S. Army Corps of Topographical Engineers, 24
U.S. Congress, 30, 91–92, 100–101, 116–17
U.S. Customs House, 116–17, *119*
U.S. Land Commission, 85, 92, 113, 136
U.S. Mint, 127, *128*
U.S. War Department, 15

V

Valentine, Henry, *81*
Vallejo, Mariano G., 26–27, 82
Van Voorhies, William, 120
vaqueros, *18, 23*
vigilance committees, 88, *89, 90,* 93–95, 102, 138
Volcano, California, 68, 72, 74

W

Wakefield, Lucy Stoddard, 95–96
Ward, Harriet Sherrill, 53
Washington City and California Company, 49, *51,* 52
Wells Fargo express, *126*
Western Association of California Pioneers, 132, 133
Whig Party, 102
Whiting, Billington C., 102
Wilkes, Lieutenant Charles, *20*
Williams, James, 84–85
Woods, Daniel, 60, 62
Wyld, James, *66*

Y

Yalisumni Nisenan Indians, 28
Yosemite, *114*
Young Whigs Club, 102
Yuba River, 58
Yurok Indians, 104